Bloom's Modern Critical Interpretations

The Adventures of
  Huckleberry Finn
The Age of Innocence
Alice's Adventures in
  Wonderland
All Quiet on the
  Western Front
As You Like It
The Ballad of the Sad
  Café
Beowulf
Black Boy
The Bluest Eye
The Canterbury Tales
Cat on a Hot Tin
  Roof
The Catcher in the
  Rye
Catch-22
The Chronicles of
  Narnia
The Color Purple
Crime and
  Punishment
The Crucible
Darkness at Noon
Death of a Salesman
The Death of Artemio
  Cruz
Don Quixote
Emerson's Essays
Emma
Fahrenheit 451
A Farewell to Arms
Frankenstein

The Grapes of Wrath
Great Expectations
The Great Gatsby
Gulliver's Travels
The Handmaid's Tale
Heart of Darkness
I Know Why the
  Caged Bird Sings
The Iliad
Jane Eyre
The Joy Luck Club
The Jungle
Lord of the Flies
The Lord of the Rings
Love in the Time of
  Cholera
The Man Without
  Qualities
The Metamorphosis
Miss Lonelyhearts
Moby-Dick
My Ántonia
Native Son
Night
1984
The Odyssey
Oedipus Rex
The Old Man and the
  Sea
On the Road
One Flew Over the
  Cuckoo's Nest
One Hundred Years of
  Solitude
Persuasion

Portnoy's Complaint
A Portrait of the Artist
  as a Young
  Man
Pride and Prejudice
Ragtime
The Red Badge of
  Courage
The Rime of the
  Ancient Mariner
The Rubáiyát of Omar
  Khayyám
The Scarlet Letter
Silas Marner
Song of Solomon
The Sound and the
  Fury
The Stranger
A Streetcar Named
  Desire
Sula
The Tale of Genji
A Tale of Two Cities
The Tempest
Their Eyes Were
  Watching God
Things Fall Apart
To Kill a Mockingbird
Ulysses
Waiting for Godot
The Waste Land
White Noise
Wuthering Heights
Young Goodman
  Brown

Bloom's Modern Critical Interpretations

Willa Cather's
My Ántonia
New Edition

Edited and with an introduction by
Harold Bloom
Sterling Professor of the Humanities
Yale University

BLOOM'S
LITERARY CRITICISM
An imprint of Infobase Publishing

Editorial Consultant Janis P. Stout

Bloom's Modern Critical Interpretations:
Willa Cather's *My Ántonia*—New Edition
Copyright ©2008 by Infobase Publishing

Introduction ©2008 by Harold Bloom

Bloom's Literary Criticism
An imprint of Infobase Publishing
132 West 31st Street
New York NY 10001

Library of Congress Cataloging-in-Publication Data

Willa Cather's My Ántonia / edited and with an introduction
by Harold Bloom.—new ed.
    p. cm. — (Modern critical interpretations)
    Includes bibliographical references and index.
 ISBN 978-0-7910-9626-0 (hardcover : acid-free paper) 1. Cather, Willa, 1873–1947.
My Ántonia. I. Bloom, Harold. II. Title: Modern critical interpretations : Willa
Cather's My Ántonia.

 PS3505.A87M8947 2008
 813'.52—dc22
                            2008007336

Bloom's Literary Criticism books are available at special discounts when purchased in
bulk quantities for businesses, associations, institutions, or sales promotions. Please call
our Special Sales Department in New York at (212) 967-8800 or (800) 322-8755.

You can find Bloom's Literary Criticism on the World Wide Web at
http://www.chelseahouse.com.

Cover design by Ben Peterson

Printed in the United States of America
Bang BCL 10 9 8 7 6 5 4 3 2 1

This book is printed on acid-free paper.

All links and Web addresses were checked and verified to be correct at the time of
publication. Because of the dynamic nature of the Web, some addresses and links may
have changed since publication and may no longer be valid.

Contents

Editor's Note

My introduction argues for Cather's aesthetic eminence, in the tradition of Walter Pater and Henry James, her critical and novelistic masters, respectively.

Blanche H. Gelfant locates the key to *My Ántonia* in the unreliability of Jim Burden as narrator, since he is a solipsist and an avoider of sexuality, attached most deeply to a vision of his own childhood.

Examining the same theme of sexuality, Deborah G. Lambert relates to Cather's lesbianism, after which Sally Allen McNall discusses the theme of immigration in the novel.

Ántonia's own art as a storyteller is analyzed by Paula Woolley, while Susan J. Rosowski emphasizes Cather's lesbian identification with nature's wildness.

The strange figure of Marek Shimerda is seen by Patrick Shaw as a counterdesign that ignites Cather's imagination.

For Steven B. Shively *My Ántonia* is a parable of yielding up expectations, after which Janis P. Stout's concern is with Cather's visual acuity.

Michael Gorman traces the American imperialism against our Indians or Native Americans, which is subtly conveyed by Cather.

The theme of national identity is handled by Diana H. Polley, while Ann Romines values *My Ántonia* for the surprising questions it keeps raising.

HAROLD BLOOM

Introduction

WILLA CATHER (1873–1947)

I

Willa Cather, though now somewhat neglected, has few rivals among
the American novelists of this century. Critics and readers frequently regard
her as belonging to an earlier time, though she died in 1947. Her best novels were published in the years 1918–31, so that truly she was a novelist of
the 1920's, an older contemporary and peer of Hemingway and of F. Scott
Fitzgerald. Unlike them, she did not excel at the short story, though there
are some memorable exceptions scattered through her four volumes of tales.
Her strength is her novels and particularly, in my judgment, *My Ántonia*
(1918), *A Lost Lady* (1923) and *The Professor's House* (1925); fictions worthy
of a disciple of Flaubert and Henry James. Equally beautiful and achieved,
but rather less central, are the subsequent historical novels, the very popular
Death Comes for the Archbishop (1927) and *Shadows on the Rock* (1931). Her
second novel, *O Pioneers!* (1913), is only just short of the eminence of this
grand sequence. Six permanent novels is a remarkable number for a modern
American writer; I can think only of Faulkner as Cather's match in this
respect, since he wrote six truly enduring novels, all published during his
great decade, 1929–39.

Cather's remoteness from the fictive universe of Fitzgerald, Heming-
way and Faulkner is palpable, though all of them shared her nostalgia for an
older America. She appears, at first, to have no aesthetic affinities with her
younger contemporaries. We associate her instead with Sarah Orne Jewett,
about whom she wrote a loving essay, or even with Edith Wharton, whom
she scarcely resembles. Cather's mode of engaging with the psychic realities

1

of post–World War I America is more oblique than Fitzgerald's or Heming-way's, but it is just as apposite a representation of the era's malaise. The short novel *A Lost Lady* (1923) is not out of its aesthetic context when we read it in the company of *The Waste Land, The Comedian as the Letter C, The Sun Also Rises, The Great Gatsby* and *An American Tragedy*. Subtler and gentler than any of these, *A Lost Lady* elegizes just as profoundly a lost radiance or har-mony, a defeat of a peculiarly American dream of innocence, grace, hope.

<h1 style="text-align:center">II</h1>

Henry James, Cather's guide both as critic and novelist, died in England early in 1916. The year before, replying to H.G. Wells after being satirized by him, James wrote a famous credo: "Art *makes* life, makes interest, makes importance." This is Cather's faith also. One hears the voice of James when, in her essay "On the Art of Fiction," she writes: "Any first-rate novel or story must have in it the strength of a dozen fairly good stories that have been sacrificed to it." Those sacrifices of possibility upon the altar of form were the ritual acts of Cather's quite Paterian religion of art, too easily misread as a growing religiosity by many critics commenting upon *Death Comes for the Archbishop*. Herself a belated Aesthete, Cather emulated a familiar pattern of being attracted by the aura and not the substance of Roman Catholicism. New Mexico, and not Rome, is her place of the spirit, a spirit of the archaic and not of the supernatural.

Cather's social attitudes were altogether archaic. She shared a kind of Populist anti-Semitism with many American writers of her own generation and the next: Sherwood Anderson, Theodore Dreiser, Ezra Pound, Thomas Wolfe, even Hemingway and Fitzgerald. Her own version of anti-Semitism is curiously marked by her related aversion to heterosexuality. She had lost her first companion, Isabelle McClung, to a Jewish violinist, Jan Hambourg, and the Jewish figures in her fiction clearly represent the aggressivity of male sexuality. *The Professor's House* is marred by the gratuitous identification of the commercial exploitation of Cather's beloved West with Marcellus, the Professor's Jewish son-in-law. Doubtless, Cather's most unfortunate piece of writing was her notorious essay in 1914, "Potash and Perlmutter," in which she lamented, mock-heroically, that New York City was becoming too Jewish. Perhaps she was learning the lesson of the master again, since she is repeat-ing, in a lighter tone, the complaint of Henry James in *The American Scene* (1907). She repeated her own distaste for "Jewish critics," tainted as they were by Freud, in the essay on Sarah Orne Jewett written quite late in her career, provoking Lionel Trilling to the just accusation that she had become a mere defender of gentility, mystically concerned with pots and pans.

This dark side of Cather, though hardly a value in itself, would not much matter except that it seeped into her fiction as a systemic resentment of her own era. Nietzsche, analyzing resentment, might be writing of Cather. Freud, analyzing the relation between paranoia and homosexuality, might be writing of her also. I am wary of being reductive in such observations, and someone perpetually mugged by Feminist critics as "the Patriarchal critic" is too battered to desire any further polemic. Cather, in my judgment, is aesthetically strongest and most persuasive in her loving depiction of her heroines and of Ántonia and the lost lady Mrs. Forrester in particular. She resembles Thomas Hardy in absolutely nothing, except in the remarkable ability to seduce the reader into joining the novelist at falling in love with the heroine. I am haunted by memories of having fallen in love with Marty South in *The Woodlanders*, and with Ántonia and Mrs. Forrester when I was a boy of fifteen. Rereading *My Ántonia* and *A Lost Lady* now at fifty-four, I find that the love renews itself. I doubt that I am falling again into what my late and honored teacher William K. Wimsatt named as the Affective Fallacy, since love for a woman made up out of words is necessarily a cognitive affair.

Cather's strength at representation gives us Jim Burden and Niel Herbert as her clear surrogates, unrealized perhaps as figures of sexual life, but forcefully conveyed as figures of capable imagination, capable above all of apprehending and transmitting the extraordinary actuality and visionary intensity of Ántonia and Mrs. Forrester. Like her masters, James and Pater, Cather had made her supposed deficiency into her strength, fulfilling the overt program of Emersonian self-reliance. But nothing is got for nothing, Emerson also indicated, and Cather, again like James and Pater, suffered the reverse side of the law of Compensation. The flaws, aesthetic and human, are there, even in *My Ántonia*, *A Lost Lady* and *The Professor's House*, but they scarcely diminish the beauty and dignity of three profound studies of American nostalgias.

Cather is hardly the only vital American novelist to have misread creatively the spirit of his or her own work. Her essential imaginative knowledge was of loss, which she interpreted temporally, though her loss was aboriginal, in the Romantic mode of Wordsworth, Emerson and all their varied descendants. The glory that had passed away belonged not to the pioneers but to her own transparent eyeball, her own original relation to the universe. Rhetorically, she manifests this knowledge, which frequently is at odds with her overt thematicism. Here is Jim Burden's first shared moment with Ántonia, when they both were little children:

> We sat down and made a nest in the long red grass. Yulka curled up like a baby rabbit and played with a grasshopper. Ántonia pointed up to the sky and questioned me with her glance. I gave her the word, but she was not satisfied and pointed to my eyes. I told her,

and she repeated the word, making it sound like "ice." She pointed
up to the sky, then to my eyes, then back to "my Ántonia."

In her ability to suggest a love that is permanent, life-enhancing, and in no
way possessive, Cather touches the farthest limit of her own strength as a
novelist. If one could choose a single passage from all her work, it would be
the Paterian epiphany or privileged moment in which Mrs. Forrester's image
returned to Niel as "a bright, impersonal memory." Pater ought to have lived
to have read this marvelous instance of the art he had celebrated and helped
to stimulate in Cather:

> Her eyes; when they laughed for a moment into one's own, seemed
> to provide a wild delight that he had not found in life. "I know
> where it is," they seemed to say, "I could show you!" He would
> like to call up the shade of the young Mrs. Forrester, as the witch
> of Endor called up Samuel's, and challenge it, demand the secret
> of that ardour; ask her whether she had really found some ever-
> blooming, ever-burning, ever-piercing joy, or whether it was all
> fine play-acting. Probably she had found no more than another;
> but she had always the power of suggesting things much lovelier
> than herself, as the perfume of a single flower may call up the whole
> sweetness of spring.

It is the perfection of Cather's difficult art, when that art was most balanced and paced, and Mrs. Forrester here is the emblem of that perfection.
Cather's fiction, at its frequent best, also suggests things much lovelier than
itself. The reader, demanding the secret of Cather's ardour, learns not to challenge what may be remarkably fine play-acting, since Cather's feigning sometimes does persuade him that really she had found some perpetual joy.

BLANCHE H. GELFANT

The Forgotten Reaping-Hook:
Sex in My Ántonia

Our persistent misreading of Willa Cather's *My Ántonia* rises from a belief that Jim Burden is a reliable narrator. Because we trust his unequivocal narrative manner, we see the novel as a splendid celebration of American frontier life. This is the view reiterated in a current critique of *My Ántonia*[1] and in a recent comprehensive study of Cather's work: "*My Ántonia* shows fertility of both the soil and human beings. Thus, in a profound sense *My Ántonia* is the most affirmative book Willa Cather ever wrote. Perhaps that is why it was her favorite."[2] Critics also elect it *their* favorite Cather novel: however, they regret its inconclusive structure, as did Cather when she declared it fragmented and unsatisfactory in form.[3] David Daiches's complaint of twenty years ago prevails: that the work is "flawed" by "irrelevant" episodes and material of "uncertain" meaning.[4] Both critical positions—that *My Ántonia* is a glorious celebration of American life and a defective work of art—must be reversed once we challenge Jim Burden's vision of the past. I believe we have reason to do so, particularly now, when we are making many reversals in our thinking. As soon as we question Jim's seemingly explicit statements, we see beyond them myriad confusions which can be resolved only by a totally new reading. This would impel us to reexamine Jim's testimony, to discover him a more disingenuous and self-deluded narrator than we supposed. Once we redefine his role, *My Ántonia* begins to resonate to new and rather shocking

American Literature, Volume 43 (1971): pp. 60–82. © 1971 Duke University Press.

meanings which implicate us all. We may lose our chief affirmative novel, only to find one far more exciting—complex, subtle, aberrant.

Jim Burden belongs to a remarkable gallery of characters for whom Cather consistently invalidates sex. Her priests, pioneers, and artists invest all energy elsewhere. Her idealistic young men die prematurely; her bachelors, children, and old folk remain "neutral" observers. Since she wrote within a prohibitive genteel tradition, this reluctance to portray sexuality is hardly surprising. What should intrigue us is the strange involuted nature of her avoidance. She masks sexual ambivalence by certainty of manner, and displays sexual disturbance, even the macabre, with peculiar insouciance. Though the tenor of her writing is normality, normal sex stands barred from her fictional world. Her characters avoid sexual union with significant and sometimes bizarre ingenuity, or achieve it only in dreams. Alexandra Bergson, the heroine of *O Pioneers!,* finds in recurrent reveries the strong transporting arms of a lover; and Jim Burden in *My Ántonia* allows a half-nude woman to smother him with kisses only in unguarded moments of fantasy. Their dreams suggest the typical solipsism of Cather's heroes, who yield to a lover when they are most solitary, most inverted, encaptured by their own imaginations. As Alexandra dispels such reveries by a brisk cold shower, their inferential meaning becomes almost comically clear. Whenever sex enters the real world (as for Emil and Marie in *O Pioneers!*),[5] it becomes destructive, leading almost axiomatically to death. No wonder, then, that Cather's heroes have a strong intuitive aversion to sex which they reveal furtively through enigmatic gestures. *In A Lost Lady,* when young Niel Herbert, who idealizes the Forrester's sexless marriage, discovers Mrs. Forrester's love affair, he vents his infantile jealousy and rage the only way he can—symbolically. While the lovers are on the phone, he takes his "big shears" and cuts the wires, ostensibly to prevent gossip, but also to sever a relationship he cannot abide. Ingenious in rationalizing their actions, Cather's heroes do not entirely conceal an underlying fear of physical love; and the connection between love and death, long undiscerned in Cather's work, can be seen as its inextricable motif. Even in her first novel, *Alexander's Bridge,* the hero's gratuitous death—generally thought to flaw the work—fulfills the inherent thematic demand to show physical passion as disastrous. Here, as in *O Pioneers!,* a later work, illicitness is merely a distracting irrelevance which helps conceal the fear of sexuality in all relationships. *O Pioneers!* reduces the interval between love and death until they almost coincide. At three o'clock, Emil races "like an arrow shot from the bow" to Marie; for the first time they make love; by evening, they are dead, murdered by the half-demented husband.

In *My Ántonia,* Jim Burden grows up with an intuitive fear of sex, never acknowledged, and in fact, denied: yet it is a determining force in his story. By deflecting attention from himself to Ántonia, of whom he can speak with utter assurance, he manages to conceal his muddied sexual attitudes. His narrative voice, reinforced by Cather's, emerges firm and certain; and it convinces. We tend to believe with Jim that his authoritative recitation of childhood memories validates the past and gives meaning to the present even though his mature years stream before him emptied of love, intimacy, and purpose. Memory transports him to richer and happier days spent with Ántonia, the young Bohemian girl who signifies *"the country, the conditions, the whole adventure of . . . childhood."*[6] Because a changing landscape brilliantly illumines his childhood—with copperred prairies transformed to rich wheatfields and corn—his personal story seems to epitomize this larger historical drama. Jim uses the coincidence of his life-span with a historical era to imply that as the country changed and grew, so did he, and moreover, as his memoirs contained historical facts, so did they hold the truth about himself. Critics support Jim's bid for validity, pointing out that *"My Ántonia* exemplifies superbly [Frederick Jackson] Turner's concept of the recurring cultural evolution on the frontier."[7]

Jim's account of both history and himself seems to me disingenuous, indeed, suspect; yet it is for this very reason highly pertinent to an understanding of our own uses of the past. In the introduction, Jim presents his memoirs as a spontaneous expression—unselected, unarranged, and uncontrolled by ulterior purpose: *"From time to time I've been writing down what I remember . . . about Ántonia. . . . I didn't take time to arrange it; I simply wrote down pretty much all that her name recalls to me. I suppose it hasn't any form, . . . any title, either"* (p. 2). Obviously, Jim's memory cannot be as autonomous or disinterested as he implies. His plastic powers reshape his experience, selecting and omitting in response to unconscious desires and the will. Ultimately, Jim forgets as much as he remembers, as his mind sifts through the years to retrieve what he most needs—a purified past in which he can find safety from sex and disorder. Of "a romantic disposition," Jim substitutes wish for reality in celebrating the past. His flight from sexuality parallels a flight from historical truth, and in this respect, he becomes an emblematic American figure, like Jay Gatsby and Clyde Griffiths. Jim romanticizes the American past as Gatsby romanticizes love, and Clyde money. Affirming the common, the prototypical, American dream of fruition, all three, ironically, are devastated—Gatsby and Clyde die violently, while Jim succumbs to immobilizing regressive needs. Their relationship to the dream they could not survive must strike us oddly, for we have reversed their situation by surviving to see the dream shattered and the Golden Age of American history impugned. Out of the past that Jim idealized comes our present stunning disorder, though Jim would deny such continuity, as Cather did. Her much-quoted statement that the world *broke* in 1922 reveals historical blindness mistaken for acuity.[8] She denied that "the beautiful past" transmitted the crassness, disorder, and violence which "ruined" the present for her and drove her to hermitic withdrawal. She blamed villainous men, such as Ivy Peters in *A Lost Lady*, for the decline of a heroic age. Like her, Jim Burden warded off broad historical insight. His mythopoeic memory patterned the past into an affecting creation story, with Ántonia a central fertility figure, "a rich mine of life, like the founders of early races." Jim, however, stalks through his myth a wasteland figure who finds in the present nothing to compensate him for the loss of the past, and in the outer world nothing to violate the inner sanctum of memory. "Some memories are realities, are better than anything that can ever happen to one again"—Jim's nostalgic conclusion rationalizes his inanition. He remains finally fixated on the past, returning to the vast and ineffaceable image that dominates his memoirs—the Nebraska prairie yielding to railroad and plough. Since this is an impersonal image of the growth of a nation, and yet it seems so personally crucial to Jim, we must be alerted to the special significance it holds for him. At the very beginning of the novel, we are told that Jim *"loves with a personal passion the great country through which his railway runs"* (p. 2). The symbolism of the railroad penetrating virgin fields is such an embarrassingly obvious example of emotional displacement, it seems extraordinary that it has been so long unnoted. Like Captain Forrester, the unsexed husband of *A Lost Lady*, Jim sublimates by traversing the country, laying it open by rail; and because he sees the land grow fertile and the people prosper, he believes his story to be a celebration.

But neither history's purely material achievement, nor Cather's aesthetic conquest of childhood material, can rightfully give Jim Burden personal cause to celebrate. Retrospection, a superbly creative act for Cather, becomes for Jim a negative gesture. His recapitulation of the past seems to me a final surrender to sexual fears. He was afraid of growing up, afraid of women, afraid of the nexus of love and death. He could love only that which time had made safe and irrefragable—his memories. They revolve not, as he says, about the image of Ántonia, but about himself as a child. When he finds love, it seems to him the safest kind—the narcissistic love of the man for himself as a boy. Such love is not unique to Jim Burden. It obsesses many Cather protagonists from early novels to late: from Bartley Alexander in *Alexander's Bridge* to Godfrey St. Peter in *The Professor's House*. Narcissism focuses Cather's vision of life. She valued above all the inviolability of the self. Romantically, she saw in the child the original and real self; and in her novels she created adult characters who sought a seemingly impossible reunion with this authentic being—who were willing to die if only they could reach somehow back to childhood. Regression becomes thus an equivocal moral victory in which the self defies change and establishes its immutability. But regression is also a sign of defeat. *My Ántonia*, superficially so simple and clear a novel, resonates to themes of ultimate importance—the theme of identity, of its relationship to time, and of its contest with death. All these are subsumed in the more immediate issue of physical love. Reinterpreted along these lines, *My Ántonia* emerges as a brilliantly tortuous novel, its statements working contrapuntally against its meanings, its apparently random vignettes falling together to form a pattern of sexual aversion into which each detail fits—even the reaping-hook of Jim's dream:

> One dream I dreamed a great many times, and it was always the same.
> I was in a harvest-field full of shocks, and I was lying against one of
> them. Lena Lingard came across the stubble barefoot, in a short skirt,
> with a curved reaping-hook in her hand, and she was flushed like the
> dawn, with a kind of luminous rosiness all about her. She sat down
> beside me, turned to me with a soft sigh and said, "Now they are all
> gone, and I can kiss you as much as I like." (p. 147)

In Jim's dream of Lena, desire and fear clearly contend with one another. With the dreamer's infallibility, Jim contains his ambivalence in a surreal image of Aurora and the Grim Reaper as one. This collaged figure of Lena advances against an ordinary but ominous landscape. Background and forefigure first contrast and then coalesce in meaning. Lena's voluptuous aspects—her luminous glow of sexual arousal, her flesh bared by a short skirt, her soft sighs and kisses—are displayed against shocks and stubbles, a barren field when the reaping-hook has done its work. This landscape of harvest and desolation is not unfamiliar; nor is the apparitional woman who moves across it, sighing and making soft moan; nor the supine young man whom she kisses and transports. It is the archetypal landscape of ballad, myth, and drama, setting for *la belle dame sans merci* who enchants and satisfies, but then lulls and destroys. She comes, as Lena does, when the male is alone and unguarded. "Now they are all gone," Lena whispers, meaning Ántonia, his threshold guardian. Keeping parental watch, Ántonia limits Jim's boundaries ("You know you ain't right to kiss me like that") and attempts to bar him from the dark unexplored country beyond boyhood with threats ("If I see you hanging around with Lena much, I'll go tell your grandmother"). Jim has the insight to reply, "You'll always treat me like a kid"; but his dream of past childhood games with Ántonia suggests that the prospect of perpetual play attracts him, offering release from anxiety. Already in search of safety, he looks to childhood, for adolescence confronts him with the possibility of danger in women. Characteristically, his statement that he will prove himself unafraid belies the drift of his unconscious feelings. His dream of Lena and the reaping-hook depicts his ambivalence toward the cycle of growth, maturation, and death. The wheat ripens to be cut; maturity invites death.

Though Jim has declared his dream "always the same," it changes significantly. When it recurs in Lincoln, where he goes as a university student, it has been censored and condensed, and transmuted from reverie to remembrance:

As I sat down to my book at last, my old dream about Lena coming
across the harvest-field in her short skirt seemed to me like the
memory of an actual experience. It floated before me on the page
like a picture, and underneath it stood the mournful line: *"Optima
dies . . . prima fugit."* (p. 175)

Now his memory can deal with fantasy as with experience: convert it to
an image, frame it, and restore it to him retouched and redeemed. Revised,
the dream loses its frightening details. Memory retains the harvest-field but
represses the shocks and stubbles; keeps Lena in her short skirt, but replaces the sexual ambience of the vision. Originally inspired by the insinuative
"hired girls," the dream recurs under the tranquilizing spell of Gaston Cleric,
Jim's poetry teacher. As his name implies, Cleric's function is to guide Jim to
renunciation of Lena, to offer instead the example of desire sublimated to art.
Voluptuous excitement yields to a pensive mood, and poetry rather than passion engages Jim: "It came over me, as it had never done before, the relation
between girls like those [Lena and "the hired girls] and the poetry of Virgil.
If there were no girls like them in the world, there would be no poetry" (p.
175). In his study, among his books, Lena's image floats before him on a page
of the *Georgics,* transferred from a landscape of death to Virgil's bucolic countryside; and it arouses not sensual desire but a safer and more characteristic
mood: nostalgia—"melancholy reflection" upon the past. The reaping-hook is
forgotten. Lena changes from the rosy goddess of dawn to an apparition of
evening, of the dimly lit study and the darkened theater, where she glows with
"lamplight" rather than sexual luminosity.

This preliminary sublimation makes it possible for Jim to have an affair
with Lena. It is brief and peculiar, somehow appropriating from the theaters
they frequent an unreal quality, the aspect of play. In contrast to the tragic
stage-lovers who feel exquisitely, intone passionately, and love enduringly,
they seem mere unengaged children, thrilled by make-believe people more
than each other. "It all wrung my heart"; "there wasn't a nerve left in my body
that hadn't been twisted"—Jim's histrionic (and rather feminine) outbursts
pertain not to Lena but to *Marguerite Gauthier* as impersonated by "an infirm
old actress." Camille's "dazzling loveliness," her gaiety and glitter—though
illusory—impassion him far more than the real woman's sensuality. With
Lena, he creates a mock-drama, casting himself in the stock role of callow
lover pitted against Lena's older suitors. In this innocuous triangle, he "drifts"
and "plays"—and play, like struggle, emerges as his memoirs' motif. Far from
being random, his play is directed toward the avoidance of future responsibil-
ities. He tests the role of lover in the security of a make-believe world where
his mistress is gentle and undemanding, his adversaries ineffectual, and his
guardian spirit, Cleric, supportive. Cleric wants him to stop "playing with this

handsome Norwegian," and so he does, leaving Lena forever and without regret. Though the separation of the stage-lovers Armand and Camille wracks them—"Lena wept unceasingly"—their own parting is vapid. Jim leaves to follow Cleric to Boston, there to study, and pursue a career. His period of enchantment has not proved one of permanent thrall and does not leave him, like Keats's knight, haggard and woebegone.

Nevertheless, the interim in Lincoln has serious consequences, for Jim's trial run into manhood remains abortive. He has not been able to bypass his circular "road of Destiny," that "predetermined" route which carries him back finally to Ántonia and childhood. With Lena, Jim seems divertible, at a crossroad. His alternatives are defined in two symbolic titles symbolically apposed: "Lena Lingard" and "Cuzak's Boys." Lena, the archetypal Woman, beckons him to full sexuality. Ántonia, the eternal Mother, lures him back through her children, Cuzak's boys, to perennial childhood.

If Jim cannot avoid his destiny, neither can he escape the "tyrannical" social code of his small town, Black Hawk, which permits its young men to play with "hired girls" but not to marry them. The pusillanimous "clerks and bookkeepers" of Black Hawk dance with the country girls, follow them forlornly, kiss them behind bushes—and run. "Respect for respectability" shunts them into loveless marriages with women of money or "refinement" who are sexless and safe. "Physically a race apart," the country girls are charged with sensuality, some of them considered "dangerous as high explosives." Through an empty conformist marriage, Jim avoids danger. He takes a woman who is independent and masculine, like Ántonia, who cannot threaten him as Lena does by her sheer femininity. Though Lena may be "the most beautiful, the most *innocently* sensuous of all the women in Willa Cather's works,"[9] Jim is locked into his fantasy of the reaping-hook.

Jim's glorification of Lena as the timeless muse of poetry and the unattainable heroine of romance requires a closer look. For while he seems to exalt her, typically, he works at cross-purposes to demean her—in his own involuted way. He sets her etherealized image afloat on pages of poetry that deal with the breeding of cattle (his memoirs quote only the last line here):

So, while the herd rejoices in its youth
Release the males and breed the cattle early,
Supply one generation from another.
For mortal kind, the best day passes first.
(*Georgics*, Book III)

As usual, Jim remembers selectively—only the last phrase, the novel's epigraph—while he deletes what must have seemed devastating counsel: "Release the males." Moreover, the *Georgics* has only factitious relevance to Lena (though I might point out that it undoubtedly inspired Cather by suggesting the use of regional material and the seasonal patterning of Book I of *My Ántonia*). If anything, the allusion is downright inappropriate, for Virgil's poem extols pastoral life, but Lena, tired of drudgery, wants to get away from the farm. Interested in fashion and sensuous pleasure, settling finally in San Francisco, she is not really the muse for Virgil.

Jim's allusion does have a subtle strategic value: by relegating Lena to the ideal but unreachable world of art, it assures their separation. Mismatched lovers because of social class, they remain irreconcilable as dream and reality. A real person, Jim must stop drifting and study; he can leave the woman while possessing Lena the dream in remembered reverie. Though motivated by fear and expediency (as much as Sylvester Lovett, Lena's fearful suitor in Black Hawk), he romanticizes his actions, eluding the possibility of painful self-confrontation. He veils his escape by identifying secretly with the hero Armand Duval, also a mismatched lover, blameless, whose fervid affair was doomed from the first. But as a lover, Jim belongs as much to comedy as to melodrama. His affair fits perfectly within the conventions of the comedy of manners: the sitting-room, Lena's "stiff little parlour"; the serving of tea; the idle talk of clothes and fashion; the nuisance pet dog Prince; the minor crises when the fatuous elder lovers intrude—the triviality. Engaged with Lena in this playacting, Jim has much at stake—nothing less than his sexuality. Through the more serious drama of a first affair, he creates his existential self: an adult male who fears a sexual woman. Through his trivial small-town comedy of manners, he keeps from introspection. He is drifting but busy, too much preoccupied with dinner parties and theater dates to catch the meaning of his drift. His mock romance recalls the words he had used years earlier to describe a childhood "mock adventure": "the game was fixed." The odds are against his growing up, and the two mock episodes fall together as *pseudo-*initiations which fail to make him a man.

Jim's mock adventure occurs years back as he and Ántonia explore a series of interconnected burrows in prairie-dog-town. Crouched with his back to Ántonia, he hears her unintelligible screams in a foreign tongue. He whirls to discover a huge rattler coiling and erecting to spring. "Of disgusting vitality," the snake induces fear and nausea: "His abominable muscularity, his loathsome, fluid motion, somehow made me sick" (p. 32). Jim strikes violently and with revulsion, recognizing even then an irrational hatred stronger than the impulse for protection. The episode—typically ignored or misunderstood—combines elements of myth and dream. As a dragon-slaying, it conforms to the monomyth of initiation. It has a characteristic "call to adventure" (Ántonia's impulsive suggestion); a magic weapon (Peter's spade); a descent into a land of unearthly creatures (prairie-dog-town); the perilous battle (killing the snake); the protective tutelary spirit (Ántonia); and the passage through the rites to manhood ("You now a big mans"). As a test of courage, Jim's ordeal seems authentic, and critical opinion declares it so: "Jim Burden discovers his own hidden courage and becomes a man in the snake-killing incident."[10] But even Jim realizes that his initiation, like his romance later, is specious, and his accolade unearned: "it was a mock adventure; the game . . . fixed . . . by chance, as . . . for many a dragon-slayer."

As Jim accepts Ántonia's praise, his tone becomes wry and ironic, communicating a unique awareness of the duplicity in which he is involved. Ántonia's effect upon Jim seems to me here invidious because her admiration of his manhood helps undermine it. Pronouncing him a man, she keeps him a boy. False to her role as tutelary spirit, she betrays him from first to last. She leads him into danger, fails to warn him properly, and finally, by validating the contest, closes off the road to authentic initiation and maturity.

Jim's exploration "below the surface" of prairie-dog-town strikes me as a significant mimetic act, a burrowing into his unconscious. Who is he "below the surface"? In which direction do his buried impulses lead? He acts out his quest for self-knowledge symbolically: if he could dig deep enough he would find a way through this labyrinth and learn the course of its hidden channels—whether "they ran straight down, or were horizontal . . . whether they had underground connections." Projecting upon the physical scene his adolescent concern with self, he speaks an analytic and rational language— but the experience turns into nightmare. Archetypal symbol of "the ancient, eldest Evil," the snake forces him to confront deeply repressed images, to acknowledge for the only time the effect of "horrible unconscious memories."

The sexual connotations of the snake incident are implicit. Later in Black Hawk they become overt through another misadventure—Wick Cutter's attempted rape of Jim, whom he mistakes for Ántonia. This time the sexual attack is literal. Wick Cutter, an old lecher, returns in the middle of the night to assault Ántonia, but meanwhile, persuaded by Ántonia's suspicions, Jim has taken her place in bed. He becomes an innocent victim of Cutter's lust and fury at deception. Threatened by unleashed male sex—the ultimate threat— he fights with primordial violence, though again sickened with disgust. Vile as the Cutter incident is—and it is also highly farcical—Jim's nausea seems an overreaction, intensified by his shrill rhetoric and unmodulated tone. Unlike the snake episode, this encounter offers no rewards. It simply reduces him to "a battered object," his body pummeled, his face swollen. His only recognition will be the laughter of the lubricious "old men at the drugstore." Again Ántonia has lured him into danger and exposed him to assault. Again he is furious: "I felt that I never wanted to see her again. I hated her almost as much as I hated Cutter. She had let me in for all this disgustingness" (p. 162). Through Wick Cutter, the sexual urge seems depraved, and more damning, ludicrous.

No male in the novel rescues sex from indignity or gives it even the interest of sheer malevolence (as, for example, Ivy Peters does in *A Lost Lady*).

Also unexempt from the dangers of sex, Ántonia is seduced, exploited, and left with an illegitimate child. When finally she marries, she takes not a lover but a friend. To his relief, Jim finds husband and wife "on terms of easy friendliness, touched with humour" (p. 231). Marriage as an extension of friendship is Cather's recurrent formula, defined clearly, if idiosyncratically, by Alexandra in *O Pioneers!*: "I think when friends marry, they are safe." Turning words to action, Alexandra marries her childhood friend, as does Cecile in *Shadows on the Rock*—an older man whose passion has been expended on another woman. At best, marriage has dubious value in Cather's fiction. It succeeds when it seems least like marriage, when it remains sexless, or when sex is only instrumental to procreation. Jim accepts Ántonia's marriage for its "special mission" to bring forth children.

Why doesn't he take on this mission? He celebrates the myth of creation but fails to participate. The question has been raised bluntly by critics (though left unanswered): "Why had not Jim and Ántonia loved and married?"[11] When Ántonia, abandoned by Donovan, needs Jim most, he passionately avers, "You really are a part of me": "I'd have liked to have you for a sweetheart, or a wife, or my mother or my sister—anything that a woman can be to a man" (p. 208). Thereupon he leaves—not to return for twenty years. His failure to seize the palpable moment seems to one critic responsible for the emotional vacuum of Jim's life: "At the very center of his relation with Ántonia there is an emptiness where the strongest emotion might have been expected to gather."[12] But love for a woman is not Jim's "strongest emotion," cannot mitigate fear, nostalgia, or even simple snobbery. Nothing in Jim's past prepares him for love or marriage, and he remains in effect a pseudo-bachelor (just as he is a pseudolover), free to design a future with Ántonia's family that excludes his wife. In his childhood, his models for manhood are simple regressive characters, all bachelors, or patently unhappy married men struggling, like Mr. Shimerda, Chris Lingard, and Ole the Swede, for and against their families. Later in Black Hawk, the family men seem merely vapid, and prophetically suburban, pushing baby-carriages, sprinkling lawns, paying bills, and driving about on Sundays (p. 105). Mr. Harling, Ántonia's employer in Black Hawk, seems different; yet he only further confuses Jim's already confused sense of sexual roles, for he indulges his son while he treats his daughter as a man, his business partner. With Ántonia, his "hired girl," Mr. Harling is repressive, a kind of superego, objecting to her adolescent contacts with men—the dances at Vannis's tent, the evening walks, the kisses and scuffles on the back porch. "I want to have my fling, like the other girls," Ántonia argues, but Harling insists she quit the dances or his house. Ántonia leaves, goes to the notorious Cutter, and then to the seductive arms of

Larry Donovan—with consequences that are highly instructive to Jim, that can only reinforce his inchoate fears. Either repression of sex or disaster: Jim sees these alternatives polarized in Black Hawk, and between them he cannot resolve his ambivalence. Though he would like Ántonia to become a woman, he wants her also to remain asexual.

By switching her sexual roles, Ántonia only adds to his confusion. As "hired girl" in Black Hawk and later as Cuzak's wife, she cooks, bakes, sews, and rears children. Intermittently, she shows off her strength and endurance in the fields, competing with men. Even her name changes gender—no adventitious matter, I believe; it has its masculine variant, Tony, as Willa Cather had hers, Willie. Cather's prototype for Ántonia, Annie Pavelka, was a simple Bohemian girl; though their experiences are similar, Ántonia Shimerda is Cather's creation—an ultimately strange bisexual. She shares Cather's pride in masculinity and projects both her and Jim's ambivalent sexual attitudes. Cather recalled that "much of what I knew about Annie came from the talks I had with young men. She had a fascination for them."[13] In the novel, however, Lena fascinates men while Ántonia toils alongside them. "I can work like mans now," she announces when she is only fifteen. In the fields, says Jim, "she kept her sleeves rolled up all day, and her arms and throat were burned as brown as a sailor's. Her neck came up strongly out of her shoulders, like the bole of a tree out of the turf. One sees that draught-horse neck among the peasant women in all old countries" (p. 80). Sailor, tree, draught-horse, peasant—hardly seductive comparisons, hardly conducive to fascination. Ántonia's illegitimate pregnancy brutalizes her even more than heavy farm-work. Her punishment for sexual involvement—and for the breezy pleasures of courtship—is thoroughgoing masculinization. Wearing "a man's long overcoat and boots, and a man's felt hat," she does "the work of a man on the farm," plows, herds cattle. Years later, as Cuzak's wife, her "inner glow" must compensate for the loss of her youthful beauty, the loss, even, of her teeth. Jim describes her finally as "a stalwart, brown woman, flat-chested, her curly brown hair a little grizzled"—his every word denuding her of sensual appeal.

This is not to deny that at one time Jim found Ántonia physically desirable. He hints that in Black Hawk he had kissed her in a more than friendly way—and had been rebuffed. But he is hardly heartbroken at their impasse, for his real and enduring love for her is based not on desire but on nostalgia. Childhood memories bind him more profoundly than passion, especially memories of Mr. Shimerda. In their picnic reunion before Jim departs for Lincoln, Ántonia recounts her father's story of transgression, exile, and death. Her miniature tale devolves upon the essential theme of destructive sex. As a young man, her father succumbs to desire for the family's servant girl, makes her pregnant, marries her against his parents' wishes, and becomes thereby an outcast. His death on the distant prairie traces back to an initial sexual act which triggers inexorable consequences. It strips him of all he values: his happy irresponsible bachelor life with the trombone-player he "loves"; his family home in beautiful Bohemia; his vocation as violinist when he takes to homesteading in Nebraska; and his joy in life itself. For a while, a few desultory pleasures could rouse him from apathy and despair. But in the end, he finds the pattern of his adult life, as many Cather characters do, unbearable, and he longs for escape. Though Ántonia implies that her poppa's mistake was to marry, especially outside his social class (as Jim is too prudent to do), the marriage comes about through his initial sexual involvement. Once Mr. Shimerda acts upon sexual impulse, he is committed to a woman who alienates him from himself; and it is loss of self, rather than the surmountable hardships of pioneer life, which induces his despair. Suicide is his final capitulation to destructive forces he could have escaped only by first abnegating sex.

Though this interpretation may sound extreme—that the real danger to man is woman, that his protection lies in avoiding or eliminating her—it seems to me the essence of the most macabre and otherwise unaccountable episode in *My Ántonia*. I refer to that grisly acting out of male aversion, the flashback of Russian Pavel feeding the bride to the wolves. I cannot imagine a more graphic representation of underlying sentiments than we find here. Like most of the episodes in Jim's memoirs, this begins innocently, with the young bride drawing Peter, Pavel, and other guests to a nearby village for her wedding. But the happy evening culminates in horror; for the wolves are bad that year, starving, and when the guests head for home they find themselves rapidly pursued through a landscape of terror. Events take on the surreality of nightmare as black droves run like streaks of shadows after the panicking horses, as sledges overturn in the snow, and mauled and dying wedding guests shriek. Fast as Pavel drives his team, it cannot outrun the relentless "back ground-shadows," images of death. Pavel's murderous strategy to save himself and Peter is almost too inhuman to imagine: to allay the wolves and lighten his load, he wrests the bride from the struggling groom, and throws her, living bait, to the wolves. Only then does his sledge arrive in safety at his village. The tale holds the paradigm for Mr. Shimerda's fate—driven from home because of a woman, struggling for survival against a brutal winter landscape, pursued by regret and despair to death. The great narrative distance at which this episode is kept from Jim seems to me to signify its explosiveness, the need to handle with care. It is told to Jim by Ántonia, who overhears Peter telling it to Mr. Shimerda. Though the vignette emerges from this distance—and through Jim's obscuring nostalgia—its gruesome meaning focuses the apparently disjunct parts of the novel, and I find it inconceivable that critics consider it "irrelevant."[14] The art of *My Ántonia* lies in the subtle and inevitable relevance of its details, even the most trivial, like the picture Jim chooses to decorate a Christmas book for Ántonia's little sister: "I took

'Napoleon Announcing the Divorce to Josephine' for my frontispiece" (p. 55). In one way or another, the woman must *go*.

To say that Jim Burden expresses castration fears would provide a facile conclusion: and indeed his memoirs multiply images of sharp instruments and painful cutting. The curved reaping-hook in Lena Lingard's hands centralizes an overall pattern that includes Peter's clasp-knife with which he cuts all his melons; Crazy Mary's corn-knife (she "made us feel how sharp her blade was, showing us very graphically just what she meant to do to Lena"); the suicidal tramp "cut to pieces" in the threshing machine; and wicked Wick Cutter's sexual assault. When Lena, the essence of sex, appears suddenly in Black Hawk, she seems to precipitate a series of violent recollections. First Jim remembers Crazy Mary's pursuit of Lena with her sharpened corn-knife. Then Ántonia recalls the story of the crazy tramp in details which seem to me unconsciously reverberating Jim's dream. Like Jim, Ántonia is relaxed and leaning against a strawstack; similarly, she sees a figure approach "across the stubble"—significantly, his first words portend death. Offering to "cut bands," within minutes he throws himself into the threshing machine and is "cut to pieces." In his pockets the threshers find only "an old penknife" and the "wish-bone of a chicken." Jim follows this anecdote with a vignette of Blind d'Arnault, a black musician who, as we shall see, represents emasculation; Jim tells how children used to tease the little blind boy and try "to get his chicken-bone away." Such details, I think, should not be considered fortuitous or irrelevant; and critics who have persisted in overlooking them should note that they are stubbornly there, and in patterned sequence.

I do not wish to make a case history of Jim Burden or a psychological document of *My Ántonia*, but to uncover an elusive underlying theme—one that informs the fragmentary parts of the novel and illuminates the obsession controlling Cather's art. For like most novelists, Cather writes out of an obsessive concern to which her art gives various and varied expression. In *My Ántonia*, her consummate work, that obsession has its most private as well as its most widely shared meanings. At the same time that the novel is highly autobiographical, it is representatively American in its material, mood, and unconscious uses of the past. In it, as in other novels, we can discover that Cather's obsession had to do with the assertion of self. This is the preoccupation of her protagonists who in their various ways seek to assert their identity, in defiance, if necessary, of others, of convention, of nature, of life itself. Biographers imply that Cather's life represented a consistent pursuit of autonomy, essential, she believed, to her survival as an artist. Undoubtedly, she was right; had she given herself to marriage and children, assuming she could, she might have sacrificed her chance to write. Clearly, she identified writing with masculinity, though which of the two constituted her fundamental drive is a matter of psychological dynamics we can never really decide. Like Ántonia, she displayed strong masculine traits, though she loved also feminine frilleries and the art of cuisine. All accounts of her refer to her "masculine personality"—her mannish dress, her deep voice, her energetic stride; and even as a child she affected boyish clothes and cropped hair. Too numerous to document, such references are a running motif throughout the accounts of Mildred Bennett, Elizabeth Sergeant, and E. K. Brown. Their significance is complex and perhaps inescapable, but whatever else they mean, they surely demonstrate Cather's self-assertion: she would create her own role in life, and if being a woman meant sacrificing her art, then she would lead a private and inviolate life in defiance of convention.

Her image of inviolability was the *child*. She sought quaintly, perhaps foolishly, to refract this image through her person when she wore a schoolgirl costume. The Steichen photograph of her in middy blouse is a familiar frontispiece to volumes of her work; and she has been described as characteristically "at the typewriter, dressed in a childlike costume, a middy blouse with navy bands and tie and a duck skirt."[15] In life, she tried to hold on to childhood through dress; in art, through a recurrent cycle of childhood, maturity, and childhood again: the return effected usually through memory. Sometimes the regressive pattern signalized a longing for death, as in *The Professor's House* and *Death Comes for the Archbishop;* always it revealed a quest for reunion with an original authentic self. In *My Ántonia*, the prologue introduces Ántonia and the motif of childhood simultaneously, for her name is linked with *"the country, the conditions, the whole adventure of . . . childhood."* The memoirs proper open with the children's journey into pristine country where men are childlike or project into life characters of the child's imagination: like Jake who "might have stepped out of the pages of 'Jesse James.'" The years of maturity comprise merely an interim period—and in fact, are hardly dealt with. For Jim, as for Cather, the real meaning of time is cyclical, its purpose to effect a return to the beginning. Once Jim finds again "the first road" he traveled as a wondering child, his story ends. Hardly discernible, this road returns him to Ántonia, and through her, to his real goal, the enduring though elusive image of his original self which Cather represents by his childhood shadow. Walking to Ántonia's house with her boys—feeling himself almost a boy again—Jim merges with his shadow, the visible elongation of self. At last, his narcissistic dream comes to fulfillment: "It seemed, after all, so natural to be walking along a barbed-wire fence beside the sunset, toward a red pond, and to see my shadow moving along at my right, over the close-cropped grass" (p. 224). Just as the magnified shadow of plow against sky—a blazing key image—projects his romantic notion of the West, so "two long shadows [that] flitted before or followed after" symbolize his ideal of perennial children running through, imaged against, and made one with the prairie grass.

Jim's return "home" has him planning a future with Cuzak's boys that will recapitulate the past: once more he will sleep in haylofts, hunt "up the Niobrara," and travel the "Bad Lands." Play reenters as his serious concern, not the sexual play of imminent manhood, but regressive child's play. In a remarkable statement, Jim says: "There were enough Cuzaks to play with for a long while yet. Even after the boys grew up, there would always be Cuzak himself!" (p. 239). A current article on *My Ántonia* misreads this conclusion: "[though] Jim feels like a boy again . . . he does not *wish* that he were a boy again. . . . He has no more need to cling to the past, for the past has been transfigured like the autumn prairie of old."[16] Such reasoning falls in naively with Jim's self-deception, that the transformation of the land to country somehow validates his personal life. Jim's need to reenter childhood never relents, becomes even more urgent as he feels adult life vacuous. The years have not enriched him, except with a wealth of memories—"images in the mind that did not fade—that grew stronger with time." Most precious in his treasury of remembered images is that of a boy of ten crossing the prairie under "the complete dome of heaven" and finding sublimity in the union of self with earth and sky. An unforgettable consummation, never matched by physical union, he seeks to recreate it through memory. Jim's ineffable desire for a child more alive to him than his immediate being vibrates to a pathetic sense of loss. I believe that we may find this irretrievable boy in a photograph of young *Willie Cather,* another child who took life from imagination and desire.[17]

In a later novel, *The Professor's House,*[18] Cather rationalizes her cathexis on childhood through the protagonist's musings, at which we might glance briefly. Toward the end of his life, Professor Godfrey St. Peter discovers he has two identities: that of his "original" self, the child; and of his "secondary" self, the man in love. To fulfill himself, "the lover" creates a meretricious "design" of marriage, children, and career, now, after thirty years, suddenly meaningless. The Professor's cyclic return to his real and original self begins with solitary retrospection. All he wants is to "be alone"—to repossess himself. For, having yielded through love to another, he has lost "the person he was in the beginning." Now before he dies, he longs for his original image as a child, an image that returns to him in moments of "vivid consciousness" or of remembrance. Looking back, the Professor sees the only escape from a false secondary life to be through premature death: death of the sexual man before he realizes his sexuality and becomes involved in the relationships it demands. This is the happy fate of his student Tom Outland, who dies young, remaining inviolate, pure, and most important, self-possessed: "He seemed to know . . . he was solitary and must always be so; he had never married, never been a father. He was earth, and would return to earth" (p. 263).

This Romantic mystique of childhood illuminates the fear of sex in Cather's world. Sex unites one with another. Its ultimate threat is loss of self.

In Cather's construct, naively and of course falsely, the child is asexual, his love inverted, his identity thus intact. Only Ántonia manages to grow older and retain her original integrity. Like Tom Outland, her affinity is for the earth. She "belongs" to the farm, is one with the trees, the flowers, the rye and wheat she plants. Though she marries, Cuzak is only "the instrument of Ántonia's special mission." Through him she finds a self-fulfillment that excludes him. Through her, Jim hopes to be restored to himself.

The supreme value Jim and other Cather characters attribute to "old friendships" reflects a concern with self. Old friends know the child immanent in the man. Only they can have communion without causing self-estrangement, can marry "safely." They share "the precious, the incommunicable past"—as Jim says in his famous final words. But to keep the past so precious, they must romanticize it; and to validate childhood, they must let memory filter its experiences through the screen of nostalgia. Critics have wondered whether Jim Burden is finally the most suitable narrator for *My Ántonia*. I submit that Cather's choice is utterly strategic. For Jim, better than any other character, could control his memories, since only he knows of but does not experience the suffering and violence inherent in his story. And ultimately, he is not dealing with a story as such, but with residual "images in the mind." *My Ántonia* is a magnificent and warped testimony to the mind's image-making power, an implicit commentary on how that creative power serves the mind's need to ignore and deny whatever is reprehensible in whatever one loves. Cather's friend and biographer said of her, "There was so much she did not want to see and saw not."[19] We must say the same of Jim Burden, who held painful and violent aspects of early American life at safe distance, where finally he could not see them.

Jim's vignette of Blind d'Arnault, the black piano player who entertains at Black Hawk, is paradigmatic of his way of viewing the past. Its factual scaffolding (whether Cather's prototype was Blind Boone, Blind Tom, or a "composite of Negro musicians") seems to me less important than its tone. I find the vignette a work of unconscious irony as Jim paints d'Arnault's portrait but meanwhile delineates himself. The motif of blindness compounds the irony. D'Arnault's is physical, as though it is merely futile for him to see a world he cannot enter. Jim's is moral: an unawareness of his stereotyped, condescending, and ultimately invidious vision. Here, in his description of the black man, son of a slave, Jim's emblematic significance emerges as shamefully he speaks for himself, for Cather, and for most of us:

> [His voice] was the soft, amiable Negro voice, like those I remembered from early childhood, with the note of docile subservience in it. He had the Negro head, too; almost no head at all, nothing behind the ears but the folds of neck under close-cropped

wool. He would have been repulsive if his face had not been so kindly and happy. It was the happiest face I had seen since I left Virginia. (p. 122)

Soft, amiable, docile, subservient, kindly, happy—Jim's image, as usual, projects his wish-fulfillment; his diction suggests an unconscious assuagement of anxiety, also. His phrase of astounding insult and innocence—"almost no head at all"—assures him that the black man should not frighten, being an incomplete creature, possessed, as we would like to believe, of instinct and rhythm, but deprived of intellect. Jim's final hyperbole registers his fear of this alien black face saved from repulsiveness only by a toothy servile smile (it might someday lose). To attenuate his portrait of d'Arnault, Jim introduced innuendoes of sexual incompetence. He recognizes d'Arnault's sensuality but impugns it by his image of sublimation: "all the agreeable sensations possible to creatures of flesh and blood were heaped up on those black-and-white keys, and he [was] gloating over them and trickling them through his yellow fingers" (p. 126). Jim's genteel opening phrase connotes male sexuality, which he must sublimate, displace from the man to the music, reduce to a *trickle*. D'Arnault "looks like some glistening African god of pleasure, full of strong, savage blood"; but superimposed is our familiar Uncle Tom "all grinning," "bowing to everyone, docile and happy."

Similarly, consider Jim's entrancing image of the four Danish girls who stand all day in the laundry ironing the townspeople's clothes. How charming they are: flushed and happy; how fatherly the laundryman offering water—no swollen ankles; no boredom or rancor; no exploitation: a cameo image from "the beautiful past." Peter and Pavel, dreadful to any ordinary mind for their murderous deed, ostracized by everyone, now disease-ridden and mindless, are to Jim picturesque outcasts: Pavel spitting blood; Peter spitting seeds as he desperately eats all his melons after kissing his cow goodbye, the only creature for him to love. And Mr. Shimerda's suicide. Jim reconciles himself to the horror of the mutilated body frozen in its own blood by imagining the spirit released and homeward bound to its beloved Bohemia. Only the evocative beauty of Cather's language—and the inevitable validation as childhood memory—can romanticize this sordid death and the squalor in which it takes place. Violence is as much the essence of prairie life as the growth of the wheat and blossoming of the corn. Violence appears suddenly and inexplicably, like the suicidal tramp. But Jim gives violence a cameo quality. He has the insistent need—and the strategy—to turn away from the very material he presents. He can forget the reaping-hook and reshape his dream. And as the novel reveals him doing this, it reveals our common usage of the past as a romance and refuge from the present. *My Ántonia* engraves a view of the past which is at best partial; at worst, blind. But our present is continuous with the whole past, as it was, despite Jim Burden's attempt to deny this, and despite Cather's "sad little refrain": "Our present is ruined—but we had a beautiful past."[20] Beautiful to one who recreated it so; who desperately needed it so; who would deny the violence and the destructive attitudes toward race and sex immortalized in his very denial. We, however, have as desperate a need for clarity of vision as Jim had for nostalgia; and we must begin to look at *My Ántonia,* long considered a representatively American novel, not only for its beauty of art and for its affirmation of history, but also, and instructively, for its negations and evasions. Much as we would like to ignore them, for they bring painful confrontations, we must see what they would show us about ourselves—how we betray our past when we forget its most disquieting realities; how we begin to redeem it when we remember.

Notes

1. Terence Martin, "The Drama of Memory in *My Ántonia,*" *PMLA,* LXXXIV (March 1969): 304–311.

2. John H. Randall, III, *The Landscape and the Looking Glass: Willa Cather's Search for Value* (Boston, 1960), p. 149.
See Cather's remark, "The best thing I've ever done is *My Ántonia.* I feel I've made a contribution to American letters with that book," in Mildred Bennett, *The World of Willa Cather* (1951; reprinted, Lincoln, Neb., 1961), p. 203.

3. Bennett, p. 212. Cather is quoted as saying, "If you gave me a thousand dollars for every structural fault in *My Ántonia* you'd make me very rich."

4. David Daiches, *Willa Cather: A Critical Interpretation* (Ithaca, N.Y., 1951), pp. 43–61.

5. 1913; reprinted, Boston, 1941, p. 259. When Emil finally approaches Marie to make love, she seems asleep, then whispers, "I was dreaming this . . . don't take my dream away!" The mergence of the real lover into the dream reminds me here of Keats's *The Eve of St. Agnes*—"Into her dream he melted." Here, too, the realization of love means facing the cold wintery world from which Madeline had been protected by her castle and her fantasy.

6. 1918; reprinted, Boston, 1946, p. 2. All italics in quotations from *My Ántonia* are in the original, and all subsequent references are to this text. I use this edition not only because it is readily available but also because the introduction by Walter Havighurst and the suggestions for reading and discussion by Bertha Handlan represent clearly the way the novel has been widely used as validating the American past.

7. James E. Miller, "*My Ántonia:* A Frontier Drama of Time," *American Quarterly,* X (Winter 1958): 481.

8. See Bennett, p. 148. Cather is quoted as saying, "The world broke in two about 1920, and I belonged to the former half." The year 1922, is given in her preface (later deleted) to *Not under Forty* (renamed *Literary Encounters,* 1937).

9. E. K. Brown and Leon Edel, *Willa Cather: A Critical Biography* (New York, 1953), p. 203. Italics mine.

10. Miller, p. 482.

11. Elizabeth Shepley Sergeant, *Willa Cather: A Memoir* (1953; reprinted, Lincoln, Neb., 1963), p. 151.

12. Brown and Edel, p. 202.

13. Bennett, p. 47.

14. Daiches says, "It is a remarkable little inset story, but its relation to the novel as a whole is somewhat uncertain" (p. 46). However, Daiches finds so many episodes and details "uncertain," "dubious," "not wholly dominated," or "not fully integrated," it might be his reading is "flawed" rather than the novel.

15. Sergeant, p. 117.

16. Martin, p. 311.

17. See the "pictures from the Wm. Cather, M.D., period of Willa's life" in Bennett, especially the photograph of Cather as a child with "her first short haircut." Note Cather's vacillating taste in clothes from the clearly masculine to feminine.

It is significant that in various plays at school and at the university, Cather assumed male roles—so convincingly that spectators sometimes refused to believe the actor was not a boy. See Bennett, pp. 175–176, 179.

18. 1925; reprinted, Boston, 1938.

19. Sergeant, p. 46.

20. Ibid., p. 121.

DEBORAH G. LAMBERT

The Defeat of a Hero: Autonomy and Sexuality in My Ántonia

My Ántonia (1918), Willa Cather's celebration of the American frontier experience, is marred by many strange flaws and omissions. It is, for instance, difficult to determine who is the novel's central character. If it is Ántonia, as we might reasonably assume, why does she entirely disappear for two of the novel's five books? If, on the other hand, we decide that Jim Burden, the narrator, is the central figure, we find that the novel explores neither his consciousness nor his development. Similarly, although the narrator overtly claims that the relationship between Ántonia and Jim is the heart of the matter, their friendship actually fades soon after childhood: between these two characters there is only, as E. K. Brown said, "an emptiness where the strongest emotion might have been expected to gather."[1] Other inconsistencies and contradictions pervade the text—Cather's ambivalent treatment of Lena Lingard and Tiny Soderball, for example—and all are in some way related to sex roles and to sexuality.

This emphasis is not surprising: as a writer who was also a woman, Willa Cather faced the difficulties that confronted, and still do confront, accomplished and ambitious women. As a professional writer, Cather began, after a certain point in her career, to see the world and other women, including her own female characters, from a male point of view. Further, Cather was a lesbian who could not, or did not, acknowledge her homosexuality and who,

American Literature, Volume 53 (1982): pp.676–690. © 1982 Duke University Press.

in her fiction, transformed her emotional life and experiences into acceptable, heterosexual forms and guises. In her society it was difficult to be a woman and achieve professionally, and she could certainly not be a woman who loved women; she responded by denying, on the one hand, her womanhood and, on the other, her lesbianism. These painful denials are manifest in her fiction. After certain early work, in which she created strong and achieving women, like herself, she abandoned her female characters to the most conventional and traditional roles; analogously, she began to deny or distort the sexuality of her principal characters. *My Ántonia,* written at a time of great stress in her life, is a crucial and revealing work, for in it we can discern the consequences of Cather's dilemma as a lesbian writer in a patriarchal society.

I

Many, if not all, achieving women face the conflict between the traditional idea of what it is to be a woman and what it is to achieve. Achievement in most fields has been reserved for males; passivity—lack of assertiveness and energy, and consequent loss of possibility of achievement—has been traditionally female. When the unusual girl, or woman, rebels, and overcomes the limitations imposed on women, she suffers from the anxiety produced by conflict. Although such a woman is, and knows she is sexually female, in her professional life she is neither female nor male. Finding herself in no-woman's land, she avoids additional anxiety by not identifying herself professionally as a woman or with other women. Carolyn Heilbrun, who diagnoses and prescribes for a variety of women's dilemmas, writes: "Sensing within themselves, as girls, a longing for accomplishment, they have, at great cost, with great pain, become honorary men, adopting at the same time, the general male attitude towards women."[2]

From childhood, Willa Cather was determined to achieve and she perceived, correctly, that achieving in the world was a male prerogative. When she decided as a child to become a doctor, she also began to sign herself "William Cather, MD," or "Willie Cather, MD," and she pursued her vocation seriously, making house calls with two Red Cloud physicians, and on one occasion giving chloroform while one of them amputated a boy's leg. She also demonstrated her clear understanding of nineteenth-century sex roles and her preference for "male" activities when she entered in a friend's album two pages of "The Opinion, Tastes and Fancies of Wm. Cather, MD." In a list that might have been completed by Tom Sawyer, she cites "slicing toads" as a favorite summer occupation; doing fancy work as "real misery"; amputating limbs as "perfect happiness"; and dressing in skirts as "the greatest folly of the Nineteenth Century."[3] At college in Lincoln, her appearance in boyishly short hair and starched shirts rather than the customary frilly blouses—like her desire to play only male roles in college dramatic productions—continued to reflect her "male" ambition. James Woodress, Cather's biographer, speaks of a "strong masculine element" in her personality, a phrase that may obscure what she saw clearly from childhood: that womanhood prohibited the achievement she passionately sought.[4]

After some measure of professional success, Cather began to identify with her male professional peers, rather than with women. Her review of Kate Chopin's novel *The Awakening* (1899) is a poignant example of the troubling consequences of this identification. First, Cather describes Edna Pontellier's struggle towards identity as "trite and sordid" and then, comparing Edna to Emma Bovary, adds contemptuously that Edna and Emma "belong to a class, not large, but forever clamoring in our ears, that demands more out of life than God put into it." In a final irony, Cather writes of Chopin that "an author's choice of themes is frequently as inexplicable as his choice of a wife." Like Flaubert and other male authors with whom she identifies, Cather fails to understand, let alone view sympathetically, the anguish that Chopin brilliantly portrays in Edna's life and death.[5]

Nevertheless, in two novels written before *My Ántonia,* she accomplished what few women authors have: the creation of strong, even heroic, women as protagonists. Cather succeeded in this because she could imagine women achieving identity and defining their own purposes. The woman author, whose struggle toward selfhood and achievement is marked by painful conflict, rarely reproduces her struggle in fiction, perhaps finding its recreation too anxiety-producing, or perhaps simply not being able to imagine the forms that a woman's initiation might take. George Eliot and Edith Wharton, to mention only two familiar examples, never created women characters who possess their own intelligence, ambition, or autonomy. Characteristically, women authors transpose their own strivings to their male characters and portray women in conventional roles. (In this case, the roles ascribed to women in fiction are the same as those ascribed to them in society.) The occasional male author—E. M. Forster, James, and Hawthorne are examples—will create an independent, even heroic, female character, perhaps because male progress toward identity, demanded and supported by society, is generally a less anxious process.

Alexandra Bergson in *O Pioneers!* (1913) and Thea Kronberg in *The Song of the Lark* (1915) are female heroes, women not primarily defined by relationship to men, or children, but by commitment to their own destinies and to their own sense of themselves. Alexandra inherits her father's farm lands and grandfather's intelligence: although her father has two grown sons, he chooses Alexandra to continue his work, because she is the one best-suited by nature to do so. Developing Nebraska farmland becomes Alexandra's mission, and she devotes herself to it unstintingly. She postpones marriage until she is nearly forty years old, and then marries Carl, the gentle and financially unsuccessful friend of her childhood. Ultimately, Alexandra has success, wealthy independence, and a marriage which, unlike passionate unions in Cather's fiction, will be satisfying rather than dangerous. In this portrait of Alexandra, Cather provides a paradigm of the autonomous woman, even while she acknowledges, through the images of Alexandra's fantasy lover, the temptations of self-abnegation and passivity.

Thea Kronberg dedicates herself to music, and her talent defines and directs her life. Born into a large frontier family, she clear-sightedly pursues her goals, selecting as friends those few who support her aspirations. Subordinating personal life to the professional, Thea, like Alexandra, marries late in life, after she has achieved success; and her husband, too, recognizes and accepts her special mission. There is never a question of wooing either of these women away from their destinies to the conventional life of women. Marriage, coming later in life, after identity and achievement, is no threat to the self; moreover, Cather provides her heroes with sensitive, even androgynous, males who are supportive of female ambition. But Alexandra and Thea are unusual, imaginative creations primarily because they embody autonomy and achievement. In these books, Cather does not transpose her struggle for success to male characters, as women authors often have, but instead risks the creation of unusual female protagonists.

What Cather achieved in these two early novels she no longer achieved in her later works. Indeed she stopped portraying strong and successful women and began to depict patriarchal institutions and predominantly male characters. Although she wrote ten more novels, in none of them do we find women like Alexandra and Thea. *Death Comes for the Archbishop* (1927) and *Shadows on the Rock* (1931) are Cather's best-known late novels, and in the former there are virtually no women, while in the latter, women are relegated to minor and entirely traditional roles. Cather's movement toward the past in these novels—toward authority, permanence, and Rome—is also a movement into a world dominated by patriarchy. The writer who could envision an Alexandra and a Thea came to be a celebrant of male activity and institutions.[6]

In this striking transformation, *My Ántonia* is the transitional novel. Given the profound anxieties that beset women authors when they recreate their search for selfhood in female characters, it is not surprising that Cather turned to a male narrative point of view. She rationalized that the omniscient point of view, which she had used in both *O Pioneers!* and *The Song of the Lark*, was not appropriate for her subject matter and continued to ignore the advice of Sarah Orne Jewett, who told her that when a woman tried to write from a man's point of view, she inevitably falsified.[7] Adopting the male persona was, for Cather, as it has been for many other writers, a way out of facing great anxiety. Moreover, it is natural to see the world, and women, from the dominant perspective, when that is what the world reflects and literature records. Thus, in *My Ántonia*, for the first time in her mature work, Cather adopts a male persona, and that change marks her transition to fiction increasingly conventional in its depiction of human experience.[8]

II

Cather was not only a woman struggling with the dilemma of the achieving woman: she was also a lesbian, and that, too, affected the fiction that she wrote. Early in life she had decided never to marry, and in reviews and letters she repeatedly stressed that marriage and the life of the artist were utterly incompatible. She seems always to have loved women: indeed her only passionate and enduring relationships were with women. Her first, and probably greatest, love was Isabel McClung, whom she met in Pittsburgh in 1898. Moving into the McClung family home, Cather lived there for five years and worked in a small room in the attic. There she wrote most of *April Twilights* (1903), her book of poems; *The Troll Garden* (1905), a short story collection; and major parts of *O Pioneers!* and *The Song of the Lark.* Her affair with McClung continued until 1916, when McClung suddenly announced that she was going to marry the violinist Jan Hambourg. At this point, Cather's world seems to have collapsed. She was first stunned and then deeply depressed. Her loss of McClung seems to have been the most painful event of her life, and it was six months before she could bring herself to see the couple. After a long visit to Red Cloud, and a shorter one to New Hampshire, she eventually returned to New York.[9] There she took up her life with Edith Lewis, with whom she was to live for forty years in a relationship less passionate than that with McClung. But clearly, throughout her life, Cather's deepest affections were given to women. During the troubled period when she felt abandoned by McClung, Cather was writing *My Ántonia:* both her sense of loss and the need to conceal her passion are evident in the text.

Cather never adequately dealt with her homosexuality in her fiction. In two early novels, the question of sexuality is peripheral: *Alexander's Bridge* (1912) and *The Song of the Lark* concern the integration of identity, and the expression of sexuality is limited and unobtrusive. Yet Cather began to approach the issue of homosexuality obliquely in subsequent novels. Many, although not all, of the later novels include homosexual relationships concealed in heterosexual guises. Joanna Russ points out that these disguised relationships are characterized by an irrational, hopeless quality and by the fact that the male member of the couple, who is also the central consciousness of the novel, is unconvincingly male—is, in fact, female and a lesbian.[10] The relationships of Claude and Enid in *One of Ours* (1922) and Niel and Marian Forrester in *A Lost Lady* (1923) are cases in point. In *O Pioneers!*, the novel which preceded *My Ántonia*, the love story of Alexandra's brother Emil and Marie, is also such a transposed relationship: to consider its treatment is to notice, from another perspective, the significant changes that occurred in Cather's writing at the time of *My Ántonia*.[11]

In the subplot of Emil and Marie's love, which unexpectedly dominates the second half of *O Pioneers!*, Cather implies the immense dangers of homosexual love. The deaths of Emil and Marie at the moment of sexual consummation suggest more than a prohibition against adultery: their story expresses both a fantasy of sexual fulfillment and the certainty that death is the retribution for this sort of passion. Seeing the story of Emil and Marie in this way, as the disguised expression of another kind of passion, becomes increasingly plausible when one examines Emil's character and behavior and observes that he is male in name only; moreover, it offers a convincing explanation for the sudden and shocking intrusion of violence in this otherwise uniformly elegiac novel. But what is most important here is that Alexandra, Cather's hero, is not destroyed by the consequences of Emil's passion; instead, passion vicariously satisfied, Alexandra retreats to the safety of heterosexual marriage. Thus the fantasy of homosexuality, and the fear of it, are encapsulated and controlled, only slightly distorting the narrative structure. Three years later, Cather's fear is pervasive and dominates the development of *My Ántonia*, so that the narrative structure itself becomes a defense against erotic expression.

The original of Ántonia was Annie Sadilek Pavelka, a Bohemian woman whom Cather had loved and admired from childhood, and with whom she maintained a lifelong, affectionate friendship. In 1921, after completion of the novel, Cather wrote of her feeling for Annie and her decision to use the male point of view:

> Of the people who interested me most as a child was the Bohemian hired girl of one of our neighbors, who was so good to me. . . . Annie fascinated me and I always had it in mind to write a story about her. . . . Finally, I concluded that I would write from the point of view of the detached observer, because that was what I had always been. Then I noticed that much of what I knew about Annie came from the talks I had with young men. She had a fascination for them, and they used to be with her whenever they could. They had to manage it on the sly, because she was only a hired girl. But they respected her, and she meant a good deal to some of them. So I decided to make my observer a young man.[12]

Here Cather suggests the long genesis of this tale and, significantly, her own replication of the "male" response to Annie, reflected in the language of the passage: "Annie fascinated me"/"She had a fascination for them." The fascination here seems to imply not only a romantic and sexual attraction, but also horror at the attraction. Cather suggests that the young men's response to Ántonia is ambivalent because Annie is forbidden; she is a hired girl, with all of that phrase's various suggestions, and so they see her "on the sly." For Cather that fascination is more complex. Identifying with the young men in their forbidden response to Annie, her impulse is that of the lesbian. Yet, when she wrote the novel and transposed to Jim her own strong attraction to Annie/Ántonia, she also transposed her restrictions on its erotic content. Although she adopts the male persona, she cannot allow him full expression of her feelings. Thus, what would seem to be Jim's legitimate response to Ántonia is prohibited and omitted: its homosexual threat is, evidently, too great, and so we find at the heart of the novel that emptiness noted by Brown.

The avoidance of sexuality (which does not extend beyond the Jim-Ántonia relationship, however) must be seen in connection with McClung's desertion of Cather, which occurred after she had composed the first two or three chapters of *My Ántonia*. During this time of grieving, she seemed not to trust herself to write of her own experience of love and sex. For the Cather persona and the beloved woman are not only separated: both are actually denied sexuality, although sexuality arises in distorted, grotesque forms throughout the novel.

During the writing of *My Ántonia*, Cather's grief coincided with the already great burden of anxiety of the woman who is a writer. After this time, her heroic stance in her fiction could not continue, and she abandons the creation of strong fictional women. In *My Ántonia* she denies Jim's erotic impulses and Ántonia's sexuality as well; and she retreats into the safety of convention by ensconcing Ántonia in marriage and rendering her apotheosis as earth mother. She abandons Ántonia's selfhood along with her sexuality: as Mrs. Cuzak, Ántonia is "a battered woman," and a "rich mine of life, like the founders of early races."[13] Interestingly, critics have recognized the absence of sexuality in Jim, although not in Ántonia, and focus their analyses on the male in the case, as though the novel had been written about a male character by a male author—or, as if the male experience were always central.

The most complex and instructive of the psychological analyses of Jim is by Blanche Gelfant, who sees Jim as a young man whose adolescence "confronts him with the possibility of danger in women."[14] He cannot accept the "nexus of love and death," and so retreats to perpetual boyhood. Noting many of the novel's ambiguous elements, Gelfant assumes that male fragility and male fear of womanhood is the crux of the problem. In her view, Jim is the protagonist and Ántonia is his guide: she is responsible for his failed initiation and, later, for his sexual humiliation and confusion.[15] Gelfant's analysis assumes traditional sex roles as normative: Jim's experience is central and Ántonia's is the subordinate, supporting role in his adventure. Yet, to understand the ambiguity in this, and perhaps in other texts by women writers, requires the reversal of such assumptions. If we assume the centrality of Ántonia and her development in the novel, we can observe the stages by which Cather reduces her to an utterly conventional and asexual character.

III

In childhood, Ántonia is established as the novel's center of energy and vitality. As a girl she is "bright as a new dollar" (p. 4) with skin "a glow of rich, dark colour" and hair that is "curly and wild-looking" (p. 23). She is always in motion: holding out a hand to Jim as she runs up a hill, chattering in Czech and broken English, asking rapid questions, struggling to become at home in a new environment. Wanting to learn everything, Ántonia also has "opinions about everything" (p. 30). Never indolent like Lena Lingard, or passive like her sister Yulka, or stolid like the Bohemian girls, Ántonia is "breathless and excited" (p. 35), generous, interested, and affectionate. By the end of her childhood, however, intimations of her future social roles appear.

When Ántonia reaches puberty, Cather carefully establishes her subordinate status in relation to three males, and these relationships make an interesting comparison with Alexandra's and Thea's. First, Ántonia's brutal brother, Ambrosch, is established as the head of the house and the "important person in the family" (p. 90). Then Jim records his need to relegate Ántonia to secondary status and receive deference, since "I was a boy and she was a girl" (p. 43), and in the farcical, pseudo-sexual snake-killing episode, he believes he accomplishes his goal. In fact, he and Ántonia enact a nearly parodic ritual of male and female behavior: in his fear, he turns on her with anger; she cries and apologizes for her screams, despite the fact that they may have saved his life; and she ultimately placates him with flattery. Forced to leave school, she soon relinquishes all personal goals in favor of serving others. No longer resentful or competitive, she is "fairly panting with eagerness to please" (p. 155) young Charley Harling, the son of her employers: "She loved to put up lunches for him when he went hunting, to mend his ball-gloves and sew buttons on his shooting coat, baked the kind of nut-cake he liked, and fed his setter dog when he was away on trips with his father" (p. 155). Cather's protagonist has been reduced to secondary status, as Alexandra and Thea were not: having challenged our expectations in earlier works, Cather retreats in this novel to the depiction of stereotypical patterns.

The second book of *My Ántonia*, with its insinuative title "The Hired Girls," dramatizes the emergence of Ántonia's intense sexuality and its catastrophic effects on her world. Now a beautiful adolescent woman, Ántonia is "lovely to see, with her eyes shining and her lips always a little parted when she danced. That constant dark colour in her cheeks never changed" (p. 223). Like flies the men begin to circle around her—the iceman, the delivery boys, the young farmers from the divide; and her employer, Mr. Harling, a demanding, intimidating, patriarch insists that she give up the dances where she attracts so much attention. When she refuses, he banishes her from his family. Next becoming the object of her new employer's lust, Ántonia loses Jim's affection and, by the end of the summer, has embarked on a disastrous affair with the railroad conductor, Donovan. Ántonia's sexuality is so powerful, in Cather's portrayal, that it destroys her oldest and best friendships and thrusts her entirely out of the social world of the novel.

Jim's intense anger at Ántonia once again reveals his fear, this time a fear of her sexuality that is almost horror. When Cutter attempts to rape her, Jim, the actual victim of the assault, returns battered to his grandmother's house. He then blames Ántonia and her sexuality for Cutter's lust, and recoils from her: "I heard Ántonia sobbing outside my door, but I asked grandmother to send her away. I felt I never wanted to see her again. I hated her almost as much as I hated Cutter. She had let me in for all this disgustingness" (p. 250). This eruption of sexuality marks the climax, almost the end, of the friendship between Ántonia and Jim, and after this, Ántonia is virtually banished from the novel.

At this point, Cather, evidently retreating from the sexual issue, broadens the novel's thematic focus. Jim and Ántonia do not meet again for two years, and all of Book III is devoted to Jim's frivolous, romanticized affair with Lena Lingard, with which he and the reader are diverted. Moreover, the events of Ántonia's life—her affair with Donovan, her pregnancy, her return home, the birth of her daughter—are kept at great narrative distance. Two years after the fact, a neighbor describes these events to Jim as she has seen them, or read about them in letters. Yet, as though banishing Ántonia and distracting Jim were not sufficient, her sexuality is diminished and then, finally, destroyed. After a punitive pregnancy and the requisite abandonment by her lover, she never again appears in sexual bloom. The metaphoric comparisons that surround her become sexually neutral, at best. In one example her neck is compared to "the bole of a tree" (p. 122), and her beauty is cloaked: "After the winter began she wore a man's long overcoat and boots and a man's felt hat with a wide brim" (p. 316). Her father's clothes, like Mr. Harling's ultimatum, seem well designed to keep Ántonia's sexuality under wraps.

After a two-year separation, during which Ántonia returns to her brother's farm, bears her child, and takes up her life of field work, Jim and Ántonia meet briefly. Dream-like and remote, their meeting is replete with nostalgia not readily accounted for by events; as Jim says, "We met like people in the old song, in silence, if not in tears" (p. 319). Inappropriately, though in a speech of great feeling, Ántonia compares her feeling for Jim to her memory of her father, who is lost to her for reasons that the text does provide:

> ". . . you are going away from us for good. . . . But that don't mean
> I'll lose you. Look at my papa here, he's been dead all these years,

and yet he is more real to me than almost anybody else. He never goes out of my life" (p. 320).

Jim's response expresses similar nostalgia and an amorphous yearning:

> "... since I've been away, I think of you more often than of anyone else in this part of the world. I'd have liked to have you for a sweetheart, or a wife, or my mother, or my grandmother, or my sister—anything that a woman can be to a man.... You really are a part of me" (p. 321).

The seductive note of sentiment may blind us as readers to the fact that Jim might offer to marry Ántonia and instead abandons her to a life of hardship on her brother's farm with an empty, and ultimately broken promise to return soon. Cather forcibly separates Jim and Ántonia because of no logic given in the text; we have to assume that her own emotional dilemma affected the narrative and to look for the reasons within Cather herself.

Following this encounter is a twenty-year hiatus: when Jim and Ántonia finally meet again, the tensions that have lain behind the novel are resolved. Ántonia, now devoid of sexual appeal, no longer presents any threat. In addition, she has been reduced to a figure of the greatest conventionality: she has become the stereotypical earth mother. Bearing no resemblance to Cather's early female heroes, she is honored by Jim and celebrated by Cather as the mother of sons. By the novel's conclusion, Cather has capitulated to a version of that syndrome in which the unusual, achieving woman recommends to other women as their privilege and destiny that which she herself avoided. While recognizing the conflict that issues in such self-betrayal, one also notes the irony of Cather's glorification of Ántonia.

Autonomy and unconventional destiny are available only to the subordinate characters, Lena Lingard and Tiny Soderball, two of the hired girls. Lena, having seen too much of marriage, child-bearing and poverty, has established a successful dress-making business and, despite her sensuous beauty, refrained from marriage. Her companion, Tiny, made her fortune in the Klondike before settling down in San Francisco. They lived in a mutually beneficial, supportive relationship: "Tiny audits Lena's accounts occasionally and invests her money for her; and Lena, apparently, takes care that Tiny doesn't grow too miserly," Jim tells us (p. 328). Both Lena and Tiny are independent and unconventional; Lena particularly understands and values the single self. In a revealing detail, she instructs her brother to buy handkerchiefs for their mother with an embroidered "B" for her given name, "Berthe," rather than with an "M" for mother. Lena, who describes marriage as "being under somebody's thumb" (p. 229), says, "It will please her for you to think about her name. Nobody ever calls her by it now" (p. 172). Although relegated to subordinate roles, these women are initially presented favorably; but, by the end of the novel, Cather simultaneously praises Ántonia's role as mother and demeans the value of their independent lives.

In her concluding gesture, Cather offers a final obeisance to convention. Her description of Lena and Tiny undercuts their achievement and portrays them as stereotypical "old maids" who have paid for their refusal of their "natural" function. Thus, Tiny has become a "thin, hard-faced woman, very well dressed, very reserved" (p. 301) and something of a miser: she says "frankly that nothing interested her much now but making money" (p. 301). Moreover, Tiny has suffered the "mutilation" of her "pretty little feet" (p. 301)—the price of her unnatural success in the Klondike. Though a little more subtly, Lena is similarly disfigured, physically distorted by her emotional abberation. Jim presents her as crude and overblown in a final snapshot: "A comely woman, a trifle too plump, in a hat a trifle too large . . . " (p. 350). So it is, too, with their friendship. Jim's barren account stresses unpleasantness about clothes and money and implies that an edge of bitterness has appeared. So much for female independence and success; so much for bonds between women. Cather, through Jim's account of them, has denigrated Tiny and Lena and their considerable achievement. In betraying these characters, versions of herself, Cather reveals the extent of her self-division.

Equally revealing is the transformation of Ántonia in the concluding segment. Now forty-four, she is the mother of eleven children, a grandmother without her former beauty. So changed is she that Jim at first fails to recognize her. She is "grizzled," "flat-chested," "toothless," and "battered" (pp. 331–332), consumed by her life of child-bearing and field work. The archetypal mother, Ántonia now signifies nourishment, protection, fertility, growth, and abundance: energy in service to the patriarchy, producing not "Ántonia's children" but "Cuzak's boys" (despite the fact that five of the children mentioned—Nina, Yulka, Martha, Anna, and Lucie—are girls). Like Cather's chapter title, Jim recognizes only the male children in his fantasy of eternal boyhood adventure, forgetting that in an earlier, less conventional and more androgynous world, his companion had been a girl—Ántonia herself.

Now Ántonia is glorified as a mythic source of life. Not only the progenitor of a large, vigorous family, she is also the source of the fertility and energy that have transformed the barren Nebraska prairie into a rich and fruitful garden. From her fruit cellar cavern pour forth into the light ten tumbling children—and the earth's abundance as well. In the images of this conclusion, she, no longer a woman, becomes Nature, a cornucopeia, a "mine of life" (p. 353). Representing for Jim "immemorial human attitudes" which "fire the imagination" (p. 353), she becomes an idea and disappears under a

symbolic weight, leaving for his friends and companions her highly individualized male children.

The conclusion of *My Ántonia* has usually been read as a triumph of the
pioneer woman: Ántonia has achieved victory over her own hard early life
and over the forces of Nature which made an immense struggle of farm life
in Nebraska. But in fact, as we have seen, Cather and her narrator celebrate
one of our most familiar stereotypes, one that distorts and reduces the lives of
women. The image of the earth mother, with its implicit denial of Ántonia's
individual identity, mystifies motherhood and nurturing while falsely prom-
ising fulfillment. Here Cather has found the means to glorify and dispose
of Ántonia simultaneously, and she has done so in a way that is consonant
with our stereotypical views and with her own psychological exigencies. The
image of Ántonia that Cather gives us at the novel's conclusion is one that
satisfies our national longings as well: coming to us from an age which gave
us Mother's Day, it is hardly surprising that *My Ántonia* has lived on as a
celebration of the pioneer woman's triumph and as a paean to the fecundity
of the American woman and American land.

Cather's career illustrates the strain that women writers have endured
and to which many besides Cather have succumbed. In order to create independent and heroic women, women who are like herself, the woman writer
must avoid male identification, the likelihood of which is enhanced by being
a writer who is unmarried, childless, and a lesbian. In the case of *My Ántonia*,
Cather had to contend not only with the anxiety of creating a strong woman
character, but also with the fear of a homosexual attraction to Annie/Ántonia.
The novel's defensive narrative structure, the absence of thematic and structural unity that readers have noted, these are the results of such anxieties. Yet,
because it has been difficult for readers to recognize the betrayal of female
independence and female sexuality in fiction—their absence is customary—it
has also been difficult to penetrate the ambiguities of *My Ántonia*, a crucial
novel in Cather's long writing career.

Notes

1. E. K. Brown and Leon Edel, *Willa Cather: A Critical Biography* (New York:
Knopf, 1953), p. 203.

2. *Reinventing Womanhood* (New York: Norton, 1979), pp. 31–32. This
essay grew out of a 1979 NEH Summer Seminar entitled "The Woman as Hero:
Studies in Female Selfhood in British and American Fiction" directed by Professor
Heilbrun.

3. Mildred Bennett, *The World of Willa Cather* (Lincoln: University of
Nebraska Press, 1961), pp. 110–114.

4. *Willa Cather: Her Life and Art* (Lincoln: University of Nebraska Press,
1970), pp. 45, 53, 176.

5. Willa Cather, rev. of *The Awakening,* in Kate Chopin, *The Awakening,* edited by Margaret Culley (New York: Norton, 1976), pp. 153–154.

6. Two lesser late novels, *Lucy Gayheart* (1935) and *Sapphira and the Slave Girl* (1940), are devoid of heroes of either gender. Instead they present women, trapped in traditional situations, who are weak or cruel and who end in suicide and paralysis. *Lucy Gayheart* can usefully be compared to *The Song of the Lark,* since it is a weaker and conventional version of similar, if not identical, subject matter.

7. Woodress, *Willa Cather,* p. 132.

8. Heilbrun, *Reinventing Womanhood,* pp. 81–92.

9. Woodress, *Willa Cather,* pp. 172–174, 178–179.

10. "To Write 'Like a Woman': Transformations of Identity in Willa Cather," unpublished paper presented at 1979 MLA meeting: Judith Fetterley argues similarly in "*My Ántonia,* Jim Burden and the Dilemma of the Lesbian Writer," unpublished paper presented at SUNY Conference, "Twentieth Century Women Writers," June 1980. Professors Russ and Fetterley were both kind enough to send me copies of their essays.

11. Referring to McClung's marriage, Leon Edel wrote in *Literary Biography* (London: Rupert Hart Davis, 1957), p. 75, that "it is from this moment that the biographer can date a change in Willa Cather's works."

12. Bennett, *The World of Willa Cather,* pp. 46–47.

13. Willa Cather, *My Ántonia* (Boston: Houghton Mifflin, 1954), p. 4. All references to this edition, and page numbers will be supplied in parentheses in the text.

14. "The Forgotten Reaping Hook: Sex in *My Ántonia,*" *American Literature,* 43 (1971: 60–82.

15. Ibid., pp. 66, 64.

SALLY ALLEN MCNALL

Immigrant Backgrounds to My Ántonia: "A Curious Social Situation in Black Hawk"

When teaching Willa Cather, I tell my students that one of her greatest strengths is her ambivalence about the cultural myths of her time—myths that have become a part of our time as well. In the case of *My Ántonia*, this statement can be applied almost indefinitely, but it is nowhere more true than in her depiction of immigrants. In Cather's day it was rare for any member of the dominant culture (and she was that) to see immigrants as subjects, as people acting in their own behalf. Her ability to do so is significant, but it is not the sole significant fact about her vision of them and of their circumstances. At the beginning of section 9 of "The Hired Girls," Jim Burden describes "a curious social situation in Black Hawk." If students are to understand the vital complexity of attitudes involved here and throughout the book, they should be given some information about the historical and cultural context of that situation.

History and Myth

My Ántonia is about the historical period during which the American frontier closed. It is also about the place where that happened, since the Great Plains were settled after the West Coast regions; the people of the Great Plains, more than those of any other region, must be thought of as immigrants (Luebke, "Regionalism" 31). In the nineties, the historian Frederick Jackson

Approaches to Teaching Cather's *My Ántonia*, edited by Susan J. Rosowski (New York: MLA, 1989): pp. 22–30. © 1989 Modern Language Association.

Turner began to expound his thesis explaining the American character in terms of the frontier. In shifting emphasis from the East to the "Great West," he also developed an idea of the frontier as a crucible, where European immigrants were "Americanized, liberated, and fused into a mixed race" (James D. Bennett 44–47). The idea of the West as melting pot was appealing in the years before World War I, but it was only one way in which Americans could think about immigrants. Three years before *My Ántonia* was published, the *Nation* printed an influential article presenting another view. According to the philosopher H. M. Kallen, each nationality should express its "emotional and voluntary life in its own language, in its own inevitable aesthetic and intellectual forms" (qtd. in Handlin, *Immigration*, 154). This currently popular idea has since been termed cultural pluralism and recently, by Carl Degler, the "salad bowl" (Howard N. Rabinowitz 27). There is no doubt that it appealed to Cather as strongly as Turner's frontier thesis could have done. Her attitude toward the immigrant is partly a matter of deeply personal identification with those who are "different," but it also may reflect Nebraska's relative noninterference with various ethnic life-styles, compared with its Great Plains neighbors (Luebke, "Regionalism" 38).

A first reading of *My Ántonia*, when it was originally published, in 1918, or today, may leave a reader with the impression of either a melting pot or salad bowl. In "Cuzak's Boys" the respectability of town (the teachings of Mrs. Burden and Mrs. Harting) and the cosmopolitanism of city (Cuzak's background) support Ántonia's role as a "rich mine of life," founding not an old but a new race: Americans, with a living cultural heritage from the Old World. Yet an examination of the book as a whole, in the context of some less benign theories and myths, will show students that Cather was equally aware of the other side of her cultural coinage.

In its most acceptable form, the earliest theory of "Americanization" was called culled assimilation. In Cather's day it deserved the description "doctrine of Anglo-Saxon Conformity," and it was a widespread response to the influx of immigration between 1880 and 1914. The years—1883 to 1895—when Cather lived in Nebraska neatly span the middle portion of the two decades during which the national question of immigration became more vexed than ever before in our history. In those decades and the two to follow, the rigid classification of social identities in the United States retched its peak (Higham, *Send These* 246). Nativism, as it was called, had been present from the beginning of the century of immigration (roughly, 1820–1920). In a society always profoundly subject to change, xenophobia was an early and persistent response to insecurity, and in the 1890s Americans were particularly insecure economically. Although immigration to the Great Plains slowed during this decade, immigration on a national level did not; in fact, xenophobia was probably exacerbated by the condition of the numerous urban immigrants. Nativism infected all sections of the country and every class, but it was not new. "If I were to put upon the printed page some of the epithets applied to . . . people from central Europe . . . by their prairie and backwoods neighbors, in the seventies and eighties," observes a Nebraska educator in 1929, "I greatly fear it would not add to the growing cordiality between this group and the rest of us" (Rosicky, *History* 16).

The growing movement for regulation of immigration argued that the arrival of cheap foreign labor was not only undesirable competition but a contribution to the widening and hardening gap between rich and poor (Warne 316). Not only labor unrest in cities but the agrarian protest movements—Cather knew well—were regularly blamed on foreign radicals (Higham, *Strangers* 73). Students should know that between 1895 and the publication of *My Ántonia*, Cather lived in Pittsburgh and (like the "I" of the introduction) in New York City, where the conditions of urban immigrants could hardly be ignored and where—as newspaperwoman and editor for a radical magazine, *McClure's*—Cather was exposed to a variety of facts and opinions on the subject.

During those years, yet another way of viewing immigrants was developing. Immigrants had begun to reach the Great Plains within the decade after the Homestead Act (1862). During that decade and in the seventies, immigrants to America were predominantly from western and northern Europe. Though the promotional activities of the railroads now brought many straight past the cities of the East to the prairies, other immigrants were moving on from earlier settlements in the East. In *My Ántonia*, the Harlings, Mrs. Gardener (nee Molly Bawn), and Mr. Jensen, the Danish laundryman, are examples of this group, soon to be called the "old immigrants." These people were more easily integrated into our society than were the "new immigrants" from eastern and southern Europe, whose numbers swelled in the eighties and nineties. The Harlings, in particular, illustrate the proposition that Scandinavian immigrants tended to be upright and cosmopolitan (Commager 6), while Lena Lingard's grandfather was a "clergyman and much respected in Norway" (200). Despite a dubious reputation, Lena does not get in trouble; rather, she is a success American-style, as is Tiny Soderball (299). Though many Czechs arrived in Nebraska at the same time as the western and northern Europeans, the national picture was different, and the Shimerdas reflect this change, arriving late, on the largest wave of Czech immigration (Roucek, "Czechoslovak Americans" and *Czechs;* Laska 29).

By the 1890s, Italians, eastern European Jews, and Slavs (a group that includes Czechs) were arriving in great numbers, and they bore the brunt of the economic insecurity of the period. During the years Cather was writing *My Ántonia*, America was making up its mind whether to go to war with Germany and Austria-Hungary. Czechs in America were eager even before our involvement to help free their homelands from the domination of the Dual Empire; early in the book Otto makes an elliptical reference to the background of this situation (21). Yet Czechs like other immigrants felt the force of the Americanization movement in the war years (Rosický, *History* 483), while Germans in America, including Nebraska, were definitely suspect; stories of their victimization can be found in almost any history of a midwestern state. The country's anxiety over the role immigrants were to play in our society did not ease, though the "tide" of immigration was stemmed, briefly, by the war; after the war years, the restrictionists won their battles, in the quota system—based on the preexisting composition of the American population—instituted in 1921 and 1924. The "new" immigrants, then, were regarded with suspicion, which took several forms, each revealing fears about American institutions. Cather misses none of them.

The Family

The most prominent anxiety in "The Hired Girls" is sexual—it concerns marriage. It is no accident that the dancing pavilion that menaces the morals of Black Hawk youth is set up by an Italian couple. Black Hawk attitudes are polarized by the dances along the lines between "old" and "new" immigrant stereotypes—the Danish laundry girls contrasted with the dangerous Bohemian Marys, and Ántonia's success at the tent the first step toward her downfall.

Students may not be aware how xenophobia in America fed, from the beginning, on a set of ideas that can only be termed racist, ideas about "mongrelization" and Anglo-Saxons' being "outbred" by inferior racial groups (see the example of E. A. Ross, a well-known sociologist of the period, and Handlin, *Immigration* 278), ideas of a "dark shadow" or a "black tide." The "new" immigrants were seen as more peasant-like than the "old"; a thread of this sort of distaste on the part of the Burdens runs through "The Shimerdas." Jim reacts with violent self-righteousness to unpleasant facts concerning Ántonia's sexuality: the rape, the first pregnancy. His reactions here ironically prefigure the way he will repeat Sylvester Lovett's pattern, will toy with Lena but marry a wealthy bloodless woman of his own ethnicity and class.

Sexuality, then, threatens both the "racial purity" and the respectability of old Black Hawk residents. It is also a threat to the immigrant, and here Cather takes considerable pains to make her point clear. In Ántonia, she writes a character whose moral isolation is all but total, who must do without the support of extended family and tradition, who must rely on herself alone to make her marital arrangements, and who at first fails disastrously. In the Old World, she would have lived, as virtually all Czech immigrants had, in a village community and would have been courted by someone like Cuzak to begin with (Kutak 10–11; Swehla 474). The absence of community is destructive to her as well as to her father. If they had come to eastern Nebraska, they would have benefited from the colony-based settlement system; Webster County's settlements were never large (Rosický, "Bohemians" 2 and *History* 207). No one is there to understand, much less sympathize with, peasant values; to the Burdens, she seems degraded by her work. Ántonia's status is precarious, then, long before the dance pavilion comes to Black Hawk, and afterward it is clear that she is regarded as "fair game," not only by Wick Cutter but, in his unconscious way, by Jim, who kisses her in a manner that is "not right" (224).

Toward the end of "The Hired Girls," an important passage tells us about the class split in Ántonia's background. Her father "lived in his mother's house," says Ántonia to Jim, "and she [Ántonia's mother] was a poor girl come in to do the work." Ántonia is the daughter of a servant who was no better than she should be, a stereotype of the undesirable immigrant, and temporarily at least Ántonia too fulfills that role.

The Church

Another influence that bound many Bohemians of Ántonia's generation into a community and preserved traditional values for more than one or two generations is all but absent from Cather's picture of the character. Bohemian immigrants, like many others, often settled in communities built around their churches, particularly in the Midwest and West (Baltensperger 77; Roucek, *Czechs* 33). Today's students are generally surprised to learn that a powerful current in American xenophobia, from the days of the Puritans, was a horror of the Catholic church. The Shimerdas (like approximately fifty percent of all Czech immigrants) are Catholic. In the 1890s, American fear of domination or at least subversion by those loyal to a foreign potentate, the pope, and fear of a religious tradition not particularly interested in the cause of temperance were aggravated by conflicts in the East and Midwest over the issue of parochial schools, where classes were often taught in the children's native languages, and which, unlike our public schools, did not "Americanize" (Curran 96–97; Higham, *Strangers* 59–60).

Twice in *My Ántonia,* Cather—most uncharacteristically—emphasizes elements of Catholicism that were, in the eyes of contemporary American Protestants, mere popish superstition. The scenes in question are Mr. Shimerda's spontaneous prayer before the Christmas tree (87)—which Grandfather Burden "Protestantizes—and Mrs. Shimerda's desire to bury her husband, a suicide and hence a mortal sinner, at a crossroads. This desire is frustrated by later (one assumes Protestant) road makers (113, 119). Cather presents Ántonia and her family as isolates, lacking a stable and coherent religious community and tradition, and therefore the sort of religious ties that could prevent the mistake she makes with Larry Donovan. Yet if the reputable Protestants of Black Hawk participated in the anti-Catholic prejudice of their times, a Catholic girl's fall (and with a Catholic young man) would not have surprised them.

Education

Although Ántonia has no religious training to help her preserve her Czech identity, she is at any rate spared the "Americanization" of the public schools. If our students take the value of public education for granted, they need to be reminded that immigrants did not invariably do so. As another member of Cather's generation in Nebraska observed of his Czech pupils, their families "wanted the children to get an English education, but corn husking took precedence over everything" (Rosický, *History* 15; see Kutak 61–62 for examples of immigrant Czechs' opposition toward schooling). In a 1923 *Nation* article, Cather comments tartly that our lawmakers "have a rooted conviction that a boy can be a better American if he speaks only one language than if he speaks two" ("Nebraska" 237). It is not necessarily Ántonia's loss that she has no time for school, and it is part of her triumph that her children grow up bilingual, speaking Czech at home and preserving Czech ways.

Ántonia's father's plea, "Te-e-ach, te-e-ach my Ántonia!" is that of an educated man helpless to pass his education on to the child who takes after him; it is not a wish that her mind should be molded to that of the New World. Cather points out that "Many of our Czech immigrants were people of a very superior type. The political emigration resulting from the revolutionary disturbances of 1848 was distinctly different from the emigration resulting from economic causes . . . in Nebraska our Czech settlements were large and very prosperous" ("Nebraska" 237). Many such settlements in fact resulted from internal migration from early Czech colonies in Wisconsin and Ohio, but this clustering argues for a considerable degree of difference perceived between the Czechs and the dominant culture (Luebke, "Regionalisim" 34 and "Ethnic" 395), and of course the Shimerdas, however superior a type Mr. Shimerda was, do not have the advantage of living in a large settlement.

For Jim, obviously, education—especially higher education—is an important indicator of class and a means of upward mobility. The relative lack of education of the "new" immigrants was one reason nativists gave for fearing them. Ántonia never gets it formal education, nor is she upwardly mobile; rather, she stays put—a "country girl" (309). Students may need to be told that by the time described in "Cuzak's Boys," farming—however prosperous—had lost the prestige it had had in America since Jefferson's day. Class and immigrant status were intertwined, even in rural Nebraska.

The Economy

In a rapidly industrializing and urbanizing America, economic dislocations between generations were inevitable, particularly for immigrant families who went to cities, but also in rural life. Mr. Shimerda is not the sort of man who can adapt to frontier conditions. As Annie Sadilek Pavelka put it in a

1955 letter, her father, a weaver in the old country, was totally unprepared for the prairies:

> he used to hear how good it was hear as he had letters from her how wonderfull it was out here that there were beautifful houses lot of trees and so on but how disapointed he was when he saw them pretty houses duged in the banks of the deep draws . . . behold our surprise . . . in the old country he was allways joking and happy. . . .

Many Bohemian villagers with crafts found them of little use in the agricultural environment (Kutak 16, 146). In Cather's novel, however, Ántonia and also her brother can and do adapt to the prairie. Cuzak, Ántonia's husband, knew little about farming to begin with, but Ántonia's strength, and the children, have made the difference. "We got plenty boys," he says (chilling any Anglo-Saxon supremacist), "we can work a lot of land" (365). This is traditional farming, and Cather has Jim look back on the stories of the immigrant girls in a way that maintains a distinction between farming and business. "Today," Jim says, "the best that a harassed Black Hawk merchant can hope for is to sell provisions and farm machinery and automobiles to the rich farms where that first crop of stalwart Bohemian and Scandinavian girls are now mistresses" (201).

Cather's vision of immigrants to central Nebraska in the crucial years retains much of the uglier furniture of the American mind at the time. Over Jim's head we see—and, with Cather, may judge—the ethnocentricity permeating every social institution. The harshness of this reality is mitigated by Jim's bemused sporadic attraction to Ántonia's very foreignness. But Ántonia is just that: Jim's romantic heroine. As Frances Harting tells him, "I expect I know the country girls better than you do. You always put a kind of glamour over them. The trouble with you, Jim, is that you're romantic" (229). Because Jim's own life, marriage, and work involve him inextricably in the world of business, as we learn in the introduction, he cannot see the contradictions in the rural lives he idealizes. Cather can, and she even has Ántonia warn Jim as a boy of his blindness: "Things will be easy for you. But they will be hard for us" (140).

Myth and the Present

While she wrote *My Ántonia*, Cather was as aware of the climate of opinion, the emphasis on being one hundred percent American, as was any major writer of her time. She wrote against universal conformity, without polemic and without oversimplification. In a world in which foreignness was the symbol of insecurity and change, she made an immigrant woman stand for permanence and stability. This trick is not the only one she played. In "Nebraska: The End of the First Cycle," she deplored the "machine-made materialism" that industrialization was producing (238). Because she confronts this issue head-on in her 1922 novel *One of Ours,* it is tempting, and certainly easier on our students, to teach *My Ántonia* as a looking back to a time and way of life uncontaminated by materialism, by capitalistic development and its imperatives. For both Jim and the narrator of the introduction, Ántonia means "the country, the conditions, the whole adventure of our childhood." Jim's vision of an immigrant woman triumphing over adversity does indeed look back, but Cather's vision, I try to show my students, examines the social conflicts beneath the mythologies of her day, looks far enough into them to suggest powerfully what our imported labor force was up against in her day.

It is still up against it today. We have not yet made up our minds what we want to do about or with immigrants. Because of this, *My Ántonia* remains a central text in our literature and can heighten our students' awareness of the history of their mythologies and attitudes.

APPENDIX:
SOME U.S. IMMIGRATION LAWS AND PROGRAMS

1891   The federal government, assuming charge of immigration, opens Ellis Island.

1903   Congress expands the list of excluded aliens (convicts, lunatics, etc.) to include radicals.

1907   Congress raises the head tax on immigrants and excludes those with physical defects and unaccompanied children.

1917   Congress establishes a literacy test.

1921   Congress (having virtually banned Asian immigrants—a ban that endured until 1943) sets it limit on European immigrants, according to quotas based on immigrant populations already here.

1924   Johnson-Reed Act: toughens quota system; it is revised downward again in 1927.

1948   Displaced Persons Act: provides for war refugees; its provisions are revised upward in 1950.

1952   McCarran-Walter Immigration and Naturalization Act: eliminates race as a barrier, continues quota system, establishes preference for family reunification.

1953–62 Congress liberalizes provisions for refugees in four successive acts.

1965   Congress abolishes quotas and establishes other limits.

1980   Refugee Act of 1980: further liberalizes policy.

1981   President Reagan proposes an Omnibus Immigration Control Act, addressing issues of illegal immigration, refugee status, and employment, among others.

1983   Senator Simpson and Representative Mazzoli propose a revised Immigration Reform and Control Act; it is adopted by the Senate but not by the House.

1986   Immigration Reform and Control Act: gives legal status to millions of illegal aliens living in the U.S. since 1 January 1982 and establishes penalties for anyone found hiring illegal aliens.

Works Cited

Baltensperger, Bradley H. *Nebraska: A Geography.* Boulder: Westview, 1985.

Bennett, James D. *Frederick Jackson Turner.* Boston: Twayne, 1975.

Cather, Willa. *My Ántonia.* Boston: Houghton, 1918.

———. "Nebraska: The End of the First Cycle." *Nation,* 5 (Sept. 1923): 236–238. Rpt. in Virginia Faulkner, 1–8.

Commanger, Henry Steele. "The Study of Immigration." *Immigration and American History.* Edited by Commanger. Minneapolis: University of Minnesota Press, 1961, pp. 3–7.

Curran, Thomas J. *Xenophobia and Immigration, 1820–1930.* Boston: Twayne, 1975.

Curtin, William M. "Willa Cather and The Varieties of Religious Experience." *Renascence,* 27 (Spring 1975): 115–123.

Handlin, Oscar. *Immigration as a Factor in American History.* Englewood Cliffs: Prentice, 1959.

Higham, John. *Send These to Me: Immigrants in Urban America.* Rev. ed. Baltimore: Johns Hopkins University Press, 1984.

Kutak, Robert I. *The Story of a Bohemian-American Village: A Study of Social Persistence and Change.* 1933. Salem: Ayer, 1970.

Laska, Vera. *The Czechs in America, 1633–1977.* Dobbs Ferry: Oceana, 1978.

Luebke, Frederick C., ed. *Ethnicity on the Great Plains.* Lincoln: University of Nebraska Press, 1980.

———. "Ethnic Minority Groups in the American West." *Historians and the American West.* Edited by Michael P. Malone. Lincoln: University of Nebraska Press, 1983, pp. 387–413.

———. "Regionalism and the Great Plains: Problems of Concept and Method." *Western Historical Quarterly,* 15 (1984): 19–38.

Rabinowitz, Howard N. "Race, Ethnicity and Cultural Pluralism in American History." *Ordinary People and Everyday Life: Perspectives on the New Social History.* Edited by James B. Gardner and George Rollie Adams. Nashville: American Association for State and Local History, 1983, pp. 23–49.

Rosický, Rose. "Bohemians in Nebraska." Address. Nebraska State Historical Society. Omaha, 30 Apr. 1926.

———. *A History of Czechs (Bohemians) in Nebraska.* Omaha: National Printing, 1929.

Roucek, Joseph. "Czechoslovak Americans." *One America*. 3rd ed. Edited by Francis J. Brown and Joseph Roucek. Englewood Cliffs: Prentice, 1952, pp. 157–168.

———. *The Czechs and Slovaks in America*. Minneapolis: Lerner, 1967.

Swehla, Frances J. "Bohemians in Central Kansas." *Kansas State Historical Collection*, 13 (1913–1914): 469–512.

Warne, Frank Julian. *The Immigrant Invasion*. 1913. Englewood: Ozer, 1971.

PAULA WOOLLEY

"Fire and Wit": Storytelling and the American Artist in Cather's My Ántonia

At the end of her groundbreaking article "The Forgotten Reaping-Hook: Sex in *My Ántonia*," Blanche Gelfant exhorts readers of Cather's novel not to perpetuate the "violence and the destructive attitudes toward race and sex" Gelfant finds in Jim Burden's narrative (81). Gelfant writes:

> We must begin to look at *My Ántonia,* long considered a representatively American novel, not only for its beauty of art and for its affirmation of history, but also, and instructively, for its negations and evasions. Much as we would like to ignore them, for they bring painful confrontations, we must see what they would show us about ourselves—how we betray our past when we forget its most disquieting realities; how we begin to redeem it when we remember. (81–82)

Since the publication of Gelfant's article in 1971 much important work has been done to address the "disquieting realities" in *My Ántonia.* Following Gelfant's lead, Elizabeth Ammons has examined Cather's racist portrayal of Blind d'Arnault, and critics such as Judith Fetterley and Sharon O'Brien have discussed Cather's use of a male narrator as a disguise for her lesbianism. Yet another "negation and evasion" hides in Jim's narrative, one that, when

Cather Studies, Volume 3, edited by Susan J. Rosowski (Lincoln: University of Nebraska Press, 1996): pp. 149–181. © 1996 University of Nebraska Press.

acknowledged, actually supports the long-held view of *My Ántonia* as a "representatively American novel," but by redefining and expanding our vision of American culture. This "negation and evasion" begins with Jim's repression of Ántonia's role as an artist. Most recent critics agree that Jim's portrayal of Ántonia at the end of the novel is reductive—she has become a "mythic" figure, an "Earth Mother"—but they differ on whether Ántonia transcends this objectification.[1] Cather does, however, offer us a way to read against Jim's narrative to find an alternative view of both Ántonia and Jim himself. Throughout the novel, Ántonia enters Jim's narrative by telling her own stories, so that, if we listen for her voice, *My Ántonia* is as much the story of Ántonia's development as an artist as it is the story of Jim's vision of her. That is, the growing recognition of the oral tradition in literary studies allows us to reread the novel with a new emphasis on Ántonia as a storyteller.[2]

Although Cather often expressed her admiration of oral storytelling and other forms of folk or "low" art, her prevailing desire to position herself within the male-dominated and male-defined literary tradition prevented her from explicitly identifying Ántonia as an artist. Instead, through her references to Virgil, Cather emphasizes Jim's role as the storyteller who seeks to "bring the Muse into [his] country" (169). Still, once we view Ántonia as an artist rather than as Jim's muse, we find that she is only one of a group of nonprivileged creators in *My Ántonia* whose work provides an alternative to the tradition of Western high art. Traits that Cather elsewhere described as signifying the "true artist" characterize not only Ántonia but also Lena Lingard, Blind d'Arnault, and the actress in *Camille*. By highlighting these usually unnoticed artists in *My Ántonia*, we can begin to see new patterns and contrasts emerge from the jumble of impressions that Cather produces by including the stories and art of others. In sharp contrast to these unrecognized artists, who celebrate life and enliven others, we notice the suicidal men—Mr. Shimerda, a tramp, and Wick Cutter—whose efforts to control or ease the harshness and formlessness of life on the prairie result in self-destruction. Each of these men is associated in his own way with art as well as with the life-denying impulses of control or repression. Their violent efforts at control not only destroy their selves but suggest the deadness of art when it is full of sentimental platitudes or overwhelmed by despair.

This motif of destructive control that underlies the presence of death and lifeless art in *My Ántonia* exemplifies Jim's (and Cather's) conflicted relation to narrative itself. By allowing the entry of other voices and other artists, Cather produces what is now considered a "feminine" text. However, in the introduction she has Jim deny the artistic quality of his narrative because it lacks "form" (2), in other words, the single voice, the linear and climactic plot, and the stable objectification of "the other," which are valued in the Western literary tradition. In an interview, Cather likewise described *My Ántonia* as full of "structural fault[s]," but she acknowledged the necessity of her divergence from the conventional form of the novel. "I know [the structural faults] are there, and made them knowingly," she said, because "I knew I'd ruin my material if I put it in the usual fictional pattern" (*Willa Cather in Person* 79, 77). In fact, through the "formlessness" of *My Ántonia*, Cather allows for a vivid contrast between the vibrant art of the marginalized artist and the lifeless, ultimately life-draining art of the masculine dominant culture (epitomized in Jim Burden), which she ambivalently desired to join.

I

The conflict between Jim's and Ántonia's narrative visions emerges most clearly during his visit with her at the end of the novel. After a twenty-year separation, Jim writes, "I did not want to find [Ántonia] aged and broken; I really dreaded it. In the course of twenty crowded years one parts with many illusions. I did not wish to lose the early ones" (211). During this visit, Jim replaces his early "illusions" about Ántonia with new ones, now seeing her as an asexual Earth Mother. But Ántonia manages to challenge Jim's narrative vision: she brings out old photographs that, as Jean Schwind points out, allow us to see Jim for the first time (51). Tellingly, he appears as "an awkward-looking boy" and as a young man "trying to look easy and jaunty" (225). Clearly, Jim's self-consciousness and lack of ease and the effort he puts into achieving the appearance of being carefree and comfortable embody the critical vision Cather has of her male narrator. The revelation that Jim has been masquerading all along encourages us to question his reliability as a narrator of both his own and Ántonia's pasts.[3]

But Jim finds that Ántonia does not simply possess pictorial representations of him. More importantly, she has made him into a character in the stories she tells her children. As she tells him, "these children know all about you and Charley and Sally, like as if they'd grown up with you" (215–216). After years of thinking of Ántonia as his own property, an "ideal" that "really [is] a part of me" (206), and above all a text for him to write, Jim finds that she has produced her own narrative. Ántonia's stories even rival Jim's own by contradicting the view of himself that he strives to assert. Although her children know "all about" Jim (and this is stressed by her sons' repetition of "we know!" in response to his feeble effort to tell them about "his" Ántonia), they are nevertheless surprised when Jim says, "I was very much in love with your mother once." To this Anton replies, "She never told us that" (222). Ántonia has probably told quite a different story, for it is clear that she has always thought of Jim as a child, from their early "nesting" together (19) to her inclusion of the adult Jim with the Harling children when she says: "I declare, Jim, I loved you children almost as much as I love my own" (215).[4]

Indeed, Ántonia's stories seem to have included the boy who killed an aged and drowsy rattlesnake but to have omitted the portrait that evolves in Jim's account: the young man who boldly scorned bourgeois conventions by associating with hired girls. The Cuzak children's familiarity with the story of his killing the snake revives Jim's uncomfortable awareness of the discrepancy between reality—the snake's age and his own fear—and Ántonia's exultation of his "manly" heroism. The children also realize that the story is a tall tale, for they tell Jim that Ántonia changes the snake's length from story to story (225). Although her story ostensibly emphasizes his "manliness," it actually portrays Jim's masculinity as a fiction. To Ántonia and her children, "Jim Burden" is still the "awkward-looking boy" whose picture elicits a giggle from Leo (225).

Feeling that Ántonia's narratives threaten his view of himself (as well as the authority of his narrative), Jim begins to distance himself from her in the final two chapters. Immediately after looking at the photographs and hearing the family legends about him, Jim refers to Ántonia only as the children's mother (226) and retires to bed with two of her sons. Although he has just left the presence of the real woman, he thinks of her as a work of art: "Ántonia had always been one to leave images in the mind that did not fade—that grew stronger with time. In my memory there was a succession of such pictures, fixed there like the old woodcuts of one's first primer" (226). After reducing her to a new, unchanging image that he can firmly stick into the photo album of his mind, Jim abandons Ántonia the woman as the center of his narrative's interest. After years of fluctuation in his opinion and approval of Ántonia and her behavior, Jim feels that she is finally controllable.[5] Once he turns his attention to her husband and sons, he sees Ántonia as a mother and housekeeper whose role as originator and accommodator of the family's life remains stable and safely behind the scenes. When he refers to her again in the novel's concluding paragraphs, "his" Ántonia is once again the little girl he knew when he was a child.

Jim's efforts to repress Ántonia's active role as an artist have been unwittingly perpetuated by critics who also overlook her artistry and see her only as the subject of Jim's art. Rather than thinking about the stories that seem to disrupt Jim's reminiscences as art produced by Ántonia and others,[6] most critics have seen them as embedded in the text merely to advance Cather's themes.[7] Although Jim enjoys Ántonia's stories, he thinks of them as "entertainment" for children (226), not as an art form. However, his description of her storytelling at the Harlings' house hints that it is something more important to Cather: "We all liked Tony's stories. Her voice had a peculiarly engaging quality; it was deep, a little husky, and one always heard the breath vibrating behind it. Everything she said seemed to come right out of her heart" (113). Instead of responding to Ántonia's stories as constructed narratives, Jim thinks only of her voice. In this way he deflects his—and the reader's—attention from her creativity and emphasizes her lack of any apparent artistic craft; her words "come right out of her heart," unshaped by the formal conventions of elite art.

However, Cather's presentation of Ántonia's storytelling allows for a more complex appreciation. Cather often links oral expression with art and artistic ability, and she values art that conveys and inspires unembellished emotion. In her earlier *Song of the Lark,* for example, the singer Thea Kronborg praises the voice specifically for being a "vessel" of "life itself":[8] "What was any art but an effort to make a sheath, a mould in which to imprison for a moment the shining, elusive element which is life itself—life hurrying past us and running away, too strong to stop, too sweet to lose? The Indian women had held it in their jars. . . . *In singing, one made a vessel of one's throat and nostrils and held it on one's breath,* caught the stream in a scale of natural intervals" (304, emphasis added). According to Thea's definition, Ántonia's apparently artless stories are a lucid vessel for life and thus represent the purest form of art.

As Sharon O'Brien has argued, Cather's reviews of female opera singers present an alternative to the traditional association of "sword/penis/pen/male/ artist" by suggesting a feminine version: "vessel/womb/throat/voice/woman/ artist" (171). In the singer's voice, Cather finds a way for the female artist to link craftsmanship with the "natural power" of the female body (O'Brien 171); likewise, we can find in the storyteller's voice a linkage of the physical body with creative power. O'Brien argues that Cather also associates the talent of the female writer with her "voice," by which she implies not only literary style and tone but also "individuality, originality, and identity" (173–174). This is seen in Cather's preface to Sarah Orne Jewett's *Country of the Pointed Firs,* where she writes that "every great story . . . must leave in the mind of the sensitive reader an intangible residuum of pleasure; a cadence, a quality of voice that is exclusively the writer's own, individual, unique" (7). Cather uses *voice* to mean more than the tone and style of the writing by stressing its independence from the words on the page: this "quality of voice" is one that the reader "can remember without the volume at hand, can experience over and over again in the mind but can never absolutely define, as one can experience in memory a melody" (Preface 7). Or, we might add, as one remembers an oral tale.

In Jim's description of Ántonia's storytelling, Ántonia's voice—both her physical voice and her artistic style and tone—is unique and striking, with its "peculiarly engaging quality" and its implied roots in her "life itself": her breath, her heart, her female body. But, interestingly, female identity is erased, for Jim describes Ántonia in masculine terms: her voice is "deep, a little husky," and he refers to her by her male nickname, Tony. This elision points, on

the one hand, to Jim's sense of Ántonia's slippery gender identity: her rough
manner, appearance, and work in the fields make her seem too much "like
a man," which (perhaps because of insecurity about his own manhood) he
finds disconcerting and "disagreeable" (81). Then again, Jim's movement away
from Ántonia's femininity when she performs her art suggests Cather's own
ambivalence about favorably portraying a nonprivileged art form performed
by an uneducated woman. By emphasizing Ántonia's masculine traits, Cather
could give her storytelling all the power of the traditionally masculine voice
of authority, but at the expense of Ántonia's identity as a female artist.[9]

Ántonia's storytelling lies between singing as performance and writing
as original composition. She belongs not to the Western literary tradition
but to a tradition of oral literature, which values communal sharing rather
than originality and solitary authorship. Cather displayed her high regard for
storytelling and its influence on her own development as a writer when, in a
Bread Loaf School lecture, she called the female storyteller of her Virginian
childhood her "first teacher in narrative" (Bennett 208). Through Ántonia and
others in My Ántonia, Cather tacitly celebrates the oral tradition of storytelling and allows other voices to enter and challenge her elite male narrator. But
even though Ántonia's role as a storyteller emerges in bits and pieces, Cather
never emphasizes it, and Jim always retreats from recognizing her as an artist; he wants Ántonia as a muse, not a rival. Ántonia's threat as a rival would
be immense exactly because she creates stories under assumptions contrary
to the tradition the adult Jim has been educated in (a tradition that, ironically, never seems to him to be as vital as his less sophisticated, "early friends"
[168]). For Cather, emphasizing Ántonia's role as an artist would have been
a bold act in 1918, for it would have aligned Cather with the folk culture of
recent immigrants; also, if Cather had taken the perspective of an uneducated
female storyteller, her novel would not have found a place within the elite,
masculine American literary tradition being defined by contemporary male
writers and professors.[10] Still, although Cather never explicitly calls Ántonia
an artist within the text of My Ántonia, her descriptions of Ántonia's storytelling and vitality clearly conform to the definition of artist that she held
both against and alongside the definitions of her time and culture.

Cather most explicitly identified Ántonia as an artist when she said of
Anna Sadilek Pavelka, the model for Ántonia, that "she was one of the truest
artists I ever knew in the keenness and sensitiveness of her enjoyment, in her
love of people and in her willingness to take pains" (Willa Cather in Person
44). Here Cather aligns the artistic personality with traits traditionally considered feminine—selflessness and sensitivity to the needs of others and with
the ability to enjoy life with enthusiasm. If in her early life Cather saw art as
a masculine endeavor, she nevertheless began to attribute "feminine" qualities
to the artist as early as the 1890s, in her college essays and reviews. In these

essays, about writers from Shakespeare and Carlyle to "Ouida," as well as in
her later comments about writers such as Jewett, Cather repeatedly describes
the creativity of writers as involving a "gift of sympathy" (*Kingdom* 46, 422;
Preface 7), which allows them to "actually [get] inside another person's skin"
(*Kingdom* 449); an "exuberant passion" or "supreme love," which is more important to genius than "supreme intellect" or perfect form (*Kingdom* 434, 52);
and a willingness to give themselves "absolutely to [their] material," to "[fade]
away into the land and people of [their] heart, [and to die] of love only to
be born again" (Preface 7). O'Brien argues that the traits Cather defines as
necessary to the creative process can be seen as feminine because "even if the
artist's social role was male and some aspects of creativity [were] metaphorically associated with paternity, the sympathy, identification, and receptive
submission to inspiration Cather attributed to male writers in the 1890s and
finally claimed for herself were considered feminine attributes by her society"
(159–160).[11] Besides being traditionally feminine, these traits clearly corre-
spond to the enthusiasm and selfless empathy that Cather praises in Anna
Pavelka and develops in Ántonia.

Ántonia's development as a storyteller begins from the moment Jim
teaches her English. She expresses her delight in language when she excitedly
wrings English words from Jim and then offers him a silver ring, an exchange
he finds "extravagant" because he does not realize the value words have for her
(19). As soon as she is able to talk "about almost anything," Ántonia tells Jim
her first stories about the badger-hunting dogs in Bohemia and Old Hata (27).
Just as many of her stories link her Bohemian past with the American prairie,
Ántonia's English remains a hybrid of her mother tongue and her new language. In contrast to Lena, who gives a new spin to American "flat common-
places," Ántonia always has "something impulsive and foreign in her speech"
(180). Her lively and original English and the energy of her enthusiasm recall
Edith Lewis's description of the storyteller to whom Cather listened as a child:
"Her talk was full of fire and wit, rich in the native idiom" (II).

Ántonia's stories are spontaneous and candid in their details of Bohemian life or the actions of people on the prairie. Jim is able to undervalue
her stories because they do not fulfill the Western definition of high art. He
thinks of her oral tales as interesting diversions rather than as an art form
involving craft and skill, talents the young Cather herself found lacking in
female writers (O'Brien 159). Unlike Jim, Ántonia is not concerned with authorial authority. She usually tells stories without manipulating their meaning, presenting people's acts in all their gruesome detail and offering her own
reaction, if at all, as only one way of thinking about the story. Her object is
always to represent what Cather calls "life itself." She does not try to assign
motivation to the characters in her stories or objectify them as reflections
of her own psyche, as Jim does. When she tells the story of the tramp who

kills himself, for example, Ántonia ends with a question rather than an interpretation: "What would anyone want to kill themselves in summer for?" (115). Thus she opens up the meaning of her story to her listeners; and the story's reverberation in Jim's memory clearly suggests the effectiveness of her method. Similarly, she does not judge Peter and Pavel when she translates their story, which Jim, out of morbid fascination, retells in his own words rather than relating it as Ántonia told it.[12] Time and again, her stories gain a new life in her listeners' minds, as when Nina Harling "interprets [Ántonia's stories about Christmas in Bohemia] fancifully, and . . . cherished a belief that Christ was born in Bohemia a short time before the Shimerdas left that country" (113).

Of course, in her stories Ántonia represents life as she remembers it, and she thus offers an alternative to Jim's narrative. The only story that she noticeably changes and interprets is that of Jim and the rattlesnake. Although she casts this story as a rite of manhood, Ántonia clearly still thinks of Jim as a child; for after he kills the snake, she tries to wipe his face with a handkerchief and "comfortingly" tells him that he is a "big mans" now (32). The story really serves as a rite of passage for Ántonia, as Jim perhaps realizes when he returns to the kitchen and finds her "standing in the middle of the floor, telling the story with a great deal of colour" (34). The killing of the snake launches Ántonia as an "epic" storyteller at the center of an audience's attention. By telling this story Ántonia actually displaces Jim as its rightful narrator, since according to the tradition of folk narratives, the narrator of a "hero story" based on real experience should be the "hero" himself (Dobos 177).[13] As the storyteller, Ántonia in effect becomes its hero, even though her role within the tale is that of a helpless female. Ántonia's position as both the teller of and a character within this story parallels the two views we can take of her in My Ántonia: as a storyteller in her own right and the object defined by Jim's narrative. Contrary to Western ideas of high art, Ántonia does not insist on solitary authorship, but allows others to tell "her" stories. She encourages her eldest son to tell the story of Wick Cutter's suicide-murder, with only "occasional promptings" (231). And, of course, she offers no resistance to Jim when he sees (and writes about) her as "anything that a woman can be to a man" (206).

The communal aspect of Ántonia's storytelling—both her responsiveness to her audience and their response to her—also reflects Cather's attribution of traditionally feminine qualities to the artist. After hearing Ántonia's story about the tramp who commits suicide, Jim thinks about the similarities between her and Mrs. Harling, both of whom have "strong, independent natures" and more nurturing characteristics: "They loved children and animals and music, and rough play and digging in the earth. They liked to prepare rich, hearty food and to see people eat it; to make up soft white beds and to see youngsters asleep in them. . . . Deep down in each of them there was a kind of hearty joviality, a relish of life, not over-delicate, but very invigorating. I never tried to define it, but I was distinctly conscious of it" (116). Instead of reflecting on Ántonia's highly disturbing tale, Jim takes refuge in more comforting thoughts, seeming to define a type of maternal nature while denying that he ever "tried to define it." However, if we read this passage in light of Cather's remarks about Anna Pavelka, it also describes the female artist. Here the sympathy, passion, and self-abandonment of the artist reappear. Most notably, Ántonia and Mrs. Harling enjoy watching others enjoy their domestic art. Because of their selflessness, Ántonia and Mrs. Harling are not bothered by the ephemeral nature of their work; instead, they work to provide pleasure for others. With their "relish of life," the two women make art from life rather than from memory and obsession, as Jim does, and without his concern about control.[14]

That Ántonia's art includes both her storytelling and her domesticity is supported by Cather's linkage, in a 1921 interview, of farmers' wives with creativity: "The farmer's wife who raises a large family and cooks for them and makes their clothes and keeps house . . . and thoroughly enjoys doing it all, and doing it well, contributes more to art than all the culture clubs" (*Willa Cather in Person* 47). Certainly, Ántonia's family life and farm express her creative vision. Her children behave so perfectly that they seem to have been raised in a utopia; she even seats them at the dinner table "according to a system" that allows the older children to care for the younger ones (223). Ántonia draws upon European culture and language as well as upon the lessons she has learned from American women to create this harmonious family life. But as her husband's controlled discontent and their triple-enclosed garden remind us, she has achieved this harmony through hard work, by constantly keeping the forces of nature or individual dissatisfaction at bay. Although the seemingly paradisiacal setting leads Jim to read Ántonia as an Earth Mother, her enclave on the prairie is ambiguously limited by its removal from society, as Katrina Irving points out, at the same time that it is peaceful and fertile (101). Ántonia's increased removal from the English language and from town life reflects her marginalization both as an immigrant and as an artist who works in a nonprivileged form. However, her children greatly appreciate her stories and display artistic talent themselves: Rudolph as a storyteller, Leo as a violinist, and Nina as a dancer. Ántonia provides American society not only with badly needed workers, as Irving argues, but with new artists.

II

Although Cather does not explicitly identify Ántonia, the other homemakers, or Lena the dressmaker as artists within the text of *My Ántonia*, her portrayal of women who do creative work without recognition realistically depicts the position of nonprivileged artists in Western society. In a culture that sees art as work created and signed by one person, and crafted according to rules deemed aesthetic by a cultural elite, the oral tales of a hired girl, the dresses of a small-town dressmaker, or the cheerful kitchen of a farmer's wife would not be valued as creative work. Even Cather, who claimed to view storytelling and domesticity as art, nevertheless strove to fulfill the standards of Western high art in her own writing. Yet the structure of *My Ántonia*, which formerly puzzled critics, is unconventional precisely because of her inclusion of the voices and tales of other storytellers; its structure could even be said to imitate the shape of Ántonia's storytelling and to realistically reproduce the effect and influence of all forms of art—high and low—on one's life.

In an interview, Cather insisted that the structure of *My Ántonia* was necessary to her subject: "*My Ántonia* . . . is just the other side of the rug, the pattern that is supposed not to count in a story. In it there is no love affair, no courtship, no marriage, no broken heart, no struggle for success. I knew I'd ruin my material if I put it in the usual fictional pattern. I just used it the way I thought absolutely true" (*Willa Cather in Person* 77). Cather's attempt to be "true" to her material recalls the value she placed on representing "life itself." Although Jim says his manuscript describes "pretty much all that [Ántonia's] name recalls to me" (2), he includes many memories in which Ántonia is only marginally important or is actually replaced by another "hired girl," Lena Lingard. The focus of *My Ántonia* moves away from Ántonia time and again, often to alight on another nonprivileged artist. If we look at some of these other artists—Lena, Blind d'Arnault, and the actress in *Camille*—we can see that they share Ántonia's lack of egoism; their attitude toward their art likewise contrasts with the Western (and highly masculine) tradition of artistic control, authority, and distinction.

Although Cather provides us with some biographical evidence that she considered Ántonia's storytelling and domestic work as undervalued forms of art, her attitude toward Lena as a figure for the female artist is less clear. Yet Lena can be seen as an artist, despite Jim's obscuring descriptions of her dressmaking as merely a business. Her interest in dressmaking obviously is not centered on financial success, which she is inept at managing, but on her enjoyment of the work itself, for the creative expression it allows. She makes the female body—both her own and her customers'—into her canvas by showing it to its best "effect" (179). From her earliest days of poverty, Lena has used whatever resources were at hand, making old clothes "over for herself very becomingly" (108). When she makes dresses for others, she abdicates some artistic control by working in a medium that becomes part of the aesthetic effect of the woman who wears it.

Lena derives sensual enjoyment from her art; Jim often finds her "in the evening . . . alone in her work-room, draping folds of satin on a wire figure, with a quite blissful expression" (179). This enjoyment is significant in light of

Cather's own attitude toward feminine attire. As an adolescent, Cather called dresses and skirts "the greatest folly of the Nineteenth Century" (Bennett 113), but as an adult she began to appreciate dresses when they were worn by other women. While living with Isabelle McClung, O'Brien writes, Cather came to see why "the female dress she found confining and unacceptable in adolescence could be redefined and reimagined along with the female iden-tity it symbolized" (237). Cather's mature interest in feminine dress, which she incorporates in Lena, thus combined her attraction to its effect and her effort to fashion her own image as a woman drawn to other women.

Yet, ironically, by celebrating a woman's appreciation of the female body, Lena's similarly female-focused art paradoxically attracts heterosexual males.[15] Like Ántonia, Lena does not assert artistic control by resisting men's efforts to "write" her into their own narratives. When she appears in Black Hawk, "a graceful picture in her blue cashmere dress and little blue hat" (103), she is the one making the picture, but Jim believes he is the one framing her. Lena is unthreatened by this appropriation of her sensuality; she recognizes that "it makes [men] feel important to think they're in love with somebody" (185). Jim responds to Lena's sensually self-confident and self-celebratory artistic power by idealizing her as his muse, just as he retreats from Ántonia's storytelling at the end of the novel by seeing her as a symbol of "immemorial human attitudes" (226).

Cather's linkage of the "true artist" with a "relish of life" and selflessness is not confined to her female characters. In the musicians Blind d'Arnault and Mr. and Mrs. Vanni we can see the same traits, for their music enlivens the stiffly conventional community of Black Hawk without being recognized as art. In a town where "the married people sat like images on their front porches," the Vannis' tent is an enabling space "where one could laugh aloud without being reproved by the ensuing silence" (125–126). The music of these "cheerful-looking Italians" (114) lowers the inhibitions of the middle-class as it echoes through the town, "call[ing] so archly, so seductively, that our feet hurried toward the tent of themselves" (126). Thus, while Cather's female art-ists inspire others with an enjoyment of the sensual pleasures of daily life, her ethnically or racially marginalized musicians temporarily enable their audi-ences to enjoy and celebrate their own sexuality as an enlivening force.

This enlivening power appears clearly in the African American pianist Blind d'Arnault, whom Jim describes as providing the only "break in the dreary monotony" of March (116). Although Jim dismisses d'Arnault's music as vio-lating Western standards of high art ("as piano-playing, it was perhaps abomi-nable"), he nevertheless feels that it is "something real, vitalized by a sense of rhythm" (121). Although Jim belittles d'Arnault's talent by describing it as instinctual, even bestial, and by calling his execution flawed, this only empha-sizes that d'Arnault is not an artist who carefully gains a desired effect through

life-draining intellectual effort, as do Mrs. Jim Burden's artists, who the unnamed narrator of the introduction dismisses as having "advanced ideas" but
"mediocre ability" (2). Instead, d'Arnault's talent is expressed as a liveliness
and a lack of rigid artistic control. Unlike Ántonia or Lena, d'Arnault has a
more ambiguous attitude toward control of his art and toward his objectification by his audience. While Jim sees him as a "docile and happy" black (123,
118), d'Arnault seems to be playing with the expectations of his white audience by putting on what Houston A. Baker Jr. calls the "mask of minstrelsy"
(47) in order to downplay the threat his powerful performance might inspire
in that audience.

The signs of that threat—to both Jim and Cather—are evident in the
defensive racism throughout the chapter devoted to d'Arnault. As Elizabeth
Ammons argues, by choosing to include d'Arnault in her novel and yet re-
sorting to racist stereotypes in her description of him, Cather ambivalently
acknowledges her debt to African American art forms (Ammons, *Conflicting Stories* 132).[16] Cather is also compelled to include a small portrait of
d'Arnault's development as an artist when, in the middle of his description of
the performance, Jim abruptly slips into an omniscient narrative recounting
the pianist's past. Although this story is filled with racist descriptions and
seems designed to dismiss d'Arnault's talent as freakish, it at times takes on
d'Arnault's perspective, relating his childhood attraction to music and his
wonder at the piano's "kind" response to his touch (120). The story must have
been told by d'Arnault at some point, but Jim—tellingly—does not allow
the black pianist's own voice to enter the narrative. Since it is impossible to
imagine that Jim would hold such an intimate conversation with d'Arnault,
it is more likely that someone else, perhaps Mrs. Harling, told Jim the story,
which further removes d'Arnault's voice and narrative control from his life
story. Instead, the story is interpreted through the distorting lens of a racist
sensibility that lessens d'Arnault's threat to Jim's (and Cather's) allegiance to
an elite Western aesthetic by obscuring his possession of the same kind of
creativity that Cather praises in her criticism and portrays in this novel.

D'Arnault's music makes possible an environment of playfulness and
sexuality among those on the fringes of Black Hawk society, bringing the
hired girls and the traveling salesmen together to dance. The pianist introduces sexuality into the text for the first time as something celebratory and
enjoyable rather than as the socially disruptive force that Jim sees in Lena's
sexuality. However, d'Arnault's role as the enabling agent of others' sexuality is highly problematic because it plays into racist stereotypes of African
Americans. D'Arnault's own sexuality is portrayed as autoerotic; we are told
that his music "worried his body incessantly" and allows him to enjoy "himself as only a Negro can. It was as if all the agreeable sensations possible for
creatures of flesh and blood were heaped up on those black-and-white keys,

and he were gloating over them and trickling them through his yellow fingers" (121). While the marginalized members of Black Hawk are able to act on these "agreeable sensations" by dancing together, d'Arnault's sexuality is only figured as self-enjoyment. Meanwhile, Jim disappears as a body during this passage and does not participate in the dancing, which leaves him impotently excited and restless (123). Threatened by the African American artist whose music elicits a sexual response in him, Jim reasserts his own narrative control by repeatedly describing d'Arnault in demeaning and dehumanizing terms. Indeed, by associating d'Arnault's music with sexuality, Jim denies that it is art; but the ability of this music to evoke passion and pleasure—which so agitates Jim—points to its status as art according to Cather's definition.

Jim is again aroused (but less troublesomely) by a less than polished artistic performance when he and Lena attend a production of *Camille* in Lincoln. His view of the actress who plays Marguerite parallels his description of d'Arnault's unschooled and unrefined yet arousing performance: she is "a woman who could not be taught . . . though she had a crude natural force which carried with people whose feelings were accessible and whose taste was not squeamish" (176). This depiction reflects Jim's ambivalence as an older man recalling his naïve and undeveloped artistic taste as a college student; yet he acknowledges that the performance, though "crude," is nevertheless powerful. While the actress is able to inspire the young Jim to "[believe] devoutly" in her performance (176), the older narrator attributes her effect to the play itself rather than to her talent: "Her conception of the character was as heavy and uncompromising as her diction. . . . But the lines were enough. She had only to utter them. They created the character in spite of her" (177). Like the music of the Vannis and d'Arnault, the play affects Jim emotionally, but by causing him to weep "unrestrainedly" and then to walk alone in the night "mourning for Marguerite Gauthier as if she had died only yesterday" (178). As Gelfant says, this emotional response is much stronger than Jim's reaction to his real-life "affair" with Lena (67); it is also notably stronger than his response to classical literature.

Importantly, both d'Arnault and the unnamed actress are very similar to real performers Cather reviewed: according to James Woodress, Blind d'Arnault is a composite of two African American performers known as Blind Tom and Blind Boone (291), and the actress in *Camille* appears to be based on Clara Morris, who played the same role in a performance Cather reviewed in 1893. Admitting that Clara Morris was "undoubtedly a loud actress" who dressed "gaudily and in bad taste" and was "coarse grained mentally and spiritually," Cather nevertheless prefers her "passion" to the "dainty" charm of other, more refined actresses (*Kingdom* 54). As she writes in another review: "The women of the stage know that to feel greatly is genius and to make others feel is art" (348). Although Jim excuses his response to these performances as the result of his immature aesthetic taste, Cather's emphasis on the importance of passion in art suggests that she includes the actress and the pianist in the novel as examples of the qualities that make a great artist. Cather's two fictional portraits of real-life performers in *My Ántonia*, when considered alongside the other unrecognized artists, point to her preoccupation with "low" art and marginalized artists who, although unrefined, are lively and sympathetic. From their sensibilities and ethnic diversity these artists create an original and undervalued American art.

III

Once we have pulled this one strand of the lively yet nonprivileged artist from the jumbled web of impressions produced by *My Ántonia*, we can see, on the one hand, a suggestive pattern of meditations on art and the artist and, on the other, a contrasting pattern of despair, the desire for death, and the controlling rigidity of repression, all of which form the dark undercurrent of the novel. Alongside her portrayal of creativity as a life force, Cather develops equally powerful images of the egoistic desire for control as a life-denying force, both in the motif of male suicides and in the appropriative hunger of Jim's narrative. Death erupts into the text in the form of mostly male suicides or murders, both premeditated acts.[17] We see this motif in the stories Jim remembers: of Peter and Pavel, who throw a bride to her death to save their own lives; the suicides of Mr. Shimerda and the tramp in Ántonia's story; and Wick Cutter's murder-suicide. This recurrence of death as a male desire illuminates Jim's narrative choices, as well as his desire to harness and control Ántonia's "meaning" in his text. Indeed, the egoism of the desire for control in art and the appeal of death are linked in *My Ántonia*, much as Cather links selflessness in art to the enjoyment of life and sensuality. By associating each of the suicides with an art form, Cather literalizes her claim that any control or form that is imposed on a narrative is deadening: "To me, the one important thing is never to kill the figure that you care for for the sake of atmosphere, well balanced structure, or neat presentation. . . . Sometimes too much symmetry kills things" (*Kingdom* 79).

Although Mr. Shimerda is the first person explicitly identified as an artist in *My Ántonia*, he stands in bleak contrast to artists such as the Vannis, Blind d'Arnault, and Ántonia, who exude liveliness and connectedness to life. In Mr. Shimerda, Cather brings together the underlying concerns of the novel: the artist, repressed sexuality, excessive nostalgia, and death. Unlike the other marginalized artists, Mr. Shimerda always seems depressed: he has "melancholy" eyes and a face that "looked like ashes like something from which all the warmth and light had died out" (18). Having lost his enthusiasm for life, after his arrival in America Mr. Shimerda never again plays his violin. The extremity of this change hints at more than homesickness. As

Ántonia explains, her father's feelings for his homeland center on the people he has left behind: "He cry for leave his old friends what make music with him. He love very much the man what play the [trombone]. . . . They go to school together and are friends from boys" (59). The loss of the man he loved seems to have led Mr. Shimerda to give up his music. In this case, his loss—or repression—of love and enthusiasm is linked with his inability to perform his art and results in his death wish.

Despite Mr. Shimerda's marginal status as an immigrant, Jim respects him and his music because of their connection to European high culture. He repeatedly thinks of Mr. Shimerda in positive terms and dissociates him from the "crowded clutter" and dirtiness of the Shimerdas' cave (57). Of a higher class than his wife, Mr. Shimerda has a "dignified manner" and reminds Jim of old portraits of Virginian gentility (18). But Mr. Shimerda's sensitive gentility and repressed sexuality work against him on the American prairie; he lacks the vitality necessary not only to create art but merely to survive the hardships of such a life. It is not his art that is dead but his ability to invest himself any longer in his music. His suicide, which is long foreshadowed, becomes a puzzle to which Jim's narrative repeatedly returns, most obviously in its echoes in the other suicides described by Ántonia and her son. Although Ántonia's stories should be viewed as her creations, they are present in Jim's narrative, of course, only because he chooses to include them. Tellingly, of all the stories Ántonia tells Jim, he includes in full only the two that concern death—the story (which Jim retells in his own words) of Pavel's grisly act of self-preservation and the story of a tramp who commits suicide.

When Jim retells the story of Peter and Pavel in his own words rather than quoting Ántonia directly, he indicates that it has become his story. Although he claims that he and Ántonia "guarded [the story] jealously—as if . . . the wedding party [had] been sacrificed, to give us a painful and peculiar pleasure" (41), it is not clear whether Ántonia shares these emotions. Instead, Jim's reaction to the story fits in with his obsession with the issues of death and control; often, as he drifts off to sleep he imagines himself being drawn along in the sledge, but whether he sees himself as Pavel or as the sacrificed bridal couple is unclear. Pavel's gruesome decision to throw the bride to the wolves—knowing that her husband would jump out after her—is interpreted by their community as markedly selfish and (at an unconscious level, perhaps) antiheterosexual. Peter and Pavel's subsequent ostracism in Russia and Peter's broken life after Pavel's death stand at the center of *My Ántonia* as a moral tale (with a perverse fascination to Jim) of the social costs of exerting self-centered control.[18]

By telling the story of the tramp, Ántonia again confronts Jim with a tale of death, but she is able to contemplate the puzzle of suicide, and by extension the horror of her father's violent death, without feeling despair herself. The tramp confronts her with this puzzle by selecting her to talk to: "He comes right up and begins to talk like he knows me already" (114). Significantly, Jim recalls that Ántonia tells this story in the middle of winter, which he describes as "bleak and desolate . . . as if we were being punished for loving the loveliness of summer" (111–112). In contrast to Jim's idealization of summer, Ántonia remembers the discomfort of the heat and the blowing chaff of the threshing machine. Yet, in her story Ántonia repeatedly counters the tramp's desire for death with the concerns of life and survival. When he says the ponds are too low to drown oneself in, Ántonia responds that "nobody wanted to drownd themselves, but if we didn't have rain soon we'd have to pump water for the cattle" (114); then, after the tramp has been "cut to pieces" by the threshing machine, she comments that "the machine ain't never worked right since"(115). While her reaction to the tramp's death wish could be an attempt to repress her own despair, Ántonia manages to ward off depression by emphasizing her bond with her community in the fight for survival.[19] She is able to sublimate the egoism that might lead to despair and accepts being "written" by the community's role for her.

Besides illustrating Ántonia's steadfast commitment to life, her story about the tramp also engages her with a mainstream American art form that is deadened by its sentimental nostalgia. Among the contents of the tramp's pocket is a "worn out" copy of a popular poem clipped from a newspaper. The poem, "The Old Oaken Bucket," by Samuel Woodworth, has as its theme a nostalgic view of childhood that recalls both Mr. Shimerda's painful homesickness and Jim's own nostalgia, which is the driving force of his narrative: "How dear to this heart are the scenes of my childhood, / When fond recollection presents them to view!"(1.1–2). By linking nostalgia with suicide, Cather implies that turning life into obsessive and falsified memory can be fatal, especially for the artist; we have already seen that Mr. Shimerda's lost love and inability to engage in his present life are deadly both to his art and to himself. Carrying this poem and a wishbone in his pocket, the tramp embodies a false and harmful American sentimentality that seeks to repress change and sexuality by glorifying childhood and the past. His comment "So it's Norwegians now, is it? I thought this was Americy" (114) reveals his chauvinistic belief in a "pure" America, free of immigrants. The drunken tramp, adhering to his bigotry and sentimental poetry, reflects the lack of vitality of American art when it strives to keep out the "foreign" influences of marginalized artists such as Ántonia and Blind d'Arnault.

Wick Cutter, the third suicide in *My Ántonia*, claims to share this sentimental view of America's past as "the good old days," but his promotion of American ideals—such as those represented in the adages from *Poor Richard's Almanack*—is clearly hypocritical (134). Cutter is not an artist, except in his construction of elaborate plots to kill his wife, to rape Ántonia, and to gain money by ruining people like Russian Peter. By taking advantage of his hired girls, his wife, and immigrants, Cutter the con artist abuses the privilege of patriarchal power. He evokes a horrible fascination in Jim by acting on the sexual urges and the opportunities for male dominance that Jim represses as negative and dangerous. Still, Cutter's narratives of control illuminate Jim's narrative strategies, for Cutter's manipulation of others' lives is a more overtly evil parallel to Jim's attempt to control Ántonia's meaning. Cutter designs his murder-suicide plot solely to assert his "will" even after his death. His need for control not only is destructive of others but is finally self-destructive as well.[20]

When Ántonia's son Rudolph tells the story of Cutter's suicide, he asks: "Did you ever hear of anybody else that killed himself for spite, Mr. Burden?" (233). Cuzak, joking that only the lawyers benefited from Cutter's death, indirectly identifies Jim, now a lawyer himself, as a beneficiary of Cutter's legacy. By placing the story of Wick Cutter's suicide at the end of the novel, Cather covertly points to a connection between the ending of Cutter's life and the ending of Jim's narrative quest. Cutter acts out not only the sexual urges that Jim represses but also Jim's urge toward suicide, which permeates his narrative despite his efforts to repress it. The story of Cutter's suicide-murder scheme illustrates the spitefulness of suicide, but perhaps more importantly, the Cuzak children's giggles and "hurrahs" in response to Rudolph's telling of it shows Jim that even an act as self-controlled as suicide can be interpreted mockingly. This lesson forces Jim to look elsewhere for relief from his unhappy adult life.

Jim's ambivalent desire for death has followed him through the novel like his shadow on the prairie, which the adult narrator "remembers" as the sign of mortality, present even in his childhood. When he describes his arrival on the prairie, he repeatedly emphasizes the erasure of his identity, as he "dissolves" into or is "blotted out" by the landscape (14, 8). Unlike women like Ántonia or Mrs. Harling, who "become a relationship" when they lose themselves in the pleasure of others (*Obscure* 115), Jim is further isolated from people when he experiences what Cather called the "erasure of personality" she felt when she was first confronted by the vast space of the prairie (*Kingdom* 448). Newly orphaned, Jim imagines that this new land is empty even of his dead parents' spirits (8). Picturing death as "happiness," a dissolution "into something complete and great" (14), Jim clearly sees death as the only way he can ever attain the pleasure of selflessness that he admires in Ántonia. In fact, Jim's furtive glimpse of Mr. Shimerda's corpse suggests that death can also be a return to the comfort of the womb, for Mr. Shimerda lies in the coffin in a fetal position, "on his side, with his knees drawn up" (75).[21] But after Jim has romanticized death as desirable and erased his memory of his dead parents, the grisly reality of willed death erupts into his narrative in the stories of the three suicides.

Included among his own memories, yet told by and about other people, the suicide stories become a part of Jim's past in which he seems to have no active role; they enter his novel as though against his conscious choice. However, that Jim also struggles with an urge toward suicide is suggested by his affinity with Mr. Shimerda. The only adult who does not take Jim "for granted" (20), Mr. Shimerda emphasizes his bond with the boy by offering him the gun that will later be used as a suicide weapon.[22] In this scene the adult narrator projects foreshadowing of his own death backward onto his childhood. Setting the scene for the encounter, he describes the autumn sunset as having "the exultation of victory . . . like a hero's death—heroes who died young and gloriously" (28). Although distinguishing Jim's view of death as an adult from his view as a child is impossible, the idea that death as a youth is heroic, even victorious, fits in with his nostalgic obsession with his childhood. He even seems to wish he had died as a child: when he and Ántonia meet as adults near Mr. Shimerda's grave Jim feels "the old pull of the earth," which makes him wish he "could be a little boy again, and that my way could end there" (207).

Despite Jim's glorification of youthful death, Cather does not portray the suicides in *My Ántonia* as "triumphant endings," but as grisly acts that are selfish and hurt others. Both Mr. Shimerda and the tramp jeopardize the well-being of others, Shimerda by leaving his family dependent on the sympathy of the community, and the tramp by damaging the threshing machine. Cutter kills not only himself but his wife just so that his money will not go to her or her family after his death. Cutter's suicide at the end of the novel counterbalances Shimerda's suicide in book 1 and ends Jim's romanticized attraction to taking one's life. Rudolph's question about the novelty of Cutter's "killing himself for spite" is answered by the cumulative contrast of the suicidal men with the nontraditional male and female artists who encourage life and sensuality. Earlier, when Mr. Shimerda offers Jim his gun, Ántonia provides an alternative to the two males' desire for death and dissolution. She carries in her hair a faintly singing insect that reminds her of Old Hata, the Bohemian beggar woman who used to sing "in a cracked voice" for "a warm place by the fire" (27). Here Ántonia views art and warmth as equal means of exchange, thus linking creative work with the work of survival, without valuing one over the other; tellingly, she dwells not on Old Hata's talent (or lack of talent) but on the children's love for her. Her emphasis on the emotional relationship of the artist to her audience shows that Ántonia feels no need to promote the greatness of her talent. She accepts as a fact of life the artist's perpetual struggle for life, fighting poverty and cold, yet (to Jim's amazement) she manages to maintain her enthusiasm and even to convey it to others. Jim interprets Ántonia's nesting of the insect not as an act of empathic identification with Old Hata but as an example of her ability to provide the nurturance the artist needs to survive the hardships of life. As an adult, Jim wants to see

Ántonia as continuing to fulfill his needs, so that he can derive the will to live as well as the material with which to create. Reaffirming his image of her as a maternal nurturer of life—an always asexual lover, mother, sister, muse, "anything that a woman can be to a man" (206)—allows him to continually circle back to his childhood without acting on his unhappiness with his adult life.[23]

IV

Jim's movement into memory to combat a tendency toward suicide is consistent with his assertion of control in creating his narrative. Since he derives his will to live from recollections of his earlier life, he attempts to force the people in his past to conform to the supportive roles he assigns them. In contrast with Ántonia and the other marginalized artists, who either imbue their audience with their "zest for life" or enable them to express their own sensuality, Jim's narrative is limited to its effect upon himself and his one chosen reader. Although he shares his finished manuscript with an old friend, its originating force is entirely personal; as Jim says in the introduction, "I've been writing down what I remember about Ántonia. . . . On my long trips across the country, I amuse myself like that, in my stateroom" (2). This image of the artist as isolated and amusing only himself more clearly fulfills the autoerotic and self-centered description Jim tries to apply to d'Arnault's piano playing.

The effect of such isolation on the artist is another of Cather's themes in her early reviews and essays. Alongside her insistence on the genius of sympathy and passion, Cather also emphasizes the loneliness of artists, whose dedication to their art requires that they separate themselves from the world and "suffer . . . the awful loneliness, the longing for human fellowship and for human love" (*Kingdom* 435). Although such isolation might be necessary for the traditionally defined Western artist, it is alien to performance artists such as Ántonia, whose art is communal by nature. As an adult married to a woman "incapable of enthusiasm" (1), Jim suppresses his longing for love by creating fictionalized characters who can fulfill his needs. When he reflects on his inability to "lose [himself]" in the "impersonal" classics as Gaston Cleric is able to do, Jim explains: "Mental excitement was apt to send me with a rush back to my own naked land and the figures scattered upon it" (168). Even when he shares his text with his friend, who also knew Ántonia, Jim controls the people of his "own naked land" exactly by making them his "own" and thus divorcing them from life: "They were so much alive in me that I scarcely stopped to wonder whether they were alive anywhere else" (168).

Jim's inability to respond to classical literature with the same enthusiasm that he feels in response to nonprivileged art points to his uneasy initiation into the Western literary tradition. Indeed, Jim's adult depression and his obsession with Ántonia and other people in his past imply that his education has separated him from the art forms that he loved during his boyhood. As a boy, Jim enjoys listening to Otto's cowboy songs or Ántonia's stories and participating in the kitchen culture of cooking and handicrafts and reads popular books such as *The Swiss Family Robinson* and *A Life of Jesse James*. Even the first "book" Jim creates—as a Christmas present for Yulka—is a mixture of pictures from popular family magazines or advertisements and circus scenes formed of pasted pieces of calico. This quiltlike piecing together of low-brow art forms and a traditionally female handicraft is a forerunner of Jim's narrative about Ántonia, which he also pieces together from the art of other, nonprivileged artists; but this first book is created to please another person.

Just as Jim does not make any value distinctions as a child between folk art and written "literature," O'Brien writes that the adolescent Cather "did not make distinctions between high- and middle-brow culture or between culturally defined 'masterpieces' and books of lesser distinction but wider popular appeal" (80). Jim's education in narrative forms follows Cather's own experience of growing up around female storytellers and then reading popular adventure stories alongside the classical literature that her male mentors taught her to read and to value. Despite her veneration for the classics, Cather often expressed in interviews and essays her appreciation of any "low" art that conveyed the liveliness, passion, and selflessness that to her represented artistic "genius." Although she railed against vulgarity and insisted on the discipline of the artist's craft, she was equally hard on elite yet lifeless art and always favored a performance or text, whether high or low art, that could "give voice to the hearts of men" (*Kingdom* 409).[24]

Cather attempts to connect Jim's depiction of Ántonia—and by extension Nebraska—with Virgil's project of turning a celebration of rural life into high art.[25] However, Jim's encounters with the vitality of nonprivileged American artists eclipse Virgil and "the world of ideas" associated with him (165). When he first studies the *Aeneid,* Jim isolates himself for the summer in "an empty room where I should be undisturbed" (147). As he recites the *Aeneid* aloud, he looks out his window at "the distant river bluffs and the roll of blond pastures between" (148). This vista, with its suggestions of female sexuality, is so much more enticing than his memorization of Virgil that Jim's narrative skips to his "one holiday that summer": a trip to that same river with the hired girls (148). In college Jim is distracted from his solitary reading of Virgil's *Georgics* by Lena's sudden appearance and his subsequent revelation that "if there were no girls like [Lena] in the world, there would be no poetry" (173). By reducing Lena and the other hired girls to his muses, he effectively erases their ability to create art themselves; they only exist to evoke his response to them. The ease with which he substitutes Lena for Ántonia as the source of his inspiration points to his desire to efface Ántonia's individuality: she is just one of the many "girls" to inspire poetry throughout time.

Still, by realizing the difficulty involved in bringing to life the supposedly universal and atemporal work of Virgil, Jim acknowledges the greater hold that the real people, who are merely objectified and marginalized by high art, have on his imagination. And, indirectly, his attraction to women such as Lena and Ántonia points to the powerful appeal of their creative work. When Jim finishes his own narrative, he supposes that it lacks "form" (2) because of his inclusion of the stories and music of all of the artists whose work enlivened his childhood. His appropriation of the energy of the female and marginalized male artists in his narrative without recognizing them as artists clearly enlivens the tale he tells. In alluding so boldly to Virgil, Cather introduces her characters, subject matter, and "formless" narrative style into the discourse of high art. However, she presents Ántonia and the other artists ambiguously, portraying them mainly as the inspiration for the narrative of a white male writer. By using the controlling vision of a male narrator, Cather unfortunately effaces the strength and clarity of the statement she might have made about art and the American artist and, as Elizabeth Ammons argues, erases the debt she owed to these nonprivileged artists and their art forms (Ammons, *Conflicting Stories* 132).

When Mr. Shimerda first moves to Nebraska, Otto Fuchs dismisses his music as useless on the prairie (16). But Cather's connection of nontraditional artists with a life force emphasizes that the community needs their enthusiasm in order to endure the hardship and monotony of prairie life. The lack of liveliness and physicality in the WASP culture of the Midwest emerges in bits and pieces in *My Ántonia:* Jim feels "surrounded by a wall of silence" in the Burden household (72), lingers in the winter twilight outside the stained-glass church window out of "hunger for colour" (112), and is amazed that Ántonia's children are "not afraid to touch each other" (224). Just as our picture of Jim emerges from the elisions of his text and from Ántonia's photographs, a picture of the starkness of Midwestern American life emerges in contrast to the ambivalently detailed descriptions Jim gives of the women and "outsiders"—whether immigrants or African Americans whose difference from him fascinates him. In such a society, the artists who break the monotony and lower the inhibitions of conventionality must come from outside the mainstream or elitist culture, from the ranks of the marginalized or disempowered. Precisely because of their lack of conventionally defined refinement and their position outside the realm of Western high art, such artists help to redefine and broaden our concept of American art. As Cather wrote of the popular comedian Nat Goodwin in 1894, nonprivileged artists like him form "a clan that is a very real part of American life and that has a strong influence in the moulding of American society, and it has a right to a representative in the great legislature of art" (*Kingdom* 129).

NOTES

1. See, e.g., Fetterley 146–150; Gelfant 63, 67; Lambert 684–690; and Rosowski 88–91.

2. At the end of her illuminating chapter on *My Ántonia,* Rosowski also attributes Ántonia's emergence "as herself" during Jim's visit to her role as "the center of 'the family legend,'" the teller of domestic tales "drawn from life" rather than literature (90). I use this moment in *My Ántonia* to support a rereading of Jim's narrative.

3. Gelfant was the first critic to discuss Jim as an unreliable narrator (60). See also Fetterley 153–158 for an invigorating discussion of Cather's own male masquerade through the "radically incomplete" transposition of her own experience and desires onto a male character.

4. Jim's response to Ántonia's mothering varies. As a boy, he feels he's superior to her because she's female and resents her "protecting manner" (30); however, once he is older, he seems happiest when she acts like a mother to him, as when he includes himself among her sons. Even during their teenage years, when Ántonia responds to his kiss as though he were breaking a taboo, Jim's pride in her reaction seems connected to his feeling that she will "always treat me like a kid" (143).

5. See, e.g., Fetterley and Irving for in-depth discussions of Jim's uneasiness about Ántonia's unconventional bending of gender and class roles. It is interesting to note that it is a story told sympathetically by the Widow Steavens that convinces Jim to "forgive" Ántonia again after she gives birth to a child out of wedlock (195).

6. In choosing to concentrate on Ántonia and the performing artists in part 2, I am neglecting other storytellers. I hope to suggest here a context in which readers might think of the many storytellers and other artists in *My Ántonia,* for example, Otto Fuchs, who often tells of his adventures (45–46); Grandmother Burden, whose kitchen and home are evidence of her "cheerful zest" despite having "very little to do with" (44); and the Widow Steavens, whose sympathetic story about Ántonia's out-of-wedlock pregnancy is the longest directly transcribed tale and serves to reconcile Jim to Ántonia (198–204). Likewise, Jim's inclusion of many stories about peripheral characters (such as Tiny Soderball, "Crazy Mary," and Ole Benson), which he seems to relate from communal knowledge, can be considered as his imitation of storytellers who tell stories about the people in their community.

7. See Daiches for an early response to the stories as having "little if any relation to the story of Ántonia's development" (47). This view was first challenged by Gelfant, who views the stories, as well as other apparent digressions in Jim's narrative, as part of the violent eruption of the sexuality Cather attempts to repress in her text. For a more recent interpretation of the stories and the work they do for Jim and Ántonia, see Peterman.

8. Cather again refers to the representation of "life itself" as the goal of the artist in her preface to Sarah Orne Jewett's *Country of the Pointed Firs and Other Stories* (7). There she praises Jewett's stories as "living things" that "melt into the land and the life of the land until they are not stories at all, but life itself" (6).

9. See O'Brien 80–81 and chs. 7–8 for an important, in-depth discussion of the effect the intersection of high art and gender had on Cather's work.

10. For a helpful history and analysis of the effort by early-twentieth-century male literature professors (and later critics) to define American literature as a

"masculine" field, see Elizabeth Ammons's introduction to her *Conflicting Stories* and O'Brien.

11. Cather did not consider the selfless sympathy and passion she praised to be the traits of most women writers; in fact, she made a clear distinction between the traits she praised and the "drivelling nonsense and mawkish sentimentality and contemptible feminine weakness" that she felt most women writers indulged in (1895 review of "Ouida" in *Kingdom* 408). In this same review, Cather distinguishes between such writers, who "only imagined and strained after effects, [and] never lived at all; . . . never laughed with children, toiled with men or wept with women," and writers who were able to "give voice to the hearts of men" because they have "known them, loved them" (409).

12. Notably, Jim thinks of Ántonia's retelling and translation of the story as a merely mirrorlike repetition of Pavel's words and does not recall how Ántonia told it. I discuss below the significance of Jim's putting the story into his own words.

13. Besides ceding this role to Ántonia, Jim also contradicts the traditional development of such stories, which usually become more exaggerated with each retelling (Dobos 177), by deflating the heroism of the actual event when he tells of it as an adult in *My Ántonia*.

14. Although Ántonia does tell stories about the past, she does not see the past as her only source, as Jim does. In contrast, Jim sees his present life as sterile and depressing and views his past as a golden time. He makes the past into a fetish, while Ántonia freely changes details in her stories about the past and draws from her present life for story material as well.

15. My view of Lena's art as a specifically female celebration of the female body, without the sole aim of attracting male attention, is indebted to Fetterley's interpretation of Lena as representing "one model of lesbian sexuality" (159).

16. For my reading of Blind d'Arnault—and, indeed, for my thoughts in this essay—I am more greatly indebted to the ideas and enthusiastic feedback of Elizabeth Ammons than a citation of any of her books or essays can convey. For a fuller analysis of d'Arnault's role and importance see Ammons, "*My Ántonia* and African American Music."

17. "Crazy Mary" is the only female character associated with intentional violence. Jealous of her husband's obsession with Lena and considered insane by her community, Mary Benson chases Lena with a corn knife (108–109). I do not include Mary in my discussion here, because the dynamics of her violence, while as important as the dynamics of the men's violence, are different from theirs. Mary's desire to "trim some of that shape off " Lena (108) and her proud exhibition of the sharpness of her knife's blade suggest that Mary's violence is a rejection of femininity and an attempt to appropriate male power.

18. James Woodress says that the story of Peter and Pavel is an actual folk tale that has been recorded by folklorists from immigrants living in Nebraska (292). That Cather claimed to have forgotten that she had borrowed the tale is highly suggestive of the influence the immigrant storytellers had on her imagination and writing.

19. As Evelyn Funda has pointed out to me, Ántonia's qualification "What would anybody want to kill themselves in summer for?" (115) suggests that she understands (and perhaps has felt) the desire to die during the winter. Since her father killed himself in the winter, Ántonia's telling of this story during that season suggests that she might associate winter with death and the desire to die.

20. It is interesting to note that the stories of Wick Cutter, Peter and Pavel, and Mr. Shimerda each link death and homosexual desire as well as art. As Fetterley notes, Cutter almost rapes Jim (157), and Peter and Pavel are a couple who have rejected heterosexuality metaphorically by killing the bridal couple (150); also, as I mentioned earlier, Mr. Shimerda gives up his music while pining for his male friend. The triangular relationship of art, homosexual desire, and death is highly suggestive.

21. His body and head covered entirely, Mr. Shimerda has been desexed as well; only "one of his long, shapely hands"—the instrument of both his death and his violin playing—is revealed (75).

22. Mr. Shimerda also expresses this bond when he first asks Jim to "te-e-ach my Ántonia!" (Sao); that Jim later makes her his Ántonia and tells her so while they sit on the older man's grave site (Sao 5–6) highlights his fascination with Shimerda.

23. See Rosowski for an insightful discussion of the circular structure of *My Ántonia* (which she describes as "[beginning] in and [returning] to childhood" 1771) as Cather's homage to and critique of the Romantic project. Ántonia—and Jim's—adult desire for a return to her nurturance might also be seen as replacing Jim's longing for his dead parents.

24. As Bernice Slow writes in her introduction to Cather's early essays, Cather made "a real effort to defend the people's choice" (*Kingdom* 55). This effort is seen, for example, in Cather's review of the comedian Nat Goodwin, whose "rare gift of reaching out to the people and appealing to them" could so delight the audience that "you almost forget that his art is not of the highest kind" (*Kingdom* 130).

25. For helpful discussions of Cather's use of Virgil in *My Ántonia*, see Fetterley 160–161; Gelfant 66–68; O'Brien 81; Schwind 59–61; and Woodress 298. Fetterley also identifies the landscape of *My Ántonia* as feminine (161), as I do below.

Works Cited

Ammons, Elizabeth. "*My Ántonia* and African American Music." *New Essays on* My Ántonia. Ed. Sharon O'Brien. New York: Cambridge University Press, forthcoming.

———. *Conflicting Stories: American Women Writers at the Turn into the Twentieth Century*. New York: Oxford University Press, 1991.

Baker, Houston A., Jr. *Modernism and the Harlem Renaissance*. Chicago: University of Chicago Press, 1987.

Bennett, Mildred R. *The World of Willa Cather*. New York: Dodd, Mead, 1951.

Cather, Willa. *The Kingdom of Art: Willa Cather's First Principles and Critical Statements, 1893–1896*. Ed. Bernice Slote. Lincoln: University of Nebraska Press, 1966.

———. *My Ántonia*. 1918. Boston: Houghton Mifflin, 1988.

———. *Obscure Destinies*. Boston: Houghton Mifflin, 1938.

———. Preface to *The Country of the Pointed Firs and Other Stories*, by Sarah Orne Jewett. Ed. Willa Cather. New York: Doubleday, 1956.

———. *The Song of the Lark*. Boston: Houghton Mifflin, 1915.

———. *Willa Cather in Person: Interviews, Speeches, and Letters*. Ed. L. Brent Bohlke. Lincoln: University of Nebraska Press, 1986.

Daiches, David. *Willa Cather: A Critical Introduction*. Ithaca: Cornell University Press, 1951.

Dobos, Ilona. "True Stories." Trans. Peter Vari. *Studies in East European Folk Narrative.* Ed. Linda Degh. Indiana University: American Folklore Society and the Indiana University Folklore Monographs Series, 1978. 167–2055.

Fetterley, Judith. "*My Ántonia*, Jim Burden, and the Dilemma of the Lesbian Writer." *Lesbian Texts and Contexts: Radical Revisions.* Ed. Karla Jay, Joanne Glasgow, and Catharine Stimpson. New York: New York University Press, 1990. 145–163.

Gelfant, Blanche H. "The Forgotten Reaping-Hook: Sex in *My Ántonia.*" *American Literature* 43 (1971): 60–82.

Irving, Katrina. "Displacing Homosexuality: The Use of Ethnicity in Willa Cather's *My Ántonia.*" *Modern Fiction Studies* 36.1 (Spring 1990): 90–102.

Lambert, Deborah. "The Defeat of a Hero: Autonomy and Sexuality in *My Ántonia.*" *American Literature* 53.4 (January 1982): 676–690.

Lewis, Edith. *Willa Cather Living: A Personal Record.* New York: Knopf, 1953

O'Brien, Sharon. *Willa Cather: The Emerging Voice.* New York: Oxford University Press, 1987.

Peterman, Michael. "Kindling the Imagination: The Inset Stories of *My Ántonia.*" *Approaches to Teaching Cather's* My Ántonia. Ed. Susan J. Rosowski. New York: MLA, 1989. 156–162.

Rosowski, Susan. *The Voyage Perilous: Willa Cather's Romanticism.* Lincoln: Univesity of Nebraska Press, 1986.

Schwind, Jean. "The Benda Illustrations to *My Ántonia*: Cather's 'Silent' Supplement to Jim Burden's Narrative." *PMLA* 100.1 (January 1985): 51–67.

Sergeant, Elizabeth Shepley. *Willa Cather: A Memoir.* 1953. Lincoln: University of Nebraska Press, Bison Books, 1963.

Woodress, James. *Willa Cather: Her Life and Art.* Lincoln: University of Nebraska Press, 1970.

Woodworth, Samuel. "The Old Oaken Bucket." *The Best Loved Poems of the American People.* Ed. Hazel Felleman. New York: Garden City, 1936. 385.

SUSAN J. ROSOWSKI

Pro/Creativity and a Kinship Aesthetic

In *The Land before Her* Annette Kolodny begins her account of women's historical responses to American frontiers and the West with a chapter titled "Dispossessed of Paradise." "By the time European women began to arrive on the Atlantic shores of what is now the United States," Kolodny writes, "the New World had long been given over to the fantasies of men." Before explorers lay "the virgin land," "a country that hath yet her maydenhead," a "*Paradise* with all her Virgin beauties." But, as Kolodny continues, "the psychosexual dynamic of a virginal paradise meant, however, that real flesh-and-blood women—at least metaphorically—were dispossessed of paradise." English-speaking women struggled to find an alternate set of images by creating "gardens in the wilderness" (3).

Willa Cather accepted no such dispossession. Instead, she sent Adam packing and claimed paradise for women, restoring to them a psychosexual identification with nature and appropriating for them the promise of nature's wildness. Rather than writing about a virgin land waiting to be despoiled, Cather conceived of the West as female nature slumbering, awakening, and roaring its independence. In her stories, and culminating in *O Pioneers!*, she gave women's fantasies to the West and cast their domestic materials on an epic scale; in doing so she reclaimed materiality for women, rewrote the captivity myth into a story of liberation, and divorced the plot of sexuality from

Birthing a Nation: Gender, Creativity, and the West in American Literature (Lincoln: University of Nebraska Press, 1999): pp. 79–92. © 1996 University of Nebraska Press.

its gendered confinements. It was all in preparation, as it turned out, to return a flesh-and-blood woman to paradise by writing about Annie Sadelik, the Bohemian hired girl of one of Cather's neighbors, celebrating her as "one of the truest artists I ever knew" (qtd. in Bohlke 44), and through her, revising the idea of creativity that she had inherited.

As Marta Weigle writes in *Creation and Procreation*, in this cosmogonical tradition procreation existed as an antithesis to creation. "Procreation is relegated to elemental or physical or biological status, while spiritual or metaphysical or symbolic creation becomes the valued paradigm for ritual custom, art, narrative, and belief systems" (xi). Women have babies; men write books. Definitions from *The Oxford English Dictionary* (1933) illustrate the difference:

> Create: Transitive. Said of the divine agent. To bring into being, cause to exist; *esp.* to produce where nothing was before, "to form out of nothing."
> Procreate. To beget, engender, generate (offspring). To produce offspring . . . to give rise to, occasion.

By structuring her novel around images of birth, Cather evoked traditional mythologies of cosmogony and parturition, then revised those traditions as she created her birth of a nation. Her descriptions of the Shimerdas living in a dugout on an unbroken frontier evoke Native American emergence mythologies; Ántonia's emerging sexuality is set within the Judeo-Christian culture of Black Hawk, and Jim Burden's awakening to ideas at the university recalls classical mythologies of creativity. Cather revised these traditions, however, by refiguring into them the Muse, the midwife, and the Earth Mother. Read sequentially, *My Ántonia* provides a historical survey of myths about and attitudes toward birth; read incrementally, Cather's narrative creates a new myth for America.

Childhood scenes in *My Ántonia* revolve around two visits to the Shimerdas in their dugout. Each visit suggests both an emergence mythology of a people's "journeying through lower or other worlds, domains, or wombs" (Weigle 7) and a people's origin in their mother, the earth. In his first visit, Jim witnesses the Shimerdas emerge from a hole in the bank as if the earth was giving birth to life itself; in the second visit, during winter and amid the apparent absence of life, Jim enters that dugout hole as if descending into an underworld to discover its secrets. To Jim, "The air in the cave was stifling, and it was very dark, too" (71). Only gradually, as his eyes adjust to the darkness, does he realize that "In the rear wall was another little cave; a round hole, not much bigger than an oil barrel, scooped out in the black earth," where Ántonia and her sister sleep (72).

Earth caves may suggest to Jim a frightening descent into a secret, sealed womblike space closely associated with death,[1] but Ántonia presents another view: "I like for sleep there," she insists, "this is warm like the badger hole" (73). Her description echoes not only emergence myths generally but the Acoma Pueblo origin myth specifically, a myth Cather likely knew from her family's copy of John M. Gunn's *Schat-Chen: History, Traditions and Narratives of the Queres Indians of Laguna and Acoma* (1917). Here she would have read of two sisters who were born underground and remained in the dark as they slowly and patiently grew until they finally emerged through a hole made by a badger.[2]

For her second stage of revisioning, Cather set Ántonia within the Judeo-Christian tradition of the Fall. Whereas the childhood scenes concerned Ántonia's genesis and birth, the Black Hawk scenes concern her awakening to a sexuality that is complicated for Western civilization because of its polarized treatment in the book of Genesis. Adam and Eve gained sexual knowledge by eating fruit from the tree of knowledge of good and evil, and as Gerda Lerner has written, "Once and forever, creativity (and with it the secret of immortality) is severed from procreativity. Creativity is reserved to God; procreativity of human beings is the lot of women. The curse on Eve makes it a painful and subordinate lot" (197). Plot lines in *My Ántonia* separate to reflect this polarized tradition when Jim aligns himself with the world of ideas while Ántonia aligns herself with that of human relationships.[3] He prepares for a creative life of the mind by excelling in high school and by studying trigonometry and beginning Virgil alone the following summer. He then leaves his family and friends to attend the university in Lincoln. During the same period Ántonia follows her script for procreativity by entering domestic service with the Harlings, going with the hired girls to the dances, and loving railway conductor Larry Donovan. Tension is inevitable when a fertility goddess from emergence myth is transplanted into Protestant Black Hawk, and Black Hawk responds by tightening its constrictions upon Ántonia until, following her lover to Denver, she disappears from the text.

Two books and two decades later, Jim returns to Ántonia, now settled with her husband and many children on a Nebraska farm. His visit builds to the most famous birth scene in American literature: "Why don't we show Mr. Burden our new fruit cave?" Ántonia's daughter asks, prompting a gathering of the family as children emerge from the house, join with other children from the yard, and run ahead to open the cellar door, so that "When we descended, they all came down after us" (326–327). The scene reaches its climax when, as Jim describes it: "We turned to leave the cave; Ántonia and I went up the stairs first, and the children waited. We were standing outside talking, when they all came running up the steps together; big and little, tow heads and gold heads and brown, and flashing little naked legs; a veritable explosion

of life out of the dark cave into the sunlight. It made me dizzy for a moment" (328). Making explicit that this scene is Cather's version of the birth
of America, Jim reflects that Ántonia is "a rich mine of life, like the founders
of early nations" (342), and thus brings the succession of birth myths to the
present. The power of the scene lies in our reading not only sequentially, but
incrementally, to recognize that the Cuzaks' fruit cave is reminiscent of the
dugout cave that first held Ántonia in the New World, and from which she
emerged as if in a first birth, and that Ántonia has fulfilled her destiny as a
natural born mother—undeniably, an Earth Mother.

Ántonia as Earth Mother? The description has become so standard that
it is easy to pass over how revolutionary is Cather's revisioning of western
myths that depict women. As Simone de Beauvoir wrote of the Earth Mother
tradition that Cather inherited, the connection of woman with nature is decidedly ambivalent. Though praises may be sung to a fecund nature, "more often
man is in revolt against his carnal state; he sees himself as a fallen god: his
curse is to be fallen from a bright and ordered heaven into the chaotic shadows of his mother's womb. . . . This quivering jelly which is elaborated in the
womb (the womb, secret and sealed like the tomb) evokes too clearly the soft
viscosity of carrion for him not to turn shuddering away. . . . The Earth Mother
engulfs the bones of her children" (144–147).[4] By Cather's account, however,
the Earth Mother tradition is no imprisonment to earth, no secret and sealed
space. Instead the nurturing womb is liberated and celebrated, fertility goddess
and Earth Mother restored into a birth myth for the New World.

Celebration takes the form of perception made finer. Having witnessed
the explosion of life out of a fruit cave, Jim now sees womblike enclosures
replicated in the larger scene, as if Ántonia's body has regenerated itself in his
perception of space. The Cuzaks' house is encircled by a roof so steep that the
eaves almost touch "the forest of tall hollyhocks" growing alongside it, and its
front yard is "enclosed by a thorny locust hedge" (328–329). Behind the house
a cherry orchard and an apple orchard are "surrounded by a triple enclosure; the
wire fence, then the hedge of thorny locusts, then the mulberry hedge. . . . The
hedges were so tall that we could see nothing but the blue sky above them. . . .
The orchard seemed full of sun, like a cup" (330–331). Movement of descent and
ascent and of in and out creates a feeling of freedom in each enclosure, and
colors establish the inestimable value of contents protected therein: the gem-
like glow of fruit preserved within the cave and the flash of gold from bodies
tumbling out of it; the silvery trees flashing from the yard and the purple-red
crabs in the orchard that have "a thin silvery glaze over them"; the handsome
drakes "with pinkish gray bodies, their heads and necks covered with irides-
cent green feathers which grew close and full, changing like a peacock's neck"
(331). Through it all, the afternoon sun pours down in a shower of gold as if
in granting grace.

Female space, liberated from the dark confines of secrecy and shame associated with birth, becomes the central and ongoing metaphor through which the world's fertility and fecundity are experienced. There is no *I* here (to refer to Ántonia's fruit cellar is to miss the point). Instead there is the *we* of family and, by implication, community and nation. "Why don't *we* show Mr. Burden *our* new fruit cellar," Anna asks; "in winter there are nearly always *some of us* around to come out and get things" Ambrosch explains; and Ántonia describes "the bread *we* bake" and the sugar it takes "for *us* to preserve with" (326–327; emphases mine) .

Enlightenment is all the more powerful because it is a release from confinement, which is so closely associated with birth as to be considered its necessary condition. Mores and laws defining and legislating procreativity undergird Black Hawk's "respect for respectability" (195), another form of confinement when, under its guise, women, bound by both class and gender, are denied sexual knowledge. "[P]hysical exercise was thought rather inelegant for the daughters of well-to-do families," Jim observes of Black Hawk society; "When one danced with them their bodies never moved inside their clothes; their muscles seemed to ask but one thing—not to be disturbed" (192–193). Country girls, on the other hand, were "physically . . . almost a race apart," for their "out-of-door work had given them a vigor which . . . developed into a positive carriage and freedom of movement," in contrast to the town girls (192).

The cultural tensions of Black Hawk reflect tensions of mythic appropriations. By moving to Black Hawk and becoming one of "The Hired Girls" (the title of book 2) Ántonia confronts a Judeo-Christian ethos by which the sexuality of the fertility goddess "was so defined as to serve her motherly function, and it was limited by two conditions: she was to be subordinate to her husband, and she would bring forth her children in pain" (Lerner 196). With Genesis in the background, a fall is inevitable—apparently Ántonia's as she suffers the cultural confinements imposed upon her and the assumptions behind those confinements.

As Ántonia develops into adolescence, the circumstances of frontier living provide her knowledge: "Ambrosch put upon her some chores a girl ought not to do, . . . and the farm-hands around the country joked in a nasty way about it" (121). The strength of her body results in hunger (eating is a metaphor for lust), and her emerging beauty attracts attention. Maturing as robustly physical and vibrantly sexual, Ántonia defies expectations that a woman be either physical *or* spiritual, sexual *or* maternal. In Black Hawk she continues going to the summer tent dances despite her employer's ultimatum that she stop because she was getting "a reputation for being free and easy." "Stop going to the tent?" Ántonia retorts; "I wouldn't think of it for a minute! My own father couldn't make me stop! Mr. Harling ain't my boss outside my work. I won't give up my friends, either!" (200). She goes to work for Wick Cutter even though she knows that previous hired girls who worked for him were ruined, and she goes to Denver to join Larry Donovan even though they are as yet unmarried.

From Fielding's Tom Jones to Fitzgerald's Nick Carroway, countless young men have left the country for the city, where they gain the knowledge of the world they will need to take their place in it; the analogous script for women is the cautionary one played out in Theodore Dreiser's *Sister Carrie*. Young women moving to the city support themselves by entering "service" and becoming "hired girls," language that doubles for prostitution and signifies the sanctions against them. Cather evokes these sanctions in "The Hired Girls," revisiting the literary version of a woman's fall into knowledge in which a young woman moves from country to city, learns sexuality, and is punished by "the nothingness that surrounds the . . . prostitute" (Michie 73).

In Black Hawk an undercurrent of gossip links a woman's independence with female sexuality and prostitution. Wick Cutter "was notoriously dissolute with women," and two Swedish girls "were the worse for the experience" of living in his house—he had taken one to Omaha "and established [her] in the business for which he had fitted her. He still visited her" (203). Lena Lingard is suspect by becoming a seamstress,[5] and Tiny Soderball by running a lodging house for sailors. "This, every one said, would be the end of Tiny" (291). Everyone knows also, one might add, that such gossip follows Ántonia.

Her punishment takes the form of silencing. Ántonia's own voice grows distant and then silent when from Denver she writes a letter, then a postcard, and then nothing. More powerfully, Jim's narrative voice erases Ántonia's presence when he admits that he scarcely thinks of her while he is at the university in Lincoln and recalls how grudging and painful references to her are in Black Hawk. "You know, of course, about poor Ántonia," Mrs. Harling says to Jim, upon which he bitterly thinks, "Poor Ántonia! Every one would be saying that now" (289). She has become a subject to be avoided, acknowledged only when necessary and then with the barest of details. Jim reports that "grandmother had written me how Ántonia went away to marry Larry Donovan at some place where he was working; that he had deserted her, and that there was now a baby" but cuts short his recollection with "This was all I knew" (289–290). When Jim remembers Frances Harling telling him tersely that "He never married her" and admitting that "I haven't seen her since she came back," Jim cuts off that reminiscence too by acknowledging flatly, "I tried to shut Ántonia out of my mind" (290).

Whereas the first half of *My Ántonia* tells of circumstances surrounding Ántonia that narrow into confinements, the second half tells of those circumstances widening into liberation. Between the two lies Jim's (and the reader's) education—not by the formal instruction of the university but by his friendship with Lena Lingard, through whom Cather rewrites the classical tradition of the Muse. Whereas allusions to Judeo-Christian traditions undergird procreativity in the Black Hawk section, classical traditions undergird the emphasis on creativity in the Lincoln section. While living in Lincoln and attending the university, Jim awakens to the world of ideas under the influence of Gaston Cleric, "a brilliant and inspiring" young classical scholar (249). The furnishings in Jim's boarding-house room reflect his teacher's influence, as do the conversations that take place there. Jim covers his wall with a map of ancient Rome ordered by Cleric, hangs over his bookcase a photograph of the Tragic Theatre at Pompeii that Cleric had given him, and buys a comfortable chair for Cleric to sit in, hoping to entice his teacher to visit and linger. Cleric "could bring the drama of antique life before one out of the shadows" (253), and with it a literary legacy held together by an authority of influence. Entranced, his forgotten cigarette burning unheeded, Cleric would speak lines of Statius who spoke for Dante of his veneration for Virgil.

Jim distinguishes himself from that tradition, however. He recognizes that, unlike Cleric, he should "never lose himself in impersonal things," and he acknowledges an alternative idea of memory for which he uses language of conception, gestation, and quickening. "I begrudged the room that Jake and Otto and Russian Peter took up in my memory," Jim reflects, "But whenever my consciousness was quickened, all those early friends were quickened within it, and in some strange way they accompanied me through all my new experiences" (254). The reflection moves him to question the separation of creativity (forming something out of nothing with an assumption of absolute, godlike authority) from procreativity (generating offspring with an assumption of giving rise to or occasioning independent life): "They were so much alive in me that I scarcely stopped to wonder whether they were alive anywhere else, or how" (254). By stopping to wonder, Jim prepares for his invocation of the Muse.

Alone, staring listlessly at the *Georgics,* Jim reads, "for I shall be the first, if I live, to bring the Muse into my country." As if invoking a spell, he repeats the phrase "bring the Muse," and then he recalls the phrase yet again—the magical third utterance (256–257). Thereupon he hears a knock at his door and, opening it, sees Lena Lingard standing in the dark hall. Admitting her, Jim leads her to the chair he had purchased for Cleric, and once she is seated he "confusedly" questions her.

Answering Jim's summons and sitting in Cleric's chair, Lena displaces Cleric as Jim's teacher and embodies Cather's answer to one of the most telling of silences, that of the Muses. Excluded by conventions that authorize the poet in creativity as the father is authorized in procreativity, Muses are to creativity as the mother is to procreativity. As standard handbooks demonstrate, the Muses are given short shrift. According to *Crowell's Handbook of*

Classical Mythology there are few myths specifically given to the Muses, who were "little worshiped, though often invoked." *The Concise Oxford Dictionary of Literary Terms* notes succinctly that the Muses are "usually represented by a female deity," and Holman and Harman's *Handbook to Literature* specifies that "In literature, their traditional significance is that of inspiring and helping POETS." In short, the Muse is the female inspiration to the male poet, and as Mary Carruthers has written in "The Re-Vision of the Muse," "he addresses her in terms of sexual rapture, desiring to be possessed in order to possess, to be ravished in order to be fruitful." Though the poet is dependent upon her, Carruthers continues, "she speaks only through him. She is wholly Other and strange, . . . an ethereally beautiful young girl in the tradition of romance." Whatever guise she assumes, however, "the basic relationship of dominance and possession is constant between her and her poet" (295).

Cather's Muse is another matter altogether. Her authority is announced by the title of book 3, "Lena Lingard." Rather than speaking only through a man, Lena speaks for herself, and rather than submitting to a relationship of dominance and possession, she invites equality in friendship. Jim's expectations are the familiar ones of the male poet to "his" Muse: he feels himself possessed, perceives the encounter as sexual, and assumes her dependency upon him. What Lena offers to him, however, is an alternative to such conventional notions of creativity. Her self-possession contrasts comically to Jim's assumptions that because she lives alone, she is lonely; that by visiting her in her room, he will compromise her; and that because she is unattached to a man, she wishes to marry.

Cather's Muse speaks for herself when she explains that men pay court to her because "It makes them feel important to think they're in love with somebody" (281) and that "men are all right for friends, but as soon as you marry them they turn into cranky old fathers. . . . I prefer to . . . be accountable to nobody" (282). Rejecting the relationship traditional to the Muse, Lena offers instead the kindness of mutual respect. When she sees Jim's hurt at hearing her say she is not dependent upon him, for example, she softens his pain by saying, "I've always been a little foolish about you" (284).

By instructing Jim in the mutuality of friendship as an alternative to dominance and possession, Lena prepares him for his return to Ántonia. Whereas the early books in *My Ántonia* depict others' attempts to control Ántonia by narrowing her confinements until she disappeared, the later ones tell of Ántonia reasserting herself into the text. "[S]uch entries for women into textuality and into language are always painful in that they always involve a shattering of the silence which enshrouds women's physical presence," observes Helena R. Michie, who in *The Flesh Made Word* (74–75) could have been describing Ántonia returning pregnant and unwed. Nobody visits her. She was "crushed and quiet," "never went anywhere," and "always looked dead weary" (306). Though afflicted with a toothache, she "wouldn't go to Black Hawk to a dentist for fear of meeting people she knew" (306), and after her daughter was born, she "almost never comes to town" (290).

The power granted to birth is apparent when Ántonia asserts her daughter against cultural erasure. Ántonia's reentry into textuality is indirect at first, accomplished by the stories that Jim hears of her. Though nobody visits Ántonia, she brings her daughter to Black Hawk to show to Mrs. Harling, and though others expect her to keep "her baby out of sight," she has the child's "picture on exhibition at the town photographer's, in a great gilt frame" (295–296). A character asserting herself against the discomfort of her own novel is the effect Cather creates when the photographer speaks of Ántonia with "a constrained, apologetic laugh" and when Jim Burden reflects, selfishly, that "I could forgive her, I told myself, if she hadn't thrown herself away on such a cheap sort of fellow" (295–296).

The stories that Jim hears are powerful, however. They work against the cultural discomfort of the text to create in Jim the "feeling that [he] must see Ántonia again" (295). Seeing again is re-visioning, and—appropriately—Jim goes to see a midwife for the re-visioning necessary to break the silence surrounding birth. Rhetoric and ritual signal that this is no ordinary visit. To reach the Widow Steavens, Jim journeys to the high country, reflecting as he travels upon the "growth of . . . a great idea" apparent in the changing face of the country, where human lives were "coming to a fortunate issue" and the flat tableland was responding by "long, sweeping lines of fertility" (298). Jim's meeting with the midwife has the ceremonial greeting of gravity: he "drew up," and the Widow Steavens "came out to meet [him]. She was . . . tall, and very strong . . . her massive head . . . like a Roman senator's. I told her at once why I had come" (299). This scene is the ritual supplication of youth to age, quester to oracle.

Further ritual, the sharing of food and withdrawing to a solemn setting, prepares for a transfer of knowledge. By such rituals Jim and the midwife eat supper and then retire to the sitting room where the moon shining outside the open windows recalls Great Goddess belief systems.[6] The Widow Steavens turns the lamp low, settles into her favorite rocking chair, then "crossed her hands in her lap and sat as if she were at a meeting of some kind" (299). As Cather proposed her version of the Muse in Lena, so she now proposes her oracle by drawing upon the ancient female tradition of a gossip/midwife serving as godparent and witness, figures "who think and act strongly about childbirth . . . [and who] must be counted among the enablers of powerful symbolic processes" (Weigle 145).

In telling a woman's version of procreativity, Cather's midwife releases birth from the secrecy that had enshrouded it, thereby setting in motion the powerful symbolic processes by which a birth story will become a national epic. By the Widow Steavens's account, rather than suffering the punishment inherited from a fallen Eve, Ántonia gave birth without confinement and apparently without pain ("without calling to anybody, without a groan, she lay down on the bed and bore her child"); rather than affirming a male line, she gave birth to a daughter; and rather than suffering shame over her child, "She loved it from the first as dearly as if she'd had a ring on her finger." "Ántonia is a natural-born mother," the Widow Steavens concludes, contradicting conventions governing the "rights" of motherhood (308–310).

As she offers a woman's version of birth, the midwife also establishes a woman's way of telling. Jim's authorial *I* that assumes possession ("*my* Ántonia") is replaced by the compassionate *I* of the Widow Steavens, and Jim's terse report of withdrawing from Ántonia contrasts with Widow Steavens's description of visiting Ántonia the morning after she returned home. Taking Ántonia in her arms and asking her to come out of doors where they could talk freely, the Widow Steavens said "'Oh, my child,' . . . 'what's happened to you? Don't be afraid to tell me'" (304); after hearing Ántonia's reply, she "sat right down on that back beside her and made lament" (305). Drawing Ántonia near, inviting her open and free speech, and then responding with compassion is the mutuality of friendship, the effect of which is suggested by the W. T. Benda drawings that Cather commissioned to accompany her text. Whereas Ántonia was previously depicted from a distance with her face averted, she now turns toward the viewer as if in response to the Widow Steavens's voice. We see her face as she walks forward, her body swelling with new life beneath her black overcoat.

In this manner expectations are reversed and conventions are overturned. Whereas the other hired girls have, like Ántonia, made places for themselves, the men have been displaced by various narrative devices. The introduction to *My Ántonia* complicates Jim's authority in matters of both procreation (he has no children) and creativity (rather than inventing the story, he wrote down stories as they returned to him in memory). Other men are killed or marginalized: Mr. Shimerda commits suicide, Peter and Pavel become outcasts, the tramp jumps into a thrashing machine, Jake and Otto vanish into the West, Mr. Harling disappears on business, and the Widow Steavens's husband is as absent as the vestigial "Mrs." from her name. Most interesting, there is Larry Donovan. Scarcely a character in his own right, he is instead a foil to Ántonia. Never pictured or described directly, Larry Donovan remains voiceless and faceless, as expendable to Ántonia's plot as the bride was to Peter and Pavel's plot.

Stories within the novel celebrate the New World as a site of miraculous births. Fuchs tells of the woman he accompanied on the boat crossing who in mid-ocean "proceeded to have not one baby, but three!" (67), and on Christmas Mr. Burden reads "the chapters from St. Matthew about the birth of Christ, and as we listened it all seemed like something that had happened lately, and near at hand. He thanked the Lord for the first Christmas, and for all it had meant to the world ever since" (81).[7]

As she releases her narrator from the desire to frame (or confine) Ántonia, Cather also liberates the reader from the desire to frame (or confine) the text. In Western paradigms, birth—like reading—is gendered and individualized. "What is it?" is the first question after birth that, once answered, determines responses to that child. Similarly, "who wrote it?" is the first question of a book that, once answered, determines our reading. As Susan Stanford Friedman has observed, "We seldom read any text without knowledge of the author's sex. The title page itself initiates a series of expectations that influence our reading throughout" (55).

From the outset Cather undermined her readers' reliance upon gender distinctions. The appearance of her name on the novel's title page initiates gender expectations that the introduction unsettles when, by appearing as the reader of Jim Burden's manuscript, Cather contradicts the most basic separation between self and other, writer and reader. Having evoked the question, "Where is the author in this text?" Cather complicates answers with a series of disclaimers. First her fictional narrator states that he didn't "arrange or re-arrange" but instead "simply wrote down what of herself and myself and other people Ántonia's name recalls to me" (xiii). Then Cather herself renounces authority by writing that "my own story was never written," saying that "the following narrative is Jim's manuscript, substantially as he brought it to me" (xiii). The effect is to undermine the premise that authority is basic to creativity.[8] This is a manuscript conceived not by a distinction between creator and created, author and subject; instead, it is conceived by the mutuality of long friendship. "We grew up together in the same Nebraska town," "we had much to say to each other," "we were talking," and "we agreed" (ix)—the exchange of conversation establishes that this text is a collaboration that grew out of continuities of life into art, of past into present, of childhood retrieved by adults, of female author and male narrator *in agreement.*

As the metaphor of birth had expanded into enlightenment, so the mutuality of friendship expands into an aesthetics of kinship in the novel's final scenes when Jim witnesses storytelling within the Cuzak family. "The distinction between female and male discourse lies not in the [childbirth] metaphor itself but rather in the way its final meaning is constituted in the process of reading," writes Friedman (61). Though she was not, Friedman could have been writing of *My Ántonia,* where Cather reconstitutes the process of reading to provide an alternative aesthetic based on an "emphasis on birth leading to a lifetime of maternal nurturance" (Friedman 62).[9]

Far from previous assumptions of possession and dominance, storytelling now proceeds by cooperation and inclusion. Ántonia's daughter Anna, for example, reveals sensitivity to her youngest brother by recognizing his need to tell his story to Ántonia: Jan "wants to tell you about the dog, mother," Anna says, whereupon Ántonia beckons her son to her and listens to him while he tells her about the dog's death, resting his elbows upon her knees as he does so (326). Ántonia then whispers to Jan, who then slips away and whispers, in turn, to his sister Nina. The principle is now of repetition. Jan repeats his mother's words to his sister, and the younger children ask Ántonia to tell the story of "how the teacher has the school picnic in the orchard every year" (330). Contrary to the convention of male author(ity) and female subject, Ántonia is at the center of storytelling by which, like the metaphor of birth, language returns to its source.

As the metaphor of birth has expanded, so does that of language's return. Coming home from a street fair in a nearby town, Cuzak says, "very many send word to you, Ántonia," then asks Jim to excuse him while he delivers their messages in Bohemian (346). As the birth scenes build to the explosion of bodies from the fruit cellar, so now storytelling builds to the reminiscences and exchanges of family stories as the Cuzaks and Jim look at photographs and then to reminiscences and exchanges at dinner. Here again storytelling is a cooperative enterprise. When at dinner Rudolph asks if Jim has heard about the Cutters, Ántonia (upon hearing that Jim hasn't), says "then you must tell him, son. . . . Now, all you children be quiet, Rudolph is going to tell about the murder." "Hurrah," they murmur, then are quiet as Rudolph tells his story "in great detail, with occasional promptings from his mother or father" (349–350).

The younger children, Anna, Jan, and Nina, the older son, Rudolph, and the parents, Cuzak and Ántonia herself—all have a voice in the family's ongoing story. What is the principle of narrative here and of the use of the word? Clearly, Ántonia is not using language in the tradition of creation (i.e., to produce where nothing was before, to form out of nothing). Instead, she is a source of the family legend in the sense that she begets, engenders, generates, produces, gives rise to, and occasions. These—the definitions of *procreate* with which I began—come together in the pro/creativity of a kinship aesthetic. In Cather's version of the Fall, Ántonia disappeared from Jim Burden's text only to return independently to claim her language and to demonstrate its power. She speaks Bohemian with her children, and around the dinner table she teaches them not only the mother tongue but also a reciprocal and communal use of language.

Cather's birth of a nation is significant for what it is not as well as for what it is. It is not a separation from or casting off of other cultures. It does not set a New World against an Old World, an American future against a European past or a Native American mythology. Instead, it offers a national identity affirming analogies and continuities. As Virgil brought the Muse to Rome by writing of his neighborhood in Mantua, so Cather would bring the

Muse to the United States by writing of her neighborhood in Nebraska. By drawing upon emergence mythologies, Cather renewed familiar figures so that the Muse inspires collaboration and the midwife sets in motion powerful symbolic processes of language and metaphor. Through Cather's revisioning, an immigrant girl she knew in Nebraska gives birth to a nation.

NOTES

1. Cather in *Death Comes for the Archbishop* creates another richly symbolic female space in the cave called Stone Lips. Latour descends into it for shelter during a storm, and Cather describes his horror over the experience as so intense that, despite the fact that it saved his life, he resolves to never again venture into such a place. Whereas Thea Kronborg, in *The Song of the Lark,* and Ántonia are nurtured by the cave spaces they inhabit, Cather's male characters characteristically feel revulsion over such direct contact with the earth and the primitive.

2. Gunn's book on Laguna and Acoma history, traditions, and narratives is now among the holdings of the Willa Cather Pioneer Memorial and Educational Foundation. For discussion of this myth see Weigle 214–218 and Hindehede.

3. Reading *My Ántonia* in terms of Homans's argument that Western metaphysics is founded on the myth that "language and culture depend on the death or absence of the mother and on the quest for substitutes for her," Ann Fisher-Wirth interprets Jim's narrative as "a form of desire, which constantly seeks but can never arrive at that lost body" (41). "In the gendered myth that informs *My Ántonia,* Ántonia represents the body of the world. The narrative of Jim's life describes his fall away from union with worldbody, into the Law of the Father. But his act of narrative itself constitutes a perpetual desirous return toward the lost motherbody from which his life necessarily departed" (67).

4. Wendy Lesser demonstrates that Beauvoir's point is still relevant. Addressing mothers as the initial subject of male artists, Lesser writes, "If to be an artist, a writer, is to fly unburdened with the weight of reality, then to think about one's mother—to attempt to think oneself *into* one's mother—is to be brought with a crash down to Mother Earth" (33).

5. *My Secret Life*'s narrator-hero, Walter, "sums up Victorian attitudes with a series of displacements: he reaches a turning point in his sexual knowledge when he has 'learnt enough . . . to know that among men of his class the term lacemaker, along with actress and seamstress, was virtually synonymous with prostitute'" (qtd. in Michie 67).

6. As Gerda Lerner writes, the Goddess's "frequent association with the moon symbolized her mystical powers over nature and the seasons" (148).

7. In discussing "biblical borrowings" in *My Ántonia,* John J. Murphy perceptively traces Cather's use of Christian iconography to describe Ántonia: "The Christmas story of Matthew and Luke echoes in Widow Steavens's account of the birth of Ántonia's child, and Jim's subsequent farewell scene with Ántonia, . . . recalls Revelation 12:1, traditionally applied to the Virgin Mary" (40); the orchard scene describes a "dells robbia image of maternity clothed in light and blossoms [that] recalls Dante's dawn-bright vision of Mary in *Paradise*" (93); and for Jim's return twenty years later, Cather "reworks the icon into a kind of Coronation of the Virgin" (103).

8. Here Cather reverses novelistic tradition of gendered authority. Whereas "The poetry of troubadours, like popular tales, stories of voyages, and other kinds of narratives, often introduces at the end the speaker as a witness to or participant in the narrated 'facts,'" writes Julia Kristeva, "in novelistic conclusions, the author speaks not as a witness to some 'event' (as in folk tales), not to express his 'feelings' or his 'art' (as in troubadour poetry); rather, he speaks in order to assume ownership of the discourse that he appeared at first to have given to someone else (a character)" (Kristeva, *Desire in Language* 63).

9. The title of book 5, "Cuzak's Boys," unsettles expectations that a patriarchal principle would be replaced by a matriarchal one. Cuzak's boys or Ántonia's? Jim's story or Cather's? Such questions are made irrelevant by a kinship aesthetics of exchange and connectivity.

Works Cited

Beauvior, de Simone. *The Second Sex.* Trans. H. M. Parshley. New York: Knopf, 1953.

Bohlke, L. Brent. *Willa Cather in Person: Interviews, Speeches, and Letters.* Lincoln: University of Nebraska Press, 1986.

Cather, Willa. *My Ántonia.* Ed. Charles Mignon with Kari Ronning. Hist. essay by James Woodress. Lincoln: University of Nebraska Press, 1994.

Friedman, Susan Stanford. "Creativity and the Childbirth Metaphor: Gender Differences in Literary Discourse." *Feminist Studies* 13 (1987): 49–82.

Kolodny, Annette. *The Land before Her: Fantasy and Experience of the American Frontiers, 1630–1860.* Chapel Hill: University of North Carolina Press, 1984.

Lerner, Gerda. *The Creation of Patriarchy.* New York: Oxford University Press, 1986.

Michie, Helena R. *The Flesh Made Word: Female Figures and Women's Bodies.* New York: Oxford University Press, 1987.

The Oxford English Dictionary. Ed. James A. H. Murray et al. Oxford: Clarendon, 1933.

Weigle, Marta. *Creation and Procreation: Feminist Reflections on Mythologies of Cosmogony and Parturition.* Philadelphia: University of Pennsylvania Press, 1989.

PATRICK SHAW

Marek Shimerda in My Ántonia: *A Noteworthy Medical Etiology*

The plot of Willa Cather's *My Ántonia* revolves around childhood, and the design of the novel is anchored in scenes depicting children, beginning with Jim Burden's childhood journey from Virginia to Nebraska and ending with the abundance of Cuzak kids bursting forth like prairie wildflowers in springtime. As Frederick J. Hoffman has reminded us, echoing Freud and Jung, the life not only of the individual but of the race is encapsulated in the child, and the artist naturally turns to the child as a symbol of artistic inspiration (19).

Underlying Hoffman's premise, however, is the assumption that the child is physically and mentally healthy. This kind of child is predominant in *My Ántonia*. For example, Ántonia's best-loved child, Leo the faun, is nearly mythological with his "tawny fleece" and "gold-green" eyes (348). Such children personify the active, inquisitive, and unrepressed child who symbolizes creativity, innocence, and a higher state of self-realization.

What, however, are we to make of Marek Shimerda, a painfully misshapen boy who conforms to none of the other childhood images in the text? The contrast between Marek and the other children is established by his being introduced immediately after Jim describes his enthusiastic first reactions to Ántonia and her sister Yulka. Ántonia's eyes are "big and warm and full of light, like the sun shining on brown pools in the wood" (23);

American Notes & Queries, Volume 13, Number 1 (2000): pp. 29–33. © 2000 Heldref Publications.

Yulka is "fair, and seemed mild and obedient" (23). Marek then appears. On seeing him, Jim says:

> Even from a distance one could see that there was something strange about this boy. As he approached us, he began to make uncouth noises, and held up his hands to show us his fingers, which were webbed to the first knuckle, like a duck's foot. When he saw me draw back, he began to crow delightedly, "Hoo, hoo-hoo, hoo-hoo !" like a rooster. (23–24)

Marek next appears when Jim visits the Shimerdas in their wintry dug-out: "The crazy boy lay under the only window, stretched on a gunny-sack stuffed with straw. As soon as we entered, he threw a grain-sack over the crack at the bottom of the door" (73). A few minutes later Jim leaves, and "Marek crawled along the floor and stuffed up the door-crack again" (74). Jim then reiterates his earlier description:

> Marek slid cautiously toward us and began to exhibit his webbed fingers. I knew he wanted to make his queer noises for me—to bark like a dog or whinny like a horse—but he did not dare in the presence of his elders. Marek was always trying to be agreeable, poor fellow, as if he had it on his mind that he must make up for his deficiencies. (77)

We do not see Marek again until the episode that is the antithesis of innocence and beauty—Mr. Shimerda commits suicide and lies frozen in the barn, and Ántonia, Ambrosch, and Mrs. Shimerda go to pray for him. Jim notes that "the crazy boy went with them, because he did not feel the cold. I believed he felt cold as much as anyone else, but he liked to be thought insensible to it. He was always coveting distinction, poor Marek!" (103).

Jim later mentions that Marek attended his father's funeral (116) and that he has been worked "hard" by Ambrosch (132). Thereafter, he disappears from the text. Only from Jim's passing comment years later do we learn that "poor Marek had got violent and been sent away to an institution a good while back" (314).

The etiology that Cather develops in these several brief scenes reveals much about her artistic processes. The malady that she assigns to Marek is known medically as syndactyly, and although medical texts historically differ about several specifics, we nonetheless can draw worthwhile information from recent descriptions of the deformity. Jim describes Marek's fingers as being webbed, like a duck's, and twice refers to him as being "crazy." He also once notes that Marek crawls, which suggests that his feet may also be "webbed" like his hands. The type of complete "webbing" and the accompanying "craziness" Cather attributes to Marek, however, are not medically precise. *The Textbook of Pediatrics* notes that syndactyly usually manifests itself in the fusion of two digits (Behrman 24). Modern medicine would most likely categorize the severe case of webbed fingers and toes such as Cather describes as Cenani Type Syndactyly. Even this type, however, does not precisely fit Cather's version. Cenani Type is not accompanied by mental retardation and can be repaired surgically with no danger to a normal life span (Buyse 1618).

That Jim Burden emphasizes Marek's being "crazy" suggests that Cather has combined two different types of the syndrome: Cenani and Filippi. Filippi Type Syndactyly has a milder form of webbing than Cenani Type, usually manifesting itself with webbing between two fingers on each hand, but it is far more damaging otherwise. It includes distorted facial appearance, mental retardation, and the inability to speak (Buyse 1619) which closely coincide with Jim's description of Marek and his animal noises. The prognosis for Filippi Type Syndactyly is a normal life span, but the mental retardation is irreversible. Little is known about the cause of the syndrome or what transmits it.

We cannot verify the source of Cather's information about syndactyly. Though she acknowledges Annie Sadilek as the prototype for Ántonia (Woodress 41) and identifies other historic characters as patterns for various personae in *My Ántonia*, nowhere does she mention an actual individual paralleling Marek. Neither do her biographers note such a person. Cather may well have encountered an instance of syndactyly in her travels with Dr. Robert Demerell, with whom as a young girl she visited patients on the Nebraska Divide (Woodress 52). More likely, given the rarity of most forms of syndactyly, Cather based Marek's case on stories she read or heard about the malady. (The most common type, Syndactyly Type 1, occurs only once in 3,000 births in North America [Buyse 1618].) Yet, whatever the source, Cather's version is more a composite of the worse possible etiology than a realistic representation of a child suffering from syndactyly.

Cather probably had little interest in developing an extensive etiology for Marek, since she quickly relegates him to an unseen role and soon dismisses him altogether from the text. Moreover, she was not particularly careful about being scientifically precise about his peculiar malady. The questions become, therefore, why Cather includes Marek in the narrative at all and why she exaggerates his syndrome into grotesquerie.

A ready explanation for Marek and his "duck" hands is that he is a continuation of a motif common to Cather's fiction—the obsession with hands and the fear of their being mutilated. This motif emanates from Cather's childhood. Edith Lewis, in *Willa Cather Living*, relates the story of the half-witted boy who slipped into Cather's bedroom and threatened to cut off her hands with a knife. The five-year-old Cather had the presence of mind to trick the boy into leaving her room, but as James Woodress says, the experience caused "a deep trauma" that left Cather with "a horror of mutilation, especially of the hands" (26). Whether Lewis's account of the boy-with-knife is accurate or apocryphal is of little consequence, since Cather's own texts are sufficient proof that she was disturbingly preoccupied with hands. Woodress, for one, summarizes the number of times mutilated or grotesque hands appear in Cather's fiction, citing instances such as the gruesome hands that protrude from the trenches in *One of Ours*. (His summary does not, however, include Marek's webbed hands.)

Moreover, Cather's obsession manifested itself in very real and painful problems with her own hands: a torn tendon in her left wrist; a hand smashed in a drugstore accident; her right hand partially paralyzed from autographing too many copies of *Sapphira and the Slave Girl*. After 1940, she periodically wore a special brace on her right hand for the rest of her life (Woodress 27). Thus, Marek clearly fits a recognized pattern. Moreover, he clearly emanates from the depths of Cather's unconscious, creative self. Our best clue to this emanation is the "violence" for which Marek is institutionalized.

Of all the symptoms attributed to syndactyly, none suggests violence. On the contrary, passivity rather than aggression seems more symptomatic. In Filippi Type, which Cather seems in part to suggest for Marek with his inarticulateness and other symptoms, the I.Q. is low (between 30 and 60) and the male genitalia remain incompletely manifested. Body size is abnormally small and bone structure can be retarded (Buyse 1619). None of these characteristics supports a pathologically violent personality.

Furthermore, textual evidence suggests Cather wanted Marek's violence attributed less to his syndactyly and more to society's reaction to it. Before Jim's offhand comment about Marek's being sent away, nothing foreshadows the violent behavior said to have caused his institutionalization. In truth, he is more the recipient of abuse than the aggressor. Marek is portrayed as obedient and kind, quick to please and to help insofar as his deformities permit, despite being underfed as a child, forbidden to speak the only "language" that he knew, severely "used" by his brother Ambrosch, and ignored by those who should be most concerned with his well-being. Even Jim, otherwise compassionate and stoic in facing the unusual, is upset by Marek's appearance. His somewhat insensitive attitude toward Marek is emphasized when he later praises the beauty of Ántonia's many children. What this scenario suggests is that Marek is driven to rebellion and thus to incarceration not because of acts of antisocial violence but because society cannot accept the abnormality that his appearance personifies.

In his attitude toward Marek and his contrasting admiration of the "normal" children, Jim reflects Cather's essential psychological tension. Through Marek, Cather conveys society's expectations of normality and her own quandary as a creative artist in conflict with those social norms. The precise causes of this conflict are not relevant to my purpose here, but years ago Bernice Slote in *The Kingdom of Art* correctly observed that from the beginning Cather "was caught in that ancient pull of the gods, torn between the Dionysian and Apollonian forces of rapture and repose, release and containment. That conflict was at the very center of her creative will" (91). More recently, Judith Fryer, in *Felicitous Space: The Imaginative Structures of Edith Wharton and Willa Cather*, recognizes that "the divided self" is a "subject central to Cather's fiction, often presented in her early works as a conflict between woman and artist, and developed with an interest, finally, not so much in reconciliation as in creating a new context in which the force, passion and energy of the creative self can be preserved" (217). If we view the child, in whatever psychological context, as the manifestation of the creative self, then clearly Marek suggests that in the writing of *My Ántonia* Cather was unconsciously revealing the conflicts that Slote, Fryer, and others have elsewhere elucidated.

For Cather, the child is not only a literary symbol of innocence and exuberance. It is an artistic extension of the essential design of her narrative, an image of guiltlessness and the time when life is enjoyed, free of what Norman O. Brown terms "the tyranny of genital organization" (29) that "normal" society demands. "Poor Marek" is the manifestation of the psychological conflict that arises when the artistic self clashes with those "normal" social demands. By subtly inserting Marek Shimerda into the fabric of her textual design, like an intentional fault in an otherwise flawlessly woven cloth, Cather demonstrates again the range of her irony and the complexity of her artistic purpose. More specifically, in the etiology of syndactyly she develops for Marek, she shows that while Nature may present a pattern that appears reliable and fundamentally reassuring, there lurks beneath that superficial perception a counterdesign that is frightening. It was this counterdesign that Cather often identified with and that fueled her creative imagination.

Works Cited

Behrman, Richard E., ed. *Textbook of Pediatrics.* 14th ed. Philadelphia: Saunders, 1992.

Brown, Norman O. *Life Against Death.* New York: Vintage, 1959.

Buyse, Mary Louise, ed. *Birth Defects Encyclopedia.* Dover: Center for Birth Defects Information Services, Inc., 1990.

Cather, Willa. *My Ántonia.* 1918; rev. 1926. Boston: Houghton, 1954.

Hoffman, Frederick J. *Freudianism and the Literary Mind.* 2nd ed. Baton Rouge: Louisiana State University Press, 1957.

Fryer, Judith. *Felicitous Space: The Imaginative Structures of Edith Wharton and Willa Cather.* Chapel Hill: University of North Carolina Press, 1986.

Lewis, Edith. *Willa Cather Living: A Personal Record.* New York: Knopf, 1953.

Slote, Bernice. *The Kingdom of Art: Willa Cather's First Principles and Critical Statements, 1893-1896.* Lincoln: University of Nebraska Press, 1967.

Woodress, James. *Willa Cather: A Literary Life.* Lincoln: University of Nebraska Press, 1987.

STEVEN B. SHIVELY

My Ántonia *and the Parables of Sacrifice*

In Willa Cather's *Death Comes for the Archbishop* (1927), Jean Marie Latour concludes that "it was the white man's way to assert himself in any landscape, to change it, make it over a little (at least to leave some mark or memorial of his sojourn)" (246). This is the traditional view of the presence of human beings in any new land, and in the American West in particular. Nine years earlier, however, Cather had offered a different story of creation. In the beginning of *My Ántonia* (1918) she dropped young Jim Burden down on the Nebraska prairie, and he was overwhelmed by feelings of insignificance and powerlessness: "I felt erased, blotted out. . . . here, I felt, what would be would be" (8). Indeed, all of the familiar consolations of life were lost to Jim: his parents were dead (even as watchful angels in heaven he did not believe they could find him here); the usual immovable, ever-present Virginia landmarks—creeks, trees, hillsides—were gone; he felt "outside man's jurisdiction" (7) and, in fact, outside of God's. Even two days later, after hearty meals in the warmth and comfort of his grandparents' home, after prayers and Bible reading, Jim sat in the garden feeling that he was nothing more than "something that lay under the sun and felt it, like the pumpkins." He had no desire "to be anything more." "[T]hat is happiness," he concluded, "to be dissolved into something complete and great" (18).

Willa Cather and the Culture of Belief, edited by John J. Murphy (Provo, Utah: Brigham Young University Press, 2002): pp. 51–62. © 2002 Brigham Young University Press.

This philosophical lapse, admittedly rather odd in a nine-year-old boy, announces one of Cather's most significant themes in this novel: loss and sacrifice, not monument-making, become essential parts of the creative act. Loss of that which is important, the sacrifice of self, even of life, the dissolution of one's self into something greater—all of these are necessary for creating a community, for bringing people together. In its form and content, *My Ántonia* shows that loss and sacrifice can be sacred and redemptive. Three times in this novel Cather uses the image of the lamb to establish her interest in sacrifice and redemption. A common symbol of renewal and innocence, the lamb is one of the most evocative of religious symbols, recalling the sacrificial lambs of the Old Testament, the lamb's blood protecting the people of Israel at Passover, and Jesus as the Good Shepherd and Lamb of God. The lamb is central to the notions of sacrifice and redemption.

The first of Cather's lambs in *My Ántonia* is Russian Peter, whom she describes thus: "His hair and beard were of such a pale flaxen colour that they seemed white in the sun. They were as thick and curly as carded wool. His rosy face, with its snub nose, set in this fleece . . ." (33). Later she calls attention to "his shaggy head and bandy legs" (34) and to the fact that Wick Cutter had "fleeced" Peter (202). Peter is a central figure in one of the most violent acts of sacrifice in the novel. Years earlier, in Russia, he was the driver of the sleigh from which his companion Pavel threw their newlywed friends to the wolves to save their own lives. Even though "Peter, crouching in the front seat, saw nothing" (57), he is implicated in the atrocity and must flee with Pavel, leaving his familiar life and his family only to endure years of difficulty in America. The newlywed couple are not the only sacrificial victims: Peter, too, is sacrificed to Pavel's act. Cather both mediates the heritage of violence and reinforces Peter's victimhood by portraying him as a lamb destroyed by Wick Cutter, a money lender who relentlessly pursues and traps his victims, who is wolfish in his pursuit of young girls, and whose "yellow whiskers, always soft and glistening," and prominent white teeth suggest his bestial nature (203).

The lamb image, with its suggestions of meekness, purity, and sacrificial victimhood, appears again in Blind d'Arnault, whom Cather describes as having short legs and folds of skin "under close-clipped wool" (178). D'Arnault's walk echoes the "funny sight" of Russian Peter, who was "fat as butter" and moved on "short, bow legs" (33–34): "[D'Arnault] was a heavy, bulky mulatto, on short legs, and he came tapping the floor in front of him" (178). D'Arnault, too, was victim to his "wolves," specifically the "big mastiff" in the kennel of his owner's plantation, but generally to his blindness and the conditions of his race. Such similarities call attention to other connections: both Peter and d'Arnault suffered horrible experiences in the past, both were turned away by their mothers, both depend on the sympathy of others, both are enveloped by Cather in an atmosphere of overwhelming loss, especially lost potential.

At the end of the novel, the lamb imagery is repeated in the next generation through Ántonia's son Leo, with his "red cheeks and a ruddy pelt as thick as a lamb's wool, growing down on his neck in little tufts" (320). Even more striking here is the echo of d'Arnault's animalistic, lamblike head, a "curious similarity" noted by John J. Murphy (76). D'Arnault's head is "almost no head at all; nothing behind the ears but folds of neck under close-clipped wool" (178). Cather writes of Leo, "He hadn't much head behind his ears, and his tawny fleece grew down thick to the back of his neck" (337). In Leo, however, a profound change accompanies the lamb imagery: now the lamb no longer marks a suffering victim, as with Russian Peter and d'Arnault, but is a symbol of the hope and promise of youth. Murphy's description of Leo as "the lamb-like son with the lion's name" suggests the transformation of the lamb into the majestic lion (92). The hope that is in Leo is all the more meaningful because it carries with it something of Russian Peter's suffering and Blind D'Arnault's passion: their losses, their sacrifices, their suffering became redemptive when these lambs are reborn in Leo. Lest we think that the lamb references are simply some sort of agricultural or pastoral allusion, the lamb Leo is born on Easter Day, the Paschal Feast Day, the celebration of the resurrection of the Holy Lamb of Christianity. The resurrection imagery attached to Leo by way of the sacrificial lamb continues when he speaks Bohemian with Ántonia and when he plays old Mr. Shimerda's violin. Mr. Shimerda, perhaps the novel's ultimate victim, reappears in the musical life of his grandson, just as for Jim he seemed present in the Burden home after his death and later inspired Jim's graduation speech.

In her telling of Mr. Shimerda's suicide, Cather further suggests the redemptive possibilities of sacrificial death, albeit suicide, with two brief but significant accounts set into the middle of the larger narrative. Just when readers are ready to accept Mr. Shimerda's suicide as the understandable act of a desperately homesick man, Cather plants doubts by inserting speculation that the gash in Shimerda's head fits Peter Krajiek's ax. With the coroner's inquest making it clear that, despite his guilty attitude, Krajiek did not murder Mr. Shimerda, the question of this swindler's guilt has the effect of extending issues of guilt and responsibility beyond the immediate narrative. Cather makes explicit that Krajiek's poor treatment of the Shimerdas contributed to the despair that finally drove Mr. Shimerda to his death—"perhaps [Krajiek] even felt some stirrings of remorse for his indifference to the old man's misery and loneliness" (108); by extension, all of those who have mistreated the immigrant family or who ignored their desperate need share the guilt. The scene suggests those familiar lines from the Bible in which Jesus discusses guilt and responsibility with his disciples, admonishing them for not feeding him when he was hungry or thirsty or lonely or naked or sick: "Inasmuch as ye did it not to one of the least of these, ye did it not to me." Jesus says that the righteous victims shall go into life eternal, but those who ignored them shall go away into everlasting punishment (Matt. 25:45–46). This potential for eternal judgment in favor of Mr. Shimerda (surely one of "the least of these") and against those who ignored his troubles is the subject of the other account set into the suicide episode. Anton Jelinek, who "came to us like a miracle" (101–102), tells the Burdens the remarkable story of when, as a boy, he helped a priest minister to wounded and sick soldiers during a cholera epidemic. Jelinek attributes their protection from the disease to the Blessed Sacrament that he and the priest carried to the dying. To the Baptist Burdens, the story is strange and mysterious; their faith does not explain it. While the story underscores Jelinek's view of suicide as "a great sin" (101), its mystery invites readers to doubt prevalent views of salvation in the novel—the conclusion of the Norwegians, for example, that Mr. Shimerda was too sinful to be buried in their cemetery—and to consider the possibility that Mr. Shimerda's soul can be saved, that who lives and dies or who is saved and who is lost is a mystery in the hands of a merciful God.

Cather reinforces the idea that the loss of Mr. Shimerda offers redemptive possibilities for affirming life through her allusions to specific biblical parables. The way the community reacts to the death of Mr. Shimerda suggests the parable of the Good Samaritan, in which a needy man on the road is ignored by a priest and by his countryman but is helped by an ancient enemy of his people (see Luke 10:30–37). Mr. Shimerda, living in a strange and foreign land, became lonely and unhappy and killed himself, leaving his family great distress and need. As in Christ's parable, those who should have been most helpful were not. The Shimerdas' fellow countryman, Krajiek, was consumed with worry and self-pity and became more of a burden than a help to the family. The neighborhood Norwegian church refused permission for the dead man to he buried in its cemetery. However, the Burdens, who lived nearby, brought food and other assistance to the bereaved family and offered prayers of mercy and comfort. Their hired hand Otto Fuchs, an Austrian for whom the ancient enmity between his people and the Czechs was like that between the Samaritans and the Jews, overcame his prejudice and made a coffin for the dead man. The parable of the Good Samaritan shifts the focus of its hearers from the injured man to the passerby; similarly, Cather uses the story of the suicide to provoke consideration of the pioneer community, of those who provide compassion and those who do not.

Cather explicitly alludes in the Shimerda episode to the parable of the Rich Man and Lazarus (see Luke 16: 19–31). Upon hearing Jake explain his understanding that "it will be a matter of years to pray [Mr. Shimerda's] soul out of Purgatory, and right now he's in torment," Jim "remembered the account of Dives in torment, and shuddered" (99–100).[1] This parable's theme of conflict between the poor and the rich, with its clear sympathy for the poor man, is echoed in the poverty of Mr. Shimerda and his family: just as Lazarus "desire[s] to be fed with the crumbs which fell from the rich man's table," so the Shimerdas eat rotting potatoes that "we get from Mr. Bushy, at the post-office—what he throw out" (72). The parable's unexpected but pleasing reversal of fortune when Lazarus rests in "Abraham's bosom" and the rich man suffers tormenting thirst in the flames of Hell affirms the novel's suggestion of peace for Mr. Shimerda's soul. By its contrast with Jake's notion of that soul's suffering in Purgatory, the parable invites the possibility of more immediate grace, of heavenly rest for Mr. Shimerda, a possibility strongly suggested by Jim's belief that the soul of Mr. Shimerda stops to rest in the quiet and comfortable Burden house, a house previously described as "heavenly" (63).

Thus at the very point when Jelinek and the Shimerdas believe his soul is in torment, Mr. Shimerda is transported by Jim to a heavenly place. Furthermore, Cather's allusion to the parable of Dives and Lazarus brings to the novel Christ's teaching that salvation is based more on spiritual goodness than financial wealth or power, a teaching especially evocative of Mr. Shimerda, whose simple but deep love for his daughters and craving for art and beauty live on far longer than the horror of his suicide. While Cather denies neither the horror nor the violence of Shimerda's suicide, nor the suffering it brings for his family, she does suggest the redemptive possibilities of his death for transformation of both individuals and the community. She provides lessons on guilt and responsibility, and she brings the survivors together in new ways that strengthen their communal understanding. She even suggests a manner of resurrection for Mr. Shimerda: his burial is immediately followed by the explosion of spring, and his powerful, long-lasting presence lives on in Ántonia, Jim, and Ántonia's children.

One of the novel's most evocative representations of how Cather's sympathetic imagination reconciles disparate, individual experiences by transforming them into something communal, something larger than they were, is the simple cedar Christmas tree decorated with frontier popcorn and gingerbread and with Otto's exotic decorations from Austria. Mixing the secular with the sacred, the Old World with the New, the ordinary with the miraculous, the tree becomes "the talking tree of the fairy tale; legends and stories nestled like birds in its branches" (80). Otto offers the brilliant Catholic figures sent by his faraway mother, and they are embraced by the Protestant Grandmother Burden, whose own memories link this tree of the New Testament to the Tree of Knowledge in the Genesis story. The decorations on the Christmas tree are, Cather writes, "full of meaning" (84), but that meaning varies with the beholder: Jim looks at them with childlike wonderment; Otto sees in them memories of his Mother; Grandmother Burden makes them symbols of her piety; and Mr. Shimerda contrasts their sacred beauty with the ugliness of his dugout. Such individual meanings, however, are secondary to the intimacy of the scene, to the connections between people: as the tree holds a variety of "legends and stories nestled like birds in its branches" (80), so too does the light from the tree's candles illuminate the bonds of sympathy between people. Cather's language explicitly encourages such an interpretation: "we" placed the tree in a corner, "*Our* tree"; "*we all* had a sense of [Mr. Shimerda's] utter content"; prayers of *all* good people are good" (79–85, emphasis added). This Christmas is "full of meaning" because Jake provides the tree, Otto decorates it, Grandmother bakes the gingerbread, Grandfather reads from the Bible, Mr. Shimerda prays, and people exchange gifts and good wishes and help each other.

The juxtaposition of contrasting elements—the foreign and the familiar, the pleasing and the disturbing, the sacred and the secular—is the essence of Cather's method. In that juxtaposing, individual, peculiar meanings of the disparate parts are subordinated and transformed into something new. This notion of subordinating the parts to create a more meaningful whole is nothing unusual for Cather, of course. She used the sacred term "sacrifice" to describe the process in writing fiction: "Any first-rate novel or story must have in it the strength of a dozen fairly good stories that have been sacrificed to it" (*On Writing* 103). In *My Ántonia* the "fairly good stories" that have been sacrificed contribute their strength to the "first-rate" story. This process seems strikingly similar to what Jim Burden experiences when he goes away to college. He realizes that he will never be a scholar because

> [w]hile I was in the very act of yearning toward the new forms that [his teacher] Cleric brought up before me, my mind plunged away from me, and I suddenly found myself thinking of the places and people of my own infinitesimal past. They stood out strengthened and simplified now. . . . I begrudged the room that Jake and Otto and Russian Peter took up in my memory, which I wanted to crowd with other things. . . . [I]n some strange way they accompanied me through all my new experiences. (254)

Cather uses the curious "Introduction" to *My Ántonia* to establish from the beginning the importance of self-sacrifice. She surrenders the role of creator, of artist, of author, to Jim Burden, presumably sacrificing her own story of Ántonia so that Jim can present "his" Ántonia. Yet, of course, Cather is not really absent, and we know it; this is, as Susan Rosowski's students call it, "a game" ("Romanticism" 66). Cather's life, her perceptions and her experiences, are the basis of this novel, yet she subordinates them to her larger purpose. Here Cather makes explicit what in *O Pioneers!* (1913) she did implicitly:

"Cather ha[s] erased her individual self," as Rosowski puts it, to let "the country and the people [tell] their own story" (*Voyage* 62). This strategy suggests something of what she admired in the work of Sarah Orne Jewett; in a phrase reminiscent of Jim's words about being "dissolved into something complete and great" (18), Cather wrote that Jewett's *Pointed Fir* sketches (1896) "melt into the land and the life of the land until they are not stories at all, but life itself" (*Not Under Forty* 78). In a 1921 interview, Cather commented on the way she employed this erasure technique in *My Ántonia:*

> In this novel I'm trying to cut out all analysis, observation, description, even the picture-making quality, in order to make things and people tell their own story simply by juxtaposition, without any persuasion or explanation on my part. Just as if I put here on the table a green vase and beside it a yellow orange. Now those two things affect each other. Side by side they produce a reaction which neither of them will produce alone. Why should I try to say anything clever, or by adding colorful rhetoric detract attention from those two objects, the relation they have to each other and the effect they have upon each other? (*Willa Cather in Person* 24)

Cather's artistic credo calls for a giving up—a surrendering of ego, of individual voice, a holding back of cleverness and description and rhetoric—to create that which lasts.

Critics have noted that in *My Ántonia* Cather further yielded her authorial role by inviting readers to be active in the story. Blanche Gelfant observes that "just as Jim appropriates Ántonia for his story, we as readers appropriate him, taking over his memories and making them so integrally part of our consciousness that we can legitimately call his Ántonia our own" (129). And Rosowski tells how she and her students discover that "by renouncing conventional authority in the narrator/writer, [Cather] has validated it in each reader" ("Romanticism" 66). Readers bring individual perceptions, experiences, and imaginations to the work of the artist and forge connections to the created story. In so doing, they become artists as well; the process is inclusive because making meaning, while necessarily an individual act, does not happen in isolation. Just as Cather subordinates herself and invites readers into the work, she expects readers to lose something, to give something up as well. Anyone who has taught this novel knows that readers bring expectations and that chief among them is that Jim and Ántonia will get together. Cather forces readers to give up that expectation, the expectation for a love story, as well as the expectation for a more traditional story of the settling of the West, or the expectation for a more precise ending. Those sacrifices are essential because without them, the larger, more human and personal meaning never gets created. Religious sacrifice, too, often involves the sacrifice of expectation: people expected Jesus to be a different kind of leader and savior, and his listeners (and most modern hearers, I suspect) expected the Prodigal Son to pay for his sins.

Critics often focus on *My Ántonia* in terms of loss. Ann Fisher-Wirth, for example, writes that "[t]he movement from possession to loss, from union to separation, is the deep and central pattern of Jim Burden's experience in *My Ántonia*" (41). David Stouck notes "the tragic realization that the past can never be recaptured" (46). Fisher-Wirth calls attention to what seems to be a relentless movement outward in "ever-widening arcs" of loss repeated and reinscribed, of a "long, slow renunciation and forfeiture" (41). I have proposed a different view of the losses in this novel—not a view that ignores or denies them, certainly, for they are a strong and certain presence—but a view that echoes Murphy's argument that the losses in the novel "become a restoration of hope and meaning" as they offer a "perspective [by] which the scattered pieces of life can be reassembled into a controllable order for purposes of meaning, survival, and future" (97). The losses experienced by characters in *My Ántonia* become more powerful, more tension-filled, more pregnant with dramatic and emotional possibility, when readers achieve an understanding of loss as sometimes sacred and as necessary to the creative act. *My Ántonia* is not relentless, not a defined movement in one direction; rather it is full of ambiguity and paradox, and surprising and unexpected moments of redemption.

One way to realize this more hopeful view of sacrifice is to compare *My Ántonia* to Cather's early story "Peter" (1892), her first incarnation of the Shimerda suicide story. In "Peter" there is neither redemption nor hope. The Old World was better than the New, the old generation better than the younger—the suicide offers no lesson, no new understanding, no emotional response, no new creation. *My Ántonia* is not so bleak. The world of *My Ántonia* is not never-never land; we do not know whether the ending will be as happy as it seems, for the world is indeed often harsh and cruel and exacts a terrible price. But it is also a world of possibility—where we do not know what is going to come out of the cave, where the Old World can merge with the New, where the lamb can become the lion. Bernice Slote has written that Willa Cather's conception and presentation of the Kingdom of Art includes the opposite realm of Philistia (32, 171–172). "Peter" is a story of Philistia, and that is all. *My Ántonia* is the story of Philistia, but it is also the story of the Kingdom of Art.

History records plenty of sacrifices that have led nowhere, that are simply loss without redemption, but from the beginning sacrifice has been a path to salvation. Sacrifice, especially sacrifice of the self, is an idea Cather explores in works other than *My Ántonia*. Alexandra Bergson and Thea Kronborg certainly know the sufferings and rewards of sacrifice. At the end of *O Pioneers!*

the stories that loomed so large—the tragedy of Emil and Marie, Alexandra's struggles, the pioneer parents—lose their individual uniqueness and become simply part of the two or three human stories that go on repeating themselves. Tom Outland and Marian Forrester and Bishops Latour and Vaillant give up much and know the cost, but each has a higher goal in sight. In *Shadows on the Rock* (1931) Father Hector tells Cecile and her father that "nothing worthwhile is accomplished except by that last sacrifice, the giving of oneself altogether and finally" (149). In *My Ántonia* Willa Cather offers a view of sacrifice in which the dissolution of self, the giving up of expectation, the sacrificial moment, can be the impetus toward something complete and great.

Notes

1. The Latin Vulgate Bible's use of the common noun *dives* (simply Latin for rich man) led to the frequent use of *Dives* as a proper name for the rich man in the parable.

Works Cited

Cather, Willa. *Death Comes for the Archbishop.* 1927. Scholarly Edition, ed. John J. Murphy, with textual editing by Charles W. Mignon. Lincoln: University of Nebraska Press, 1999.

———. *My Ántonia.* 1918. Scholarly Edition, ed. Charles W. Mignon with Kari Ronning. Lincoln: University of Nebraska Press, 1994.

———. *Not Under Forty.* New York: Knopf, 1936.

———. *On Writing.* 1949. Lincoln: University of Nebraska Press, 1988.

———. "Peter." *Willa Cather's Collected Short Fiction.* Ed. Virginia Faulkner. Lincoln: University of Nebraska Press, 1970, pp. 541–543.

———. *Shadows on the Rock.* 1931. New York: Vintage, 1971.

———. *Willa Cather in Person.* Ed. L. Brent Bohlke. Lincoln: University of Nebraska Press, 1986.

Fisher-Wirth, Ann. "Out of the Mother: Loss in *My Ántonia.*" *Cather Studies* 2. Ed. Susan J. Rosowski. Lincoln: University of Nebraska Press, 1993, pp. 41–71.

Gelfant, Blanche H. "Art and Apparent Artlessness: Self-Reflexivity in *My Ántonia.*" *Approaches to Teaching Cather's "My Ántonia."* Ed. Susan J. Rosowski. New York: MLA, 1989, pp. 126–133.

Murphy, John J. *"My Ántonia": The Road Home.* Boston: Twayne, 1989.

Rosowski. "The Romanticism of *My Ántonia*: Every Reader's Story." *Approaches to Teaching Cather's "My Ántonia."* Ed. Rosowski. New York: MLA, 1989, pp. 65–70.

———. *The Voyage Perilous: Willa Cather's Romanticism.* Lincoln: University of Nebraska Press, 1986.

Slote, Bernice. *The Kingdom of Art: Willa Cather's First Principles and Critical Statements, 1893–1896.* Lincoln: University of Nebraska Press, 1966.

Stouck, David. *Willa Cather's Imagination.* Lincoln: University of Nebraska Press, 1975.

JANIS P. STOUT

The Observant Eye, the Art of Illustration, and Willa Cather's My Ántonia

In early 1919 Willa Cather wrote to her friend from childhood, Carrie Miner Sherwood, inquiring whether Carrie had received the gift she had sent her for Christmas, a print of Albrecht Dürer's watercolor of a hare.[1] The painting shows a single animal on an empty white ground. It is rendered with such clarity that one can distinguish individual hairs in the animal's coat (see fig. 1). Cather's choice of this particular painting for her gift was, it seems to me, entirely characteristic of her way of seeing the world, which was also her way of rendering the world in her fiction. Like Dürer's painting, her writing was focused, finely but selectively detailed, and freed of background clutter. As Eudora Welty discerningly pointed out a number of years ago, Cather's fiction typically occupies either far panoramas or a clear foreground, while tending to be vacant in the middle distance. Again like the hare in Dürer's watercolor (with opaque white touches), her selected details are characteristically surrounded by blankness, the unsaid or the disregarded. Throwing the bulk of the furniture out the window, as she proclaimed a desire to do in "The Novel Démeublé" (42), she allows the reader's eye along with her own to focus on the few selected pieces that are kept in the room. It is largely this isolation of individual details against an uncluttered middle ground—perhaps like the microscopic views she would have

Cather Studies, Volume 5, edited by Susan J. Rosowski (Lincoln: University of Nebraska Press, 2003): pp. 128–152. © 2003 by the Board of Regents of the University of Nebraska Press.

experienced as a budding scientist in her adolescent years—that accounts for
the effect of visual acuity in Cather's writing.

As Welty's remark about the locus of Cather's vision, either in the far
perspective or in close focus, implies, she does not so much amass details as
focus on a few specific details one at a time. For example:

- In *Ántonia*, out of what must have been a prairieful of
grasshoppers, we see one specific grasshopper up close as Ántonia
cups it in her hand, then slips it into her hair for safekeeping (40).
- In *A Lost Lady*, we see the "pointed tip" of the last poplar in a
row—just that last one, and not the whole poplar but only its tip,
with the "hollow, silver winter moon" poised above it (40).
- In *Lucy Gayheart*, the "point of silver light" of the evening's one
first star (10).

There are many other examples that could be cited. Critics have often noted
that these specific, isolated presences gain a luminous significance. They
also gain visual clarity from being set alone against a blankness. When
Cather wished to convey to Elizabeth Shepley Sergeant the sense of her new
heroine as she was beginning *My Ántonia*, she reached for a single glazed jar
and placed it by itself on the clear space of Elsie's desk (149). In this anecdote illustrating the visual nature of Cather's thought processes, the concrete
image of the jar established in the reader's mind becomes emblematic of the
abstract idea of the heroine's centrality in the novel. It makes the idea real.

Cather's own association of reality with visual experience is evident in
letters that she wrote to Dorothy Canfield in 1902 during her first trip to
England. Writing from Ludlow, in Shropshire, she said that she had been
tracking A. E. Housman through the scenes of his poetry and had seen with
her own eyes the Severn River reflecting nearby steeples, the "lads" playing
football, the nearness of the jail to the railroad switchyard in Shrewsbury,
precisely as these details are reported in "Is my team ploughing" and "On
moonlit heath and lonesome bank." Having seen these things, she said, she
now realized that Housman's poetry was even truer than she had previously
thought. *Truth* is linked with *seeing*. What made Housman's poetry truer
for her was visual verification. She had seen the specific details recorded in
his poems, verified poem against sight, and on that basis judged the poems
true.[2] Visual accuracy makes truth. What this means for the *writing* of poetry
is that the poet must be able to evoke clear visual images in language. But
before that can happen the poet must possess the power of observation, the
ability to see clearly. If Housman had lacked that power, he would not have
been able to carry these details into his poetry, and it would presumably have
been less true.

Cather seems to have seen the world very much as Housman saw it—very clearly indeed. She seems to have possessed, as he did, close powers of observation that are translated into clear visual images conveying, as such images do in Housman's poetry, rich resonance. Recognition of the visual quality of her style is, of course, one of the staples of Cather criticism. Whether we think in terms of powerful symbolizing pictures like the plow against the setting sun or in terms of small visual details like the ring of dirt around the sink in the opening chapter of *One of Ours* (3) or the "thread of green liquid" oozing from the crushed head of the snake in *My Ántonia* (45), we recognize that her writing has the power to make us see. It also has the power to convince us of the keenness with which Cather herself saw.

More direct evidence of the sharpness of Cather's powers of observation is provided by a small treasure found at the Harry Ransom Humanities Research Center at the University of Texas, her personal copy of F. Schuyler Mathews's *Field Book of American Wild Flowers* (1902). Looking through this book that bears the evidence of Cather's observation of her natural surroundings is an enlightening experience—and moreover a very moving one; between the pages is a tiny clover, threadlike stem, tiny root ball, and all still intact, that she must have placed there. This is the field guide to wildflowers that she carried on her nature walks for over twenty years, from 1917 to 1938. It is heavily annotated in her distinctive hand with checkmarks or lines in the margin beside entries (for some 156 distinct varieties) and comments in the margin beside others. These annotations provide abundant demonstration that Cather was a remarkably close observer of plant life.

A number of entries in the *Field Book* record the dates and places where she saw particular plants. Mostly these indicate Jaffrey, New Hampshire, the rustic resort town at the foot of Mount Monadnock where she spent her autumns for many years, or Grand Manan, the island off the coast of New Brunswick where she and Edith Lewis had a cabin. Three times she records having seen certain plants—the calamus or sweet fig, the flowering dogwood, and the pinxter flower or wild honeysuckle—in Virginia during her visit in 1938, during the writing of *Sapphira and the Slave Girl*. Several times, as if Mathews's descriptions had jogged her memory, she notes that she had seen such-and-such a plant in Nebraska. But the most striking entries are those in which she actually adds details to the book's already detailed descriptions. These are astonishingly precise. When Mathews describes the "small dense clusters" of flowers on the arrow-leafed tearthumb (108), Cather adds that the clusters are club-shaped. When Mathews describes the "generally smooth stem" of the Canada hawkweed (526), she insists that the branches and stem were joined in sharp angles. When he describes the leaves of the white woodland aster as "smooth," she notes that on the underside they are bristly along the veins (484). On the back of one of the plates she wrote a long description of the habitat and characteristics of the exiguous, with its sawtooth-edged, sessile leaves (486)—*sessile* meaning attached to the main stem at the base rather than with an intermediate stem.

We see in these annotations Cather's effort to observe the natural world as closely as she could and to describe it as minutely, in as accurate language, as she could. This practice of close observation that she brought to her experience of her various natural environments as she walked, hiked, and climbed translates itself, through the medium of her lucid prose, into precision of rendered details. Her descriptions evince a remarkable eye-hand coordination: a linkage of visual experience and verbal virtuosity.

• • •

A similar clarity and focus, as well as another kind of linkage of the visual and the verbal, characterize the illustrations of the first edition and (until recently) most subsequent editions of *My Ántonia*. It is these illustrations and, even more, the process of their conception and development for the text that I am primarily interested in here. We know that it was Cather herself who conceived the idea for the eight spare pen-and-ink drawings and selected the artist to do them, after having tried to make suitable drawings herself. My central questions are: Why did she choose W. T. Benda and why did she want illustrations of precisely this kind, which are actually quite different from Benda's usual work?

In the textual commentary to the Scholarly Edition of *My Ántonia* Charles Mignon states that Cather wanted Benda "because he knew both Europe and the American West" (512). That is indeed the reason she indicated on 24 November 1917, in a letter to Ferris Greenslet, her editor at Houghton Mifflin. W. T. Benda was in fact an immigrant from Bohemia (the national group primarily emphasized in *My Ántonia*) who had lived in the West and painted Western subjects.[3] Cather was aware of his work from her days as editor at *McClure's;* Benda illustrations appeared in a dozen or more issues of the magazine between 1906 and 1912.[4] The letter to Greenslet of 24 November 1917 goes on to say that another reason she wants Benda, besides his familiarity with both Europe and the American West, is that he has imagination and has been willing to work with her to get precisely the effects she wanted. My conjecture, which I will go into below, is that there was still another reason, which she doesn't mention.

What Cather wanted was very different from what Houghton Mifflin initially wanted. The publisher proposed illustrating the book with a frontispiece (WC to Greenslet, 24 November 1917). Cather was determined not to have so conventional a decoration and one that would necessarily have generalized. Not only did she prefer that the drawings be attached narratively to specific moments or ideas in the text, as the Benda drawings are, but she was intent on having a series of drawings that would give the impression of the minimalist line techniques of woodcuts. Her correspondence with editors Greenslet and Scaife is striking in its revelation of just how emphatic her determination was and the extent to which visual design was a part of her creative act of authorship. She conceived the appearance of the book while she was still conceiving, or at any rate executing, the verbal text. Mignon comments that as early as 13 March 1917, "even before she had completed a first draft" of the novel, Cather was "thinking as a designer might about how to present her work" (483). In Jean Schwind's words, she "acted as artistic director of the project" (53). At various points in the correspondence she specified the kind of paper that should be used for the illustrations, their sizing, their placement in the text, and even their placement on the page (WC to Miss [Helen] Bishop, Secretary to F. Greenslet, "Saturday," 2 February 1918).

Cather justified her determination *not* to have a conventional frontispiece in conjunction with explaining why she wanted Benda (WC to R. L. Scaife, 1 December 1917). She had seen his pen-and-ink drawings in Jacob Riis's 1909 book *The Old Town*. (We might note that *The Old Town* is a book that evokes a lost but nostalgically remembered European setting—a congenial theme as Cather thought about *My Ántonia*.) It is significant that in referring to Benda's work in the Riis book Cather specified the drawings. She did not use the more general term "illustrations" because in fact most of the illustrations (both a frontispiece and full-page glossies scattered through the volume) are not pen-and-ink drawings at all, but charcoal halftones. These were Benda's usual kind of work. But Cather indicated explicitly that they were what she did *not* want. She told Scaife that she considered Benda's halftones stilted (WC to R. L Scaife, 7 April 1917). In addition to the full-page illustrations for Riis's book, however, Benda had done a number of simpler, more open pen-and-ink head-and-tail pieces. Even these are more filled up with details than the drawings he would do for *Ántonia*, as we can see from his headpiece to chapter 4, "Christmas Sheaf" (78, see fig. 2) and his mid-chapter ornament from chapter 2, "Fanö Women" (21, see fig. 3). Yet we can see how she might have discerned in such drawings the potential for achieving what she had in mind, through simplifying and "un-cluttering" them even further.

Benda in fact captured in these spare drawings much of the essence of Cather's spare style. They have the visual equivalence of her selective focus on a few details set against a far prospect with an emptied middle ground—that quality of isolated detail that Welty designated as the elimination of the middle ground. Benda captured these qualities not only because he read the text in typescript, and as a capable professional was able to vary his style accordingly, but because Cather worked closely with him on his conceptualization of the drawings. Indeed, as I have pointed out, she established for him the kind of illustrations she wanted by first trying to draw them herself. Having tried to make her own head-and-tail pieces, she told Greenslet, she wanted an artist who would emulate her efforts (WC to Greenslet, 18 October 1917). *She* was in control. A little over a month later she reported that Benda was indeed seeking to capture her precise intentions (WC to Greenslet, 14 November 1917).

There are eight drawings in all. Originally there were to have been twelve, but Houghton Mifflin's skimpy production budget would not pay for more (WC to Greenslet, 14 November 1917). This would seem to account for their concentration in the early parts of the text.

The illustrations are familiar to most readers of *My Ántonia,* but will bear reviewing in order to emphasize certain features. As Cather herself said, they capture the tone of the novel admirably.

Drawing 1 comes in the first chapter, Jim Burden's narration of his train trip to Nebraska. We see, much as Jim would have seen, an immigrant family waiting among their bundles on what we assume, from the textual context, to be a train platform (see fig. 4). These are, of course, the Shimerdas arriving in Nebraska. The man's downward gaze and the darkness of the drawing, quite unlike the others in the series, speak of discouragement. The girl whose bright eyes will be celebrated gazes out beyond the reader. Central emphasis is on the woman's cradling grasp of a treasured possession. Benda's practiced technique is greatly in evidence here both in mood and in composition.

Drawing 2 shows Mr. Shimerda again, tall and lanky, still with bowed head suggestive of discouragement. Ántonia and Jim have spied her father out hunting, and Ántonia has confided to Jim that he is unhappy in the new country (see fig. 5). Despite conveying discouragement, this picture strikes the outdoor note that will characterize all the rest. For the first time we gain a visual impression of the vastness of the prairie and especially the spaciousness of its sky. Scattered curving lines indicate the prairie grass, and the sinking sun sends its long beams up into the sky, disappearing into blank page.

Drawing 3 is equally narrative in import, echoing the incident of the dried mushrooms given to Grandmother Burden by Mrs. Shimerda. It hints at far-off places, with a woman gathering mushrooms in the old country (see fig. 6). The woman's figure is generalized, with perhaps the clearest details being her rolled-up sleeve, conveying the idea of physical work, and a cluster of mushrooms clearly seen in the foreground. There seems to be quiet and isolation all around.

Drawing 4 shows the hired man bringing home the Christmas tree (see fig. 7). With notable minimalism, the drawing indicates the empty countryside, the narrow trail, and a few weeds. The big, absolutely empty sky is indicated by blank paper.

Drawing 5 shows another big sky, an effect Cather sought to emphasize by having the illustrations lowered on the page so as to create a sense of sunlight and air at the top (WC to Miss Bishop, "Saturday," 2 February 1918, see fig. 8). This time summer thunderheads are indicated. Once again there is emptiness all around, with a strong central focus on Ántonia herself, the plow, the horses, and the heavy horse collar.

Drawing 6 is reminiscent of drawing 2, with its sunrays (see fig. 9). In this case, it is the striking sun that will magnify the plow on the horizon. We see companionable young people, a head scarf implying immigrant identity, one sunflower plant, and empty prairie all around. This drawing demonstrates particularly well the idea of the vacant middle distance, with nothing intervening between its depictions of horizon and close-up details.

Drawing 7 shows another big summer sky with the merest indication of cumulus clouds (see fig. 10). The rows of Lena's knitting are clearly seen, along with her two knitting needles, her bare feet, and the line of a nipple inside her tight bodice—clear focus indeed! Cather gloated over this drawing that Lena was fairly bursting out of her clothes (WC to Greenslet, 7 March 1918).

Drawing 8, the last in the series, starkly shows Ántonia struggling through the snow into the wind (see fig. 11). The dark tones of coat, hat, and boots, and the bent position of her head, are reminiscent of the first picture, of the Shimerdas waiting on the train platform. A single line outlines the top of the cloud, closing in the top of the picture in contrast to those in which either the clear sky or the hinted shape of cumuli opens the top. Again Benda captures the emptiness of the prairie, which he emphasizes by isolating a few strong details: snow in the air, tracks, the whip in the hand. It is another masterful example of minimalist design executed with line techniques reminiscent of woodcuts.

• • •

We have accounted for Cather's selection of W. T. Benda as her illustrator by citing several factors: his familiarity with both the Old World and the West, her prior acquaintance with him (i.e., a reason of convenience), her admiration of some (but not all) of his work in Jacob Riis's *The Old Town*, and the fact that he was willing to work with her to catch her conception of the drawings. But where did she get that conception? Here my essay becomes frankly conjectural—offering, however, a conjecture supported by both biographical evidence and visual comparison. I believe that Cather was seeking to emulate the illustrations to Mary Austin's *The Land of Little Rain* (1903), done by E. Boyd Smith.

The Austin-Cather connection has been recognized for some time. It is well documented that they knew each other personally, and connections between their work have been demonstrated by several critics.[5] For the most part, it is *The Song of the Lark* and Austin's *A Woman of Genius* that have been linked, though in fact the connections extend much further, reaching both forward and considerably backward. To my knowledge, no one has suggested any connection of Cather's work to *The Land of Little Rain*, or even any indication that she was aware of the book. Yet it is quite clear that Cather was familiar with Austin and her writings long before she wrote *My Ántonia*. David Stouck has identified a likely borrowing by Cather even before 1900, in the 1893 story "A Son of the Celestial." The two were personally acquainted by at least 1910, and in 1917 specifically, the year when Cather was corresponding with Greenslet and Scaife about the Benda illustrations, her awareness of Austin remained sufficiently keen to prompt a brief comment on Austin's newly published novel *The Ford* in a letter to Elizabeth Shepley Sergeant.[6]

Considering the mass of evidence that Cather was aware of Austin as early as the 1890s and that she remained both personally and professionally conversant with her up until Austin's death in 1934, it seems overwhelmingly likely that she knew *The Land of Little Rain*, the book that launched Austin's career and is usually regarded as her finest work. Probably she would have been aware of its serialization in *Atlantic Monthly*. Cather was keenly aware of periodical literature and more than once during her years as editor at *McClure's* advised correspondents to send their manuscripts to *Atlantic Monthly*. When she did, her dearly specified reasons show that she had more than a reputational acquaintance with that prestigious magazine. The publisher of Austin's series of sketches in book form, in 1903, was Houghton Mifflin, which in less than a decade would also be Cather's publisher and whose acquisitions editor, Ferris Greenslet, would be an acquaintance even sooner. The archive of correspondence between Cather and Greenslet reveals that they at times discussed Austin. There was ample and varied opportunity, then, for her to be acquainted with Austin's book and perhaps with behind-the-scenes information about its production history.

Perhaps when Lather looked through Riis's *The Old Town*—which we know she had seen at least by December 1917 but probably much earlier, perhaps even drawing on it early in the work on *My Ántonia* for the atmosphere of remembered European origins—Benda's pen-and-ink drawings there reminded her of Smith's in *The Land of Little Rain*. As we have noted, these were only the head-and-tail pieces and a few small inserts; the full-page illustrations in Riis's book were the halftones she disliked. And in fact Benda's drawings in *My Ántonia* more closely resemble Smith's pen-and-ink drawings in Austin's book than they do Benda's own earlier work.

Design is a significant element in *The Land of Little Rain*. Visual elements, by which I mean primarily the illustrations but also layout, might well be called, as Schwind calls the Benda illustrations of *My Ántonia*, a "silent supplement" to the text. Unlike its magazine version, the book was set with abundant white space and was adorned with pen-and-ink drawings, most but not all of them narrative in nature, that is, directly linked to the text. E. Boyd Smith, the artist who did the drawings, was a well-established and prolific illustrator and would later do the illustrations for Austin's *The Flock* and *The Ford* as well.[7]

We recall that Cather initially meant to have head-and-tail pieces and emphatically did not want a frontispiece (WC to Greenslet, 18 October 1917). The Smith illustrations of *The Land of Little Rain* are of two sorts, full-page line drawings and head-and-tail pieces. Choosing just one of many possible examples of the latter (from p. 15), we might note how it shows the operation of a precise eye, an eye having keen powers of observation (see fig. 12). In its precision, this drawing, like the other small drawings in *The Land of Little Rain,* stands as a correlative for Austin's prose in this book (though not all of her writing): precise, warm, and personal, tending to address the reader directly in the second person. It is a style that may remind us of Cather's in *Ántonia.*

It is Smith's full-page and most-of-page drawings, however, that are most strikingly comparable to the Benda illustrations of *My Ántonia.* The first is one of a single crow or raven sitting on a cow skull with empty desert space all around, a few wisps of dust devils, and a distant horizon indicated simply by a couple of lines (4, see fig. 13). Like the Benda drawings, this one is placed relatively low on the page, allowing it to open up into white space above—an indication of a big sky. A big sky characterizes, indeed, all of the larger drawings in *Little Rain.* Another good example is one of a vanishing row of fence posts with one bird in the sky and one bird catching a little shade in the foreground (10, see fig. 14). Notice, as well, the drawing showing the litter left in the land by people, a smoking camp-fire or perhaps cigarette, and a single disgusted-looking bird (38, see fig. 15). Here and in the one that follows, showing a "pocket hunter" camping for the night, with his campfire, two cooking implements, and two burros (53), there is no horizon line at all (see fig. 16). This is true bareness, a true minimalist style. I would stress, again, the big sky that is so evident in the Benda illustrations of *My Ántonia.*

In 1926, when she and Greenslet were contemplating a new edition of *Ántonia* (the edition in which the preface was reduced), Cather said that the Benda illustrations were one of the few instances she could think of in which pictures materially assisted the narrative (WC to Greenslet, 15 February 1926). That is, they were essentially a part of the text. Here, again from *The Land of Little Rain,* is a remarkable instance in which the line drawing is actually interwoven with the text (21), so that the two, picture and text, demonstrably assist each other (see fig. 17). The words printed on the page become a part of the landscape separating the coyote from the rising moon that he looks at apprehensively over his shoulder.

• • •

My conjecture that the original source of Cather's conception for the visual "'silent' supplement" to *My Ántonia* lay in the illustrations of Austin's *The Land of Little Rain* is based entirely on readerly and visual comparison, though bolstered by biographical evidence and a considerable archive establishing her intentions. Demonstrably, Cather and Austin experienced the natural world in much the same sorts of ways. They shared habits of hiking, close observation of plant life, and the use of notebooks to record their field observations. For all their differences *as novelists*, if we compare Cathers writing with Austin's in *The Land of Little Rain*, we see a similar minimalism of prose style at work, a style keenly focused on selected details, rendered in terse descriptive language. The two books are similar in their employment of illustrations of a precise, minimalist kind: pen-and-ink line drawings making notable use of empty space to isolate details and to suggest the West's big sky.

If my conjecture about the impact of Smith's drawings on Cather's vision for the illustrations of her own book is correct, the critical judgment of at least one art historian that Smith "had few followers and made no major impact on American illustration" (Best 28) may merit revision. Another implication is a further expansion of our understanding of the aesthetic sisterhood between Cather and Austin, as well as perhaps an increased estimate of the importance to Cather of visual experience itself. And perhaps, too, it would evoke a more thorough study of the Harold von Schmidt illustrations for the second edition of *Death Comes for The Archbishop*, which, as Mignon has established (520), were also developed with active involvement by Cather. It is a linkage, then, of considerable significance and one that I hope may yet be conclusively established through archival records not presently known. Not only does Smith's beautiful work in the drawings for *The Land of Little Rain* extend beyond itself into the work of Benda—transformed, for this project, from his usual heavily shaded style—but the combination of Smith's drawings and Austin's style is carried forward into the minimalist aesthetic that would characterize much of Cather's fiction and which she would formulate in "The Novel Démeublé." It was an aesthetic that, as the notes in her field guide to wildflowers demonstrate, derived in large measure from her own visual acuity, plus what might be called a highly developed eye-hand coordination: a precise writerly hand working in perfect coordination with a precise eye for detail.

NOTES

I want to express my gratitude to Molly McBride Lasco for her assistance in locating information about W. T. Benda and E. Boyd Smith.

1. WC to Carrie Miner Sherwood, 11 February [prob. 1929], Willa Cather Pioneer Memorial, Red Cloud, Nebraska.

2. WC to Dorothy Canfield, 6 July 1902, Bailey-Howe Library, University of Vermont.

3. See Schwind, especially n. 4; also Samuels and Samuels, cited by Schwind. The letters to Ferris Greenslet and Roger L. Scaife on which I am drawing for the production history of *My Ántonia* are at the Houghton Library, Harvard University, bMS Am 1925 (341).

4. Benda's illustrations had also appeared in *Century, Scribner's,* and *Cosmopolitan,* as well as in books.

5. Archival evidence of Cather's and Austin's personal acquaintance is to be found at the Houghton Library and at the Huntington Library. T. M. Pearce's edition of selected letters of Austin, *Literary America,* prints a short letter to Austin from Cather. See McNall; Porter; and Stout, "Willa Cather and Mary Austin." Regarding biographical parallels, see Gelfant; also Stout, *Through the Window Out the Door.*

6. WC to Elizabeth Shepley Sergeant, 23 June [1917?], Alderman Library, University of Virginia.

7. Surprisingly, in a letter written in 1907, when Austin was making arrangements for publication of *Lost Borders,* she wrote, "I sincerely hope you will not insist upon illustrating it. I am strongly prejudiced against illustrated fiction except for children"; MA to W. I. Booth, 27 April 1907, Houghton Library, Harvard, bMS Am 1925 (83).

WORKS CITED

Austin, Mary. *The Land of Little Rain.* 1903. Albuquerque: University of New Mexico Press, 1974.

———. Letters. Houghton Library, Harvard University.

Best, James J. *American Popular Illustration: A Reference Guide.* Westport CT: Greenwood, 1984.

Cather, Willa. Letters. Alderman Library, University of Virginia; Bailey-Howe Library, University of Vermont; Houghton Library, Harvard Uuniversity; and Willa Cather Pioneer Memorial, Red Cloud, Nebraska.

———. *A Lost Lady.* 1923. Ed. Susan J. Rosowski et al. Willa Cather Scholarly Edition. Lincoln: University of Nebraska Press, 1997.

———. *Lucy Gayheart.* 1935. New York: Vintage Books, 1995.

———. *My Ántonia.* 1918. Ed. Charles Mignon and James Woodress. Willa Cather Scholarly Edition. Lincoln: University of Nebraska Press, 1994.

———. *One of Ours.* 1922. New York: Vintage Books, 1991.

Gelfant, Blanche. *Women Writing in America: Voices in Collage.* Hanover NH: University Press of New England, 1984.

Mathews, F. Schuyler. *Field Book of American Wild Flowers.* 1902. Personal copy belonging to Willa Cather. Harry Ransom Humanities Research Center, University of Texas.

McNall, Sally Allen. "The American Woman Writer in Transition: Freeman, Austin, and Cather" In *Seeing Female: Social Roles and Personal Lives.* Ed. Sharon S. Brehm. Westport CT: Greenwood, 1988. 43–52.

Mignon, Charles, and Kari Ronning. Textual Commentary. *My Ántonia.* By Willa Cather. Willa Cather Scholarly Edition. Lincoln: University of Nebraska Press, 1994.

Pearce, T. M. *Literary America, 1903—1934: The Mary Austin Letters.* Westport CT: Greenwood, 1979.

Porter, Nancy. Afterword. *A Woman of Genius*. By Mary Austin. Old Westbury NY: Feminist Press, 1985.

Riffs, Jacob. *The Old Town*. New York: Macmillan, 1909.

Samuels, Peggy, and Harold Samuels. *The Illustrated Biographical Encyclopedia of Artists of the American West*. Garden City NJ: Doubleday, 1976.

Schwind, Jean. 'The Benda Illustrations to *My Ántonia*: Cather's 'Silent' Supplement to Jim Burden's Narrative." *PMLA* 100 (1985): 51–67.

Sergeant, Elizabeth Shepley. *Willa Cather: A Memoir*. 1953. Athens: Ohio University Press, 1992.

Stouck, David. "Mary Austin and Willa Cather." *Willa Cather Pioneer Memorial Newsletter* 23.2 (1979): n.p.

Stout, Janis P. *Through the Window, Out the Door: Women's Narratives of Departure, from Austin and Cather to Tyler, Morrison, and Didion*. Tuscaloosa: University of Alabama Press, 1998.

———. "Willa Cather and Mary Austin: Intersections and Influence." *Southwestern American Literature* 21 (1996): 39–60.

Welty, Eudora. "The House of Willa Cather." *The Eye of The Story: Selected Essays and Reviews*. New York: Random House, 1977. 41–60.

MICHAEL GORMAN

Jim Burden and the White Man's Burden:
My Ántonia *and Empire*

Recent harvests in American history and letters have yielded an almost
universal acknowledgment: the pioneer myth of the American West has
been cultivated in a soil broken and furrowed by the colonizing impulse of
empire. Each narrative of western settlement is rooted in a "legacy of conquest" (Limerick) informing the text, and exposing this legacy demands
recovering lost texts and rereading familiar works within their ideological
contexts. Nowhere is this challenge more complex—or more reward-
ing—than in reading Willa Cather, a writer simultaneously celebrated
for her depiction of pioneers and respected for her historical authenticity.
The bounty from this garden has been sampled often in the last decade
and a half. Mike Fischer has unearthed the "burden of imperialism" in
Cather's pioneer texts; Joseph Urgo has considered Cather's acceptance
of America's imperial stance; and Deborah Karush has discussed the
"nostalgic vision" with which Cather viewed the frontier. These studies
demonstrate the veracity and continuing vitality of Guy Reynolds's assertion that "Cather's novels fictionalize the transfer of European empires
to America and the subsequent growth of American empire" (46). My
trespass into this field attempts to reveal how Cather's most enduring
pioneer text—*My Ántonia*—reconciles the insular conception of the
nineteenth-century United States with the post-Spanish-American War

Cather Studies, Volume 6, edited by Steven Trout (Lincoln: University of Nebraska Press,
2006): pp. 28–57. © 2006 Board of Regents of the University of Nebraska.

117

reality, reflecting America's transition from continental to global power. I argue in particular that with the Great War as its immediate subtext, this novel reaches back to the closing years of the American frontier and the influx of European immigrants to the Plains states, projecting an image of the nation and legitimizing its status as "European" power.

The original introduction (1918) to *My Ántonia* is an intricate frame for what some critics regard as a simple country novel. Like the openings to Daniel Defoe's *Robinson Crusoe* and Nathaniel Hawthorne's *The Scarlet Letter*, it operates as a narrative of transmission establishing a fictionalized origin for the text. The most obvious effect of the introduction is the distance it establishes between Cather and her story. In the opening pages, an unnamed female narrator credits Jim Burden, a childhood acquaintance, for writing the tale. By making Jim "legal counsel for one of the great Western railways" (x), Cather complicates his perspective through its association to the controversial role the railroad played in Indian-white relations, western settlement patterns, and resource exploitation.

The introduction situates the production of Jim's manuscript in the immediate present (1916–1918), synchronous to the novel's actual composition. As the dates of its composition suggest, *My Ántonia* is a highly charged exercise of political memory. Written as the First World War ravaged Europe and cast as the reminiscence of middle-aged Jim Burden, it is a "prehistory" reconstructing the 1880s and early 1890s from the verge of America's entrance into the Great War. Cather further complicates the account by making its teller a rural Nebraskan turned successful New York attorney and infusing the memory of his prairie childhood with a whole-hearted acceptance of progress (the Yankee credo) and a fair share of romantic yearning:

> As for Jim, no disappointments have been severe enough to drill his naturally romantic and ardent disposition. This disposition, though it often made him seem very funny when he was a boy, has been one of the strongest elements in his success. He loves with a personal passion the great country through which his railway runs and branches. His faith in it and his knowledge of it have played an important part in its development. He is always able to raise capital for new enterprises in Wyoming or Montana, and has helped young men out there to do remarkable things in mines and timber and oil. If a young man with an idea can once get Jim Burden's attention, can manage to accompany him when he goes off into the wilds hunting for lost parks or exploring new canyons, then the money which means action is usually forthcoming. Jim is still able to lose himself in those big Western dreams. (xi)

The speaker in the introduction claims that Jim "loves with a personal passion the great country through which his railway runs and branches," yet his infatuation for this territory is clearly an obsession to exploit its resources for material gain like the despicable Wick Cutter of *My Ántonia* and other characters appearing in Cather's oeuvre (e.g., Bayliss Wheeler in *One of Ours* and Ivy Peters in *A Lost Lady*). While described as one who loves exploring "lost parks" or "new canyons," Jim appreciates these marvels with a mercenary eye like the Spanish conquistador Francisco Vasquez de Coronado (1510–1554), who figures so prominently in his adolescent figuration of Nebraska. Notwithstanding the "naturally romantic" character attributed to James Quayle Burden, the "big Western dreams" in which he loses himself equal not innocent adventure but economic conquest: raising capital for ventures that "do remarkable things in mines and timber and oil." Like Coronado's famed 1540–1541 expedition from New Spain to present-day Kansas in search of the legendary Seven Cities of Gold, Jim's frequent travels to the West are speculative in nature and rooted in colonialism.

Cather plants U.S. expansionism squarely in Jim's retrospective, which allegorizes America's displacement of the Plains Indians and the Spanish Empire. Although they do not figure explicitly in the novel, the history and culture of the Plains Indians form a palimpsest occasionally—and tellingly—exposed in the text, especially when considering the impact federal policies like the 1862 Homestead and Pacific Railroad acts and the 1887 Dawes Act had upon the original inhabitants of Nebraska. Equally significant are suggestive allusions in the novel to Spain's presence in North America. Such rhetoric and imagery hints to America's wresting the mantle of empire from Spain in the 1898 Spanish-American War and suggest that, in addition to absorbing Spain's colonial holdings in the Caribbean and Pacific, the United States has inherited Spanish obligations in Europe. In other words, within the pastoral and nostalgic account ascribed to Jim, Cather traces the United States' cultural heritage and its rise to global power—a genealogy suggesting that America has a duty, as de facto European state, to participate in the Great War.

Taking Possession

Despite the sentimentality with which this novel has been received traditionally, Cather scholars—reflecting America's long history of distrusting jurists—have treated Jim's narrative as a suspect document. While narratologists have pointed to the intricate layering involved in the tale's construction and transmission, feminist readings have focused on the relationship between Jim and his subject, Ántonia. Among the vanguard in questioning Jim's reliability as a narrator is Susan J. Rosowski, who asserts in *The Voyage Perilous: Willa Cather's Romanticism* (1986) that Jim's allegiance as an adult is not to Ántonia but to his own ideas; when the circumstances in Ántonia's life conflict with his beliefs or intentions, he "denies the reality" (89).

What Rosowski perceives in Jim's treatment of Ántonia can also he witnessed in his construal of western American history; just as Cather builds tension into Jim's thoughts about Ántonia in order to deconstruct the myths about women to which he subscribes (Rosowski 89), she undermines his interpretation of history. Although *My Ántonia* accurately projects an image of the United States as empire, statements attributed to Jim consistently disregard the political maneuvers—most obviously the incidents involving the removal and genocide of the American Indians—contributing to his nation's hemispheric ascendancy and growing global prominence.

Jim's initial observation about the rolling grasslands reveals the superficial understanding of Plains history Cather imposes on him. On the ride from the train station in Black Hawk to his grandparents' homestead, the orphaned traveler peers from the wagon bed into the dark night and concludes, "There seemed to be nothing to see; no fences, no creeks or trees, no hills or fields. If there was a road, I could not make it out in the faint starlight. There was nothing but land: not a country at all, but the material out of which countries are made. No, there was *nothing* but land" (7, italics added). In subtle strokes, Jim Burden erases the inhabitants preexisting the arrival of European settlers from his memoir. The black night, which he suggestively labels "utter darkness" (5) and later "empty darkness" (7), functions like a geopolitical tabula rasa, an ideological blackboard with the previous record wiped clean and awaiting the next lesson to be inscribed.

Jim's language echoes a common sentiment in American literature and political ideology: that of the frontier as a virgin land waiting to be settled. On one level his reflections about the prairie's barrenness suggest the youthful ignorance of a ten year old on his inaugural visit to the Plains. Yet beneath this childish observation lurks the willful blindness that Cather writes into the adult narrating this episode. Deborah Karush notes that Cather's novels promote a "fantasy of unrestrained expansion" by using child narrators to impart nostalgic accounts of "the frontier as a vast, empty space . . . conveniently devoid of Native Americans" (30). Jim's reflections certainly fit this pattern. He specifically equates the emptiness of the prairie landscape to its lack of infrastructure and agrarian development. Progress requires improvement to the land: it demands fences, fields, and roads. At the time he is credited with writing the story of Ántonia, Jim is implicitly involved in the exigencies of progress. As a railroad attorney, his career would entail what Patricia Nelson Limerick cleverly calls "the drawing of lines and the marking of borders" (55): through legal sleight of hand, he would have turned *land* into *property*. Successful performance of his duties would necessitate an intimate familiarity with the territorial statutes, congressional legislation, and military involvement making the land grants to the railroads possible.

Competing experiences of dispossession and possession figure prominently in the early chapters of My Ántonia. In one sense, Cather's entire tale charts Jim's individual journey from banishment and divestiture to acquisition, and, accordingly, in its earliest appearance, Nebraska is Jim's Paradise Lost. Upon disembarking from the train at Black Hawk, Jim and the immigrant family he sees huddling together on the station platform are enveloped by cold and "utter darkness" despite the red glow emanating from the locomotive firebox. The night's imposing blackness and the steam engine's smoldering fire evoke Miltonic images of Hell encountered by Satan and his minions after being exiled from Heaven to a "Dungeon horrible, on all sides round / As one great Furnace flam'd, yet from those flames / No light, but rather darkness visible / [. . . .] / As far remov'd from God and light of Heav'n / As from the Center thrice to th' utmost Pole" (*Paradise Lost,* Book I, ii. 61–74). Disoriented by his new surroundings, Jim gazes toward Heaven and contemplates his fate. As he looks up at the unfamilar expansive sky, "the complete dome of heaven all there was of it," Jim concludes "that the world was left behind, that we had got over the edge of it, and outside man's jurisdiction" (7). His remarks a few lines later extend upon this phrasing: "Between that earth and that sky I felt erased, blotted out. I did not say my prayers that night: here, I felt, what would be would be" (8). The orphaned boy feels that he has traveled not merely beyond the authority of men but beyond the influence of Heaven—no need for prayers since they can no longer be heard, let alone answered.

Cather's wording—being "erased and blotted out"—indicates a profound sense of alienation. Though his initial thoughts reflect the idea of being exiled, Jim's views about his new surroundings soon move from the nihilistic toward the existential. His life in the West will be what he *makes* of it—what he takes and claims title to, including Ántonia. His determination to make his own world is reflected in the final lines of the introduction, when the speaker points out how he corrected the working title of the manuscript by adding "My" to the original inscription, "Ántonia" (xiii). Before his narrative even begins, Cather establishes not only Jim's impulse to acquire but also his awareness of the role semantics play in acquisition. Of course, this is a lesson a successful railroad attorney in an age of phenomenal railway expansion would know well: to procure anything legitimately it must be first recognized and named. Ántonia Shimerda, "this girl [who] seemed to mean . . . the country" (xi–xii), embodies the West. By having Jim prefix the title of his manuscript with the first-person singular possessive pronoun, Cather deepens the parallel between Jim's judicious claim to Ántonia and the territory absorbed by his burgeoning nation throughout the nineteenth century.

The convergence of verbal expression and possession makes its most conspicuous appearance in the novel when Jim and his grandmother visit the primitive dugout homestead of their new neighbors. Shortly after they arrive, Ántonia Shimerda takes Jim's hand and they race away from the adults to the edge of a ravine, followed by Yulka, Ántonia's younger sister. The ensuing encounter is incredibly Edenic. "'Name? What name?' she asked, touching me on the shoulder. I told her my name, and she repeated it after me and made Yulka say it. She pointed into the gold cottonwood tree behind whose top we stood and again, 'What name?'" (25). Hidden from everyone and everything but the red grass, blue sky, and yellow cottonwood, Jim names the things around him on that breezy autumn afternoon with the assurance of Adam in the Garden. While an exercise in discovery for Ántonia, this lesson displays Jim's powers of recognition and identification, deliberately recalling Genesis 1:28–2:19, where God bestows dominion over the earth to humankind and has Adam christen "every living creature." As he confidently identifies all Ántonia points to, Jim verbally demonstrates his familiarity with the prairie environment, a territory to which he initially felt alien, and proves himself less a stranger to the surrounding landscape than the oldest daughter of the Bohemian family.

Teaching English to the Shimerda girls plays a pivotal role in Jim's recovery of what he lost, namely, his identity associated with a sense of place, after being orphaned and moving from the lush wooded hills of Virginia to the open, wine-colored grassland of Nebraska. At the entreaty of Ántonia's father, Jim continues the English tutorials until she turns fifteen, when events (including her father's suicide) force her to abandon language learning and attend to chores at the farm (116–117). Jim's thoughts about teaching Ántonia read like a parody of George Bernard Shaw's *Pygmalion*. During the lessons Jim attempts to exercise authority over Ántonia in a fashion similar to the way phonetics Professor Henry Higgins lords over Eliza Doolittle in Shaw's 1913 comedy.[1] "Much as I like Ántonia," Jim writes, "I hated a superior tone that she sometimes took with me. She was four years older . . . and had seen more of the world; but . . . I resented her protecting manner. Before the autumn was over she began to treat me more like an equal and to defer to me in other things than reading lessons" (41). Like Professor Higgins, Jim wants to influence his student in more than language matters, and he soon gets his wish.

The desired change in Ántonia's opinion of him was brought about by an event of mock-epic proportions. With Ántonia to act as his damsel in distress, Jim instinctively reenacts the legend of St. George and slays "a circus monstrosity" of a rattlesnake with a borrowed spade (44). Though he and Otto Fuchs, the Burdens' Austrian farmhand, later realize the cold autumn day and the age of the snake took away its "fight," Jim is pleased with the immediate result: it "was enough for Ántonia. She liked me better," he notes happily, "she never took a supercilious air with me again. I had killed a big snake—I was now a big fellow" (47–48). Once recognized by Ántonia as both linguistic and prairie authority, Jim is empowered to mold her to the extent possible, not *in* his own *image* but *through* his own *imagination*. At this point, she has become both his inspiration and his invention and, like other resources in the West, will become subject to his exploitation.

The Dead Snake: Commemoration and Appropriation

In addition to enhancing Jim's esteem in Ántonia's eyes, the dead snake links Nebraska's agricultural present to its frontier past. During the post-mortem examination of the unfortunate rattler, Jim uses all "five and a half feet" of its carcass to instruct Ántonia in rudimentary herpetology and Plains history: "He had twelve rattles, but they were broken off before they began to taper, so I insisted that he must once have had twenty-four. I explained to Ántonia how this meant that he was twenty-four years old, that he must have been there when white men first came, left on from *buffalo and Indian times*. As I turned him over I began to feel proud of him, to have a kind of respect for his age and size. He seemed like the ancient, eldest Evil" (45–46, italics added).

This seemingly insignificant episode where Jim kills a rattlesnake with a spade borrowed from the Russian immigrants Pavel and Peter functions on a figurative level. Jim's victory allegorizes America's decimation of the American Indians and Spanish colonial enterprise.

Not only does this passage reflect the legacy of what Werner Sollors in *Beyond Ethnicity* (1986) has deemed the "cult of the vanishing Indian," it also echoes the rhetoric of the "black legend," the defamatory discourse criticizing Spain's colonial enterprise during the Spanish-American War. Metaphorically, the rattlesnake Jim encounters symbolizes the obstacles facing American continental expansion and hemispheric hegemony. Competing claims to the land and the armed resistance formed by parties opposed to the United States realizing its manifest destiny constituted the chief impediment to the new nation's growth in size and influence. The snake denotes the challenges Plains Indians (primarily the Lakota Sioux) and Spain (including its former colony Mexico) posed to American territorial advances, while Jim's violent method of dispatching the reptile reflects federal strategies employed to achieve hemispheric supremacy.

As Jim marvels at the size and the age of the rattler, concluding that it was "left on from buffalo and Indian times," Cather somewhat uncannily (if incidentally) evokes Henry H. Cross's 1898 oil painting *Victim of Fate,* in which a seriously wounded buffalo has climbed to the crest of a hill to stand near the contorted body of a recently deceased Plains Indian warrior (see fig. 1 on p. 52). Depictions of dying indigenes, like the fallen hunter in Cross's canvas, were widespread in the nineteenth century. In the final decades of the

1800s, "epitaphs" for the Lakota and other Great Plains tribes were especially
popular in painting, sculpture, popular literature, and Wild West shows. Despite its sentimentality and conventional theme, Cross's painting reflects a
reality exploited by American expansionists: the fortunes of the bison and the
Plains cultures were inextricably linked. The decimation of the great herds,
expedited by hunters hired by the railroads to provide meat for the construction crews, precipitated the decline in the power of the Arapaho, Cheyenne,
Kiowa, Lakota, Pawnee, and other Plains nations.

Relegating buffalo and Indians to extinction is a logical extension of
Jim's earlier conclusion regarding the "emptiness" of the landscape. Informing
his utterance is the erroneous—but popularly accepted and widely promoted—assumption that the American bison and the Plains Indians are extinct,
that their times have passed in the scant twenty-four years since the arrival of
the "white men." The phrasing Cather attributes to Jim reflects racist under-
pinnings allowing Americans to dismiss Plains cultures and seriously endan-
gered herding animals in the same breath and betrays his acceptance of the
popular representation of native peoples collectively as a "vanishing" race .[2]

Jim's slaying of the serpent gains further significance by considering the
term "Sioux," a name Cather never allows him to utter. According to its ety-
mology, "Sioux" is an abbreviated form of "Naddouessioux," the French trans-
literation of the Ojibwa epithet for their principal enemies to the west.[3] Since
its earliest appearance in seventeenth-century French documents, "Sioux" has
been regarded by whites as a synonym for a venomous snake.[4] Popular and
scholarly sources at the time of My Ántonia's release in 1918 also accepted
this interpretation. In Native American studies the decade prior to the publication of My Ántonia, few scholars and studies were as influential as ethnolo-
gist Frederick Webb Hodge and the Handbook of American Indians North of
Mexico, which he edited from 1907 to 1910. The Handbook defines "Sioux" as
"a French-Canadian abbreviation of the Chippewa Nadowe-is-iw, a diminutive of nadowe, 'an adder,' hence 'an enemy.' Nadoweisiw-eg is the diminutive
plural. The diminutive singular and plural were applied to the Dakota, and
to the Huron to distinguish them from the Iroquois proper, the true 'adders'
or 'enemies'" (1: 376, 2:577). Notwithstanding the significant regional and
cultural distinctions differentiating the speakers of three mutually intelligible
dialects, they became known collectively and derogatively as Sioux, a frozen
curse derived from an Ojibwa expression denoting a venomous snake.[5]

At the time of European contact, the Dakota, Nakota, and Lakota
peoples inhabited territory ranging from the upper reaches of the Mississippi River to the eastern slopes of the Big Horn Mountains. The Pawnee
may have been the most numerous people in Central Nebraska when Spanish and French first arrived, but in the second half of the nineteenth century,
the Lakota (Teton Sioux) of western Nebraska, South Dakota, and eastern

Wyoming came to represent the greatest threat to American expansion. Not only did they comprise the largest contingent in the force that defeated Custer at the 1876 Battle of Little Bighorn, the three most famous Indian figures in America at that time—Sitting Bull, Crazy Horse, and Red Cloud—were Lakota. By declining to name specific tribes in Jim's account, Cather further delineates Jim's character. Jim's usage of the misnomer "Indian" in *My Ántonia* suggests his disinterest in issues affecting the native peoples of western Nebraska and North America in general, betraying instead an acceptance of the wider U.S. Indian policy directed toward the containment and cultural assimilation of the Plains Indians as well as the allotment of "surplus" tribal lands.

Jim's slaughter of the rattlesnake resembles the dirty political reality in which his future employer, the railroad, was complicit. In other words, Jim's vicious beating and near beheading of the aged sidewinder corresponds to the manner in which the U.S. military and railway industry colluded to eliminate Native American claims to territory in the Central Great Plains. While the rattlesnake serves as the namesake for all members of the Great Sioux Nation (and, by extension, other Plains Indians), the spade represents the superior technology and complex strategy—involving homesteading, railroad grants, and Indian policy—used to eliminate the native presence and supplant it with European settlement, agricultural development, and exploitation of natural and mineral resources.

As Richard Slotkin recognizes in *The Fatal Environment* (1985), particularly close ties were established between the railroad and the U.S. military; in fact, General Philip Sheridan vociferously promoted extending the railroads west, for he theorized that the railroad would contribute to the elimination of the buffalo and the eventual decimation of the Sioux and other native inhabitants of the Plains who depended on buffalo as a source of food, shelter, and clothing (408, 427). Sheridan's theory was deadly accurate; nothing contributed more to the erosion of the Plains Indian cultures than the railroad, which not only brought meat and hide hunters west but also led to settlement and agricultural development that disrupted migration patterns of the buffalo and divided the great bison herds into lesser northern and southern herds.

The future railroad attorney's mortal wielding of the spade also mirrors the devastating effect of federal legislation designed to appropriate native lands. The deleterious legacy of the 1887 Dawes Allotment Act on America's native population is well documented. Even more devastating for the Plains cultures was congressional passage of the Homestead and Pacific Railroad acts in 1862. These remain for Native Americans two of the most insidious bills ever drafted and passed since they worked in tandem to expropriate Indian lands and to populate the West with European immigrants and Americans willing to migrate. In *Native American History* (1996), Judith Nies declares these acts of legislation to be the "two most influential laws in overturning

Indian treaties and opening western Indian lands to settlement," making special note of the 174 million acres of "public lands" and subsequent land char-
ters granted to transcontinental railroad companies (168). The railroads, in
turn, promoted the settlement and development of the Great Plains, eventually pushing to extend into lands—notably Paha Sapa, the sacred Black Hills,
which Red Cloud's Lakota Sioux along with their Cheyenne and Arapaho
allies were assured by the 1868 Treaty of Fort Laramie.

Throughout the narrative, the language Cather assigns to Jim hints to
the violent history of the Central Plains that preceded large-scale settlement,
reminding readers of the recent campaign to contain the western tribes and appropriate the land they formerly controlled. Once, after concluding an English
lesson and escorting her home as far as Squaw Creek, Jim and Ántonia stood
in silence mesmerized by the beauty of the setting sun upon the stubble fields
and stacks of hay—evidence of European occupation and agrarian development of the Plains: "As far as we could see, the miles of copper-red grass were
drenched in sunlight that was stronger and fiercer than at any other time of
the day. The blond cornfields were red gold, the haystacks turned rosy and
threw long shadows. The whole prairie was like the bush that burned with fire
and was not consumed. That hour always had the exultation of victory, of triumphant ending, like a hero's death—heroes who died young and gloriously.
It was a sudden transfiguration, a lifting-up of day" (38–39). Jim has come to
view the settlement of the Plains in quasi-religious terms. For him, the developed landscape offers a covenant as sacred as the one revealed to Moses. Nebraska itself is evidence of the "manifest destiny" awaiting a new generation
of chosen people.[6] Close scrutiny of this passage indicates that realizing this
destiny will only come after much sacrifice and migration—for immigrants
and native inhabitants alike. The name of the creek running between the Burden and Shimerda farms is an oblique reminder of western Nebraska's former
inhabitants relegated to Pine Ridge and Rosebud reservations just across the
border in South Dakota. In this context, the glorious deaths Jim envisions are
likely to be those of Custer and his Seventh Cavalry troops, who died at the
1876 Battle of Little Bighorn in a recent effort to eliminate the native threat
to "progress." Along with 211 soldiers, the man known as the "Boy General"
lost his life in the campaign waged to open the Black Hills to mining and
settlement interests.[7] Posthumously, Custer achieved his goal: the Black Hills
were opened, and the European culture and industry transfigured the former
"savage" land, just as John Gast depicted in *American Progress,* his 1872 canvas
personifying Progress on her westward course.

"As I turned him [the dead snake] over," Jim recalls, "I began to feel
proud of him, to have a kind of respect for his age and size" (45). The respect
that Jim accords the rattler after killing it mirrors the nobility American writers and artists, since Washington Irving's essay "Philip of Pokanoket" (1814),

had projected upon dead or dying Indians.[8] Although nominally appearing to lament the passing of the American Indians, the art and literature devoted to Native American themes, in Jill Lepore's words, "mourned these losses as inevitable and right" (210). Case in point: the antebellum art and literature lamenting the elimination or removal of eastern tribes had virtually no effect on the treatment of Native Americans encountered by U.S. citizens and federal agencies in the trans-Mississippi West after the Civil War. Moreover, at the close of the century, when the First Nations of the Great Plains and the Southwest had been removed or contained and American expansionists began coveting Hawaii and Spain's colonial possessions, Indian subjects in art were still represented heroically as a doomed race, perhaps culminating in *The End of the Trail* (1894), James Earle Fraser's award-winning sculpture depicting a slouching Plains Indian rider upon his equally exhausted mount. Although the Indians were portrayed as vanishing, the popular motif was not, nor, as its presence in *My Ántonia* indicates, did it appear likely to vanish in the twentieth century.[9]

In the nineteenth century, commemorating the "vanishing American" and celebrating European territorial supremacy merged in the practice of naming American communities. Innumerable European settlements across the United States in the nineteenth century were named for Indian tribes (like Omaha, Nebraska, and Cheyenne, Wyoming) or for famed American Indian leaders (like Red Cloud, Nebraska, and Pontiac, Michigan). Cather, reflecting this cultural phenomenon, names the nearest community to the Burden farm Black Hawk, after the Sauk (Sac) leader, Ma-ka-tai-me-she-kia-kiak, who unsuccessfully resisted the influx of European settlers and miners into his people's territory. As scholars have long recognized, the community Cather names Black Hawk is a fictional version of her Nebraskan hometown, actually named Red Cloud for the talented Teton Sioux strategist who forced the United States to sign the 1868 Treaty of Fort Laramie after effectively closing the Bozeman Trail to American advancement.[10] Renaming her south-central Nebraskan community Black Hawk displaces the most recent struggles between the United States and American Indians (the Plains Wars) in time and locale, making it seem like the Indian wars were concluded several decades earlier (1832) east of the Mississippi (Illinois Territory). *My Ántonia*, therefore, literally removes the nations known generically by the whites as the Plains Indians from the territory they occupied less than a decade before Jim Burden's (and Cather's own) arrival.

Cather allows Jim only a vague acknowledgment of the people formerly living on the prairie surrounding Black Hawk: "Beyond the pond on the slope that climbed to the cornfield, there was, faintly marked in the grass, a great circle where the *Indians* used to ride" (60, italics added). By limiting Jim's description of the people formerly living in Nebraska to the abstract term

"Indian," Cather eliminates specific controversies affecting the Lakota and other Plains natives from his narrative. Specifically, she diminishes the controversy surrounding the 1887 Dawes Act, which, in favor of promoting further agricultural and industrial development of the Central Plains, reduced title to lands granted Plains Indians by treaty. The West, then, can be seen as settled, the indigenous inhabitants as "vanished" or subsumed as Domestic Dependent Nations under the aegis of the Republic. *My Ántonia* is rhetorically freed to pursue its economic interests and cultural obligations in Europe in the midst of the Great War.

The Snake as Reflection of Spain
Despite the romanticism with which Jim initially celebrates his annihilation of the snake, experience has provided him a more accurate lens to view the episode. In hindsight, he interprets his vanquishing of the reptile more pragmatically, as a keen legal professional who wisely understands that myriad capricious elements contribute to every victory:

> Subsequent experiences with rattlesnakes taught me that my first encounter was fortunate in circumstance. My big rattler was old, and had led too easy a life; there was not much fight in him. He had probably lived there for years, with a fat prairie dog for breakfast whenever he felt like it, a sheltered home, even an owl-feather bed, perhaps, and he had forgot that the world doesn't owe rattlers a living. A snake of his size, in fighting trim, would be more than any boy could handle. So in reality it was a mock adventure; the game was fixed for me by chance, as it probably was for many a dragon-slayer. I had been adequately armed by Russian Peter; the snake was old and lazy; and I had Ántonia beside me, to appreciate and admire. (47–48)

As an adult, Jim recognizes that several factors irrelevant to his martial skill contributed to the lopsided defeat of the serpent. The corpulent snake had become complacent and corrupt, undeserving of the bounty from which it benefited for so long. Jim's characterization of the snake as lazy hunter echoes the reasoning of American leaders like Senator Dawes who believed the traditional hunting economies of Plains nations unsuitable to the goal of assimilation and designed legislation to force the native inhabitants to adopt an agricultural lifestyle. At the same time, Jim's unsympathetic description of the rattlesnake resembles rhetoric the American press and politicians voiced of Spain during the Spanish-American War.

Wartime understanding of the Spanish Empire was shaped by a defamatory discourse that can be traced to sixteenth-century anti-Spanish sentiment based in religious differences (Protestants versus Papists) and competition to control the seas and acquire territory in the New World. In "American Ideology: Visions of National Greatness and Racism" (1992), Michael H. Hunt describes the influence the "black legend" and "its condemnatory view of the Spanish character" exercised on the American consciousness, noting its prominence in textbooks, comics, "political rhetoric," and national policy (20). Simply put, according to the tradition, Spain was backward, negligent, and cruel: an imperial bower that never grew out of feudalism. "More broadly understood," Hunt writes, "the legend stood for all those undesirable characteristics that were Spain's unfortunate legacy to much of the New World" (21).

The impact of this rhetoric relied upon the contrast drawn between the republican virtues of Anglo-Saxon powers like Great Britain and the United States and the tyranny of the Spanish Empire. Empires who fail to profit their colonial subjects have no legitimacy. Consequently, U.S. involvement in the Spanish-American War was predicated on America's duty to confer abstract benefits namely, democracy and progress—on Spain's former colonies. Before and after the Spanish-American War, the War Hawks including future president Teddy Roosevelt, Republican senators Henry Cabot Lodge and Albert J. Beveridge, and naval mastermind Alfred Thayer Mahan—invoked the "black legend" to rationalize America's "crusade" against Spain. The following excerpt from an 1898 justification for the war serves as a vivid example of the centuries-old Spanish rhetoric: "Spain has been tried and convicted in the forum of history. Her religion has been bigotry, whose sacraments have been solemnized by the faggot and the rack. Her statesmanship has been infamy: her diplomacy, hypocrisy: her wars have been massacres: her supremacy has been a blight and a curse, condemning continents to sterility, and their inhabitants to death" (qtd. in Hunt 21). Most commonly levied against Spain were accusations of brutality, vampirism, and neglect of her colonial possessions—charges justifying America's participation in the war. Likewise, inherent iniquity and indolence contribute to the perdition of the rattlesnake in *My Ántonia*. It is characterized as evil (42) and lazy (43), having preyed too long among its hapless victims, the prairie dogs and burrowing owls, through a parasitical living arrangement that mirrors the *reconcentrado* strategy instituted and maintained in rural Cuba by the Spanish military.

In *The Reckless Decade* (1995), popular historian H. W. Brands describes *los reconcentrados* as "Spanish established fortified camps and towns into which Cuban peasants were herded from the countryside; access to these camps was strictly controlled, with the idea that any guerrillas who came into the camps would be unable to get out and cause mischief and any person who stayed outside must be a guerrilla and therefore would be subject to capture or killing" (305). With an eye on Cuba's sugar industry, expansionists in the United States criticized Spain's handling of the rebellion, expressly attacking the policy of the concentration camps and casting the commander of Spanish forces in Cuba, General Valeriano Weyler, as the epitome of the "black legend." Weyler was depicted by William Randolph Hearst's *New York Journal* as a "brute" who could not contain "his carnal, animal brain from running riot with itself in inventing tortures and infamies of bloody debauchery," while Joseph Pulitzer's *New York World* pleaded for a "nation wise . . . brave . . . and strong enough to restore peace in this bloodsmitten land" (qtd. in Brands 307). Such one-sided accounts of the Cuban Insurrection pressured the United States to deliver Cuba from Spanish villainy, specifically the cold-blooded conduct of General Weyler. When it finally entered the fray, the United States accomplished the task in four months (April to August 1898). In the papers at least, the United States liberated Cuba and the Philippines from Spanish despotism. The war with Spain proved to be, like Jim's encounter with the sidewinder, a "mock adventure" against a once formidable adversary no longer in "fighting trim."

The imagery and language employed in the snake episode draw powerfully on the legacy of nineteenth-century American imperialism. An attentive reading of the passage reveals compelling figurative parallels to American removal/containment of the Plains tribes and U.S. participation and successful resolution of the Spanish-American War. By crushing the idle serpent with a simple sod-breaking tool used by industrious homesteaders, Jim reenacts the United States' displacement of Native Americans and Spaniards, peoples Americans have traditionally regarded as obstacles to expansion and dismissed as shiftless.

Spain's Bequest: Unearthing the Legacy of Conquest

While child narrators (like Jim Burden) in Cather's fiction help authenticate the myth of manifest destiny, Cather's frequent reference to archeology and history legitimate America's position as a global power and heir to the Spanish Empire. Through allusion to archeology and invocation of epic, *My Ántonia* actually reinforces former Spanish claims to the American West, now inhabited by American and European settlers, only to support the transfer of imperial responsibility.[11]

In "Selling Relics, Preserving Antiquities" (1995), Howard Horwitz, recognizes that "ethnology, anthropology and archaeology—overlapping emergent disciplines—were nationalist enterprises dedicated to discovering the fundamental racial and cultural characteristics of America and Americans" (362). Jim's manuscript, likewise, serves nationalist enterprises by reflecting America's European inheritance while dismissing native influences. Although Cather introduces "the great circle where the Indians used to ride" (60) into Jim's reminiscence, he remains unable or unwilling to assign it to a specific Plains Indian people. His lack of specificity suggests an indifference to indigenous civilizations as well as an ignorance of current practices in anthropology promoted by Columbia University professor Franz Boas. By 1915 the Boasian approach, stressing intensive study of localized cultures, had begun to supplant comparative methods in anthropology that reified scientific racism so popular after Darwin. The result, as Robert F. Berkhofer Jr. notes in "White Conception of Indians," was that indigenous Americans were studied "as tribes and as cultures not as the Indian" (543). The absence of native artifacts, combined with Jim's inability to interpret traces left by Plains Indian tribes, weakens indigenous claims to the land now inhabited by definable groups of European settlers—Austrians, Bohemians, Danes, Norwegians, Russians, and Swedes—that Jim befriends in Nebraska.

In a break from study the summer before enrolling at the University of Nebraska, Jim Burden attends a picnic with "the hired girls"—Ántonia Shimerda, Lena Lingard, Tiny Soderball, and Anna Hansen—and entertains the four young immigrant women with a myth Ántonia characterizes as "how the Spanish *first* came here [to Nebraska], like you and Charley Harling used to talk about" (235, italics added):[12]

> They sat under a little oak, Tony . . . and the other girls . . . listened to the little I was able to tell them about Coronado and his search for the Seven Golden Cities. At school we were taught that he had not got so far north as Nebraska, but had given up his quest and turned back somewhere in Kansas. But Charley Harling and I had a strong belief that he had been along this very river. A farmer in the county north of ours, when he was breaking sod had turned up a metal stirrup of fine workmanship, and a sword with a Spanish inscription on the blade. He lent these relics to Mr. Harling, who brought them home with him. Charley and I scoured them, and they were on exhibition in the Harling office all summer. Father Kelly, the priest, had found the name of the Spanish maker on the sword, and an abbreviation that stood for the city of Cordova.
>
> "And that I saw with my own eyes," Ántonia put in triumphantly. "So Jim and Charley were right, and the teachers were wrong!" (235–236)

As in the definitive judgment he forms upon his strained first "sight" of the prairie landscape, Jim denies the thinking that conflicts with his own "strong belief[s]" by telling his eager listeners of a Spanish stirrup and a sword unearthed by a local farmer and explaining—again, despite teachings to the contrary—that the sixteenth-century expedition of the Spanish conquistador Francisco Vasquez de Coronado had come as far north as present-day Nebraska in his search for fabled riches.[13] In a manner echoing Virgil's tracing Roman civilization to the Trojan refugee Aeneas, Cather has Jim weave a tale recognizing Coronado as the mythological father of Nebraska.

To lend credence to his interpretation of history, Jim refers to the assistance he receives restoring and interpreting the artifacts from Father Kelly and his friend Charley Harling. Mentioning these two figures lends more than an air of authenticity to his tale; it invokes the long and convoluted history of cultural imperialism. In a strategy Cather would employ later in *The Professor's House*, she uses a Roman Catholic priest—a living tribute to Western civilization and Christianity—to make sense of the archeological finds. Father Kelly's facility with Latin reinforces the preeminence of European culture, especially the legacy of the Roman Empire as well as the global reach of the Roman Catholic Church and, more importantly, establishes the United States as a European state culturally.

By naming Charley Harling, who entered the U.S. Naval Academy and would have been a junior officer during the Spanish-American War, Cather evokes the U.S. Navy, the deciding factor in America's 1898 defeat of Spain and its inheritance of former Spanish colonies.[14] As Cather would have been intimately familiar with from her days as telegraph editor for the *Pittsburgh Leader* during the Spanish-American War, George Dewey's naval victories in the Philippines were far more instrumental in winning the war than the battles won by land forces in Cuba. Cather shapes Jim's Eurocentric sense of national and cultural identity through his association with Father Kelly and Charley Harling, champions of cultural and martial imperialism, as well as his interest in the recovered Spainish antiquities that point to a once-great European empire's former presence in Nebraska—an empire, no less, that America has now largely relieved of its colonial holdings.

My Ántonia invokes the popularity of archaeology in turn-of-the-century America and uses the recovered artifacts to suggest Spanish occupation of the West predating European contact with the native inhabitants. By doing so, Cather effectively frees Jim from concern about military and political actions during the Plains Indian Wars, including the breaking of the 1851 and 1868 Treaties of Fort Laramie and Colonel Chivington's notorious attack on unarmed Cheyennes at Sand Creek in November 1864. Jim's account can be read, therefore, as an intricate piece of sophistry ascribing intermediate possession of the American West to the Spanish. The only interpreted artifacts suggest a prima facie case for Spanish claim to Nebraska by right of discovery. America's problematic relations with the indigenous civilizations of the West can be dismissed then as historically immaterial since the December 1898 Treaty of Paris (ratified in February 1899) concluding the Spanish-American War grants to the United States possession of Spain's territories in the Western Hemisphere and the Pacific.

Immediately after Jim finishes relating the legend about Coronado, he and the girls witness a curious phenomenon: a plough framed by the "molten red" of the setting sun (237). The timely vision of the silhouetted piece of farm equipment figuratively turns the swords of the conquistadors into ploughshares and triumphantly punctuates Jim's account of the wandering Spaniard, effectively reinforcing European "discovery," immigration, settlement, and agrarian development of North America with no mention of the dispossession or genocide of the indigenous population.

Alongside passages of archeological and anthropological import in *My Ántonia*, Cather makes several allusions to epic reinforcing the celebratory tone of this novel. Book II ("The Hired Girls") opens with a description of Jim's preparations for college, including his solitary reading of Virgil's *Aeneid*, Cather's hint that conventions, motifs, or formal elements of epic will be used to link late-nineteenth-century settlement to a mythic past." Cather's invocation of mythic elements is particularly effective but hardly unique among American writers in the late nineteenth and early twentieth centuries. Virgil, especially in his *Aeneid* as Sollars notes, "shaped the form of American epics" by "lending itself to a sanctioning of the further transporting west of empires" (*Beyond Ethnicity* 239), so it is hardly surprising that his verse appears frequently in Jim's account, strategically invoked in reverse-chronological order. The last of Virgil's poems, the *Aeneid*, figures most prominently in relation to Jim Burden's college preparation, while the earlier-composed *Georgics* are mentioned later, during Jim's first year at college. As these two texts are brought together, so are the ideas informing them: the *Aeneid* and its epic concern with the westward migration of empire (from Ilium to Latium) and the *Georgics*, with its pastoral focus on "patria," which Jim is informed by his classics professor, Gaston Cleric, should be interpreted locally, "not [as] a nation or even a province, but the little rural neighborhood on the Mincio where the poet was born" (256).

In his lessons on Virgil's *Georgics*, Cleric emphasizes the significance of the local communities and landscapes subsumed by the Roman Empire; Virgil was less concerned with empire than a localized setting and culture contained within the larger state. As Jim puts it, by writing the *Georgics*, Virgil brought the muse to his country along the Mincio River (256). Though it seems natural that *My Ántonia* is Jim's attempt to do the same, he does not. Rather than bringing the muse to his country, he very literally extracts her (Ántonia and the land she personifies) like the resources and profits he draws from his interests in mines, timber, and oil. Jim's concern in *My Ántonia* is with nation in a global age. Cather cleverly has Jim invert Cleric's lesson by merging his patria—the farmland surrounding Black Hawk—into the "world's cornfields" that his grandfather foresaw: "It took a clear, meditative eye like lily grandfather's to foresee that they would enlarge and multiply until they would be, not the Shimerda's cornfields, or Mr. Bushy's, but the

world's cornfields; that their yield would be one of the great economic facts,
like the wheat crop of Russia, which underlie all the activities of men, in peace
or war" (132). Jim celebrates the political power reflected in the economic fact
of the American West. Like the ledgers kept for his various enterprises, *My
Ántonia* charts the nation's realization of its economic and political potential.

Conclusion: Nebraska in the Time of Nations

In the passage about the "world's cornfields" Jim comments on his grandfather's ability to collapse history and see the farmland generations later.
Although regarded as an uncommon ability, this destinarian vision was
not peculiar to Grandfather Burden. At a fundamental level, it is the most
American of capacities. As essential a contribution to success as investment
capital, this prescience provides the psychological impetus and comfort
necessary to undertake any new venture in peace and war, especially homesteading. Only because Jim inherited this disposition from his grandfather
can he tell the story of *My Ántonia*.

In fashioning Jim Burden Cather renders a sophisticated performance
of rurality meant to embody the contradictions of the age in which he lives.
As such, the narrator of *My Ántonia* resembles no American more than Theodore Roosevelt, a figure deeply associated with America's territorial expansion
at home and abroad. Roosevelt took office in the greatest age of American
imperialism, shortly after the United States assumed possession of Spanish
territories in the Caribbean and the Pacific—an event he ardently participated in, first as undersecretary of the navy in Washington DC, and finally
as lieutenant colonel in the First U.S. Volunteer Cavalry serving in Cuba.
As he was inaugurated twenty-sixth president of the United States, American troops engaged guerrillas in the Philippines, who were happily rid of
Spain but resented America's presence. Roosevelt would make no apologies
for these activities, as is evident in the foreword he wrote for the presidential
edition of *The Winning of the West*:

> Many decades went by after Spain had lost her foothold on the
> American continent, and she still held her West Indian empire.
> She misgoverned the continent; and in the islands, as once upon
> the continent, her own children became her deadliest foes. . . . At
> last, at the close of one of the bloodiest and most brutal wars that
> even Spain ever waged with her own colonists, the United States
> intervened, and in a brief summer campaign destroyed the last
> vestiges of the mediaeval Spanish domain in the tropic seas alike
> of the West and the remote East.
>
> We of this generation were but carrying to completion the work
> of our fathers' fathers. (ix)

In this statement, Roosevelt presents U.S. participation in the Spanish-American War as the logical conclusion to generations of westward migration and cultural conflict initiated by the first Dutch and English settlers in North America. By preceding a history of American migration and settlement with an argument defending U.S. involvement in the Spanish-American War, Roosevelt merges domestic and international concerns, continental expansion and overseas colonialism. So too does *My Ántonia*. Cather uses Jim to frame an account of America's rise to world power, which he describes literally in realizing the vision of his "father's father," Josiah Burden.

It takes a person with a "clear, meditative eye" and "big Western dreams" to make sense of the contradictions implicit in American imperialism. Cather created Jim Burden to reconcile the nation's global mandate and its pastoral pose. The imagery and language employed throughout *My Ántonia* draw powerfully on the legacy of nineteenth-century American imperialism and forecast its twentieth-century consequences. Attentive readings reveal compelling figurative parallels to American treatment of Plains tribes and U.S. participation in the Spanish-American War. The snake episode, for example, parodies Theodore Roosevelt's "Big Stick Policy," his warning to powers threatening American interests in the Western Hemisphere. Jim's elimination of the aged serpent with a spade reenacts the United States' displacement of American Indians and Spaniards in the New World. Similarly, Josiah Burden's prediction of the United States becoming the "world's cornfields" reflects America's global economic and political status on the eve of the Great War—a reality the United States will eventually enter World War I to defend when unlimited German submarine warfare makes feeding, the world impossible.

In *Imagined Communities: Reflections on the Origin and Spread of Nationalism* (1991), Benedict Anderson asserts, "All profound changes in [a nation's] consciousness bring with them characteristic amnesias. Out of such oblivions, in specific historical circumstances, spring narratives" (204). The period from the end of the Plains Indian Wars to the beginning of World War I marks one such oblivion in American history. The United States changed drastically between Wounded Knee (December 1890) and the assassination of Archduke Ferdinand (June 1914). Clearly, new cultural and mythological "maps" would have to be drafted to address the changes brought about by America's acquisition of overseas territories. Cather's *My Ántonia* is one such map or mythology. From references to the political reasons for the Bohemians "natural distrust" of Austrians (*My Ántonia* 20) to the violence reflecting the war consciousness at the time of the novel's composition (Stout 165), the Great War asserts its presence in this narrative. But more than that, *My Ántonia* charts the course of American empire, from its occupation of the Central Plains in the nineteenth century to its twentieth-century obligations as a world power.

Notes

I am grateful to Susan J. Rosowski, Kyoko Matsunaga, and James Kelley for reading and commenting upon earlier drafts of this article.

1. Written between 1912 and 1913, *Pygmalion* was first performed in England on April 11, 1914, at His Majesty's Theatre in London and in the United States on October 12, 1914, at the Park Theatre in New York while Cather lived there. Based on her favorable reviews of Shaw's earlier plays—Cather reviewed *The Devil's Disciple* (1897) and *A Perfect Wagnerite* (1898) (Woodress 134, 236, 260; Lee 53, 132)—it is possible that Cather saw or read *Pygmalion* (published in New York by Brentano in 1916) before completing *My Ántonia.*

2. For detailed discussions of this motif before and up to the nineteenth century, see Lepore, *The Name of War* (1998). For its invocation in the nineteenth century, see Sollors, *Beyond Ethnicity* (1986), and Berkhofer, "White Conceptions of Indians" (1988). For discussion of this motif in relation to the twentieth century, see Michaels, *Our America* (1994) and Berkhofer. While Sollors calls the popularity of this image "the cult of the vanishing Indian," Michaels refers to it as the "Vanishing American," a phrase taken from Zane Grey's 1925 novel of the same name. It is likely that Grey was inspired by other art such as *The Vanishing Race* (1904), one of Edward Curtis's famous photographs of his Native American subjects.

3. Ojibwa, Ojibway, Ojibwe, and Chippewa (variants of the Algonquian term "puckered moccasin"—a feature distinguishing its wearers from their neighboring tribes) all refer to the same Algonquian-speaking people, who refer to themselves as Anishinabe.

4. Although considerable debate exists as to the original meaning of the name today, most current academic resources, including *Red Cloud: Warrior-Statesman of the Lakota Sioux* (Larson 1997) and the *Atlas of the North American Indian* (1985, 2000), maintain "Sioux" to be derived from the Ojibwa word for adder or snake (9; 177). Some scholars insist Naddowessioux first meant "lesser enemy" before being applied to snakes, while others believe it originally designated the Eastern Massasauga rattlesnake. Douglas R. Parks and Raymond J. DeMallie (2001) in "The Sioux" (Vol 13, pt. 2 of *The Handbook of North American Indians* 749) and Guy Gibbon in *The Sioux* (2002) are among current scholars who do not accept "Sioux" as an abbreviated synonym for snake. However, both sources rely upon the research of Ives Goddard, who based his study on Ottawa rather than Ojibwa (Chippewa). Ottawa and Ojibwa are closely related, but distinct, Algonquian dialects.

5. In *Beyond Ethnicity,* Sollors recognizes that "many names . . . originated in frozen curses" (193). I am indebted to him for this term.

6. According to Anders Stephanson, this famous phrase was initially coined in 1845 by John O'Sullivan, the editor of the *Democratic Review;* he defined it as America's mission "to overspread the continent allotted by Providence for the free development of our yearly multiplying millions" (xi).

7. Slotkin notes that this nickname was given by the *New York Herald* (*The Fatal Environment* 390). The number of U.S. soldiers believed killed at the Battle of the Little Bighorn varies considerably. Nies claims 211 to 225 soldiers died alongside Custer (282, 283).

8. Such images pervaded drama, fiction, history, poetry, painting, sculpture, and song throughout the nineteenth century. The art stands witness. The titles of antebellum works treating this subject are instructive, if not very imaginative.

In drama and fiction, "last of the" was an extremely popular modifying phrase, invoked in 1823 by Joseph Doddridge for his play *Logan: The Last of the Race of Shikellemus, Chief of the Cayuga Nation* and later (1829) by John Augustus Stone in his award-winning drama *Metamora; or, The Last of the Wampanoags,* and perhaps most famously in 1826 by James Fennimore Cooper in *The Last of the Mohicans,* the most popular of his *Leatherstocking Tales.* In antebellum sculpture—at least in 1856—"dying" was the modifier of choice, employed both by Thomas Crawford in his marble *The Dying Indian Chief* and somewhat more specifically by Ferdinand Pettrich in *The Dying Tecumseh,* his neo-classical interpretation of the great Shawnee leader's final moments.

9. In *Manifest Manners: Narratives on Postindian Survivance* (1994, 1996), Gerald Vizenor argues convincingly that the name "Indian" has always implied what Sollors and Michaels see as "vanished." For Vizenor, "*indians* are immovable simulations, the tragic archives of dominance and victimry" (ix–x). In other words, "Indian" is a misnomer applied by Europeans to the peoples of the New World; shaped by misinformed European notions (and Orientalizing discourse), this term can never represent a dynamic and evolving civilization. Vizenor uses the term "postindian" to connote the viability of Native American cultures.

10. In an interview for the *Philadelphia Record* (August 10, 1913), Cather described Red Cloud as "still wild enough and bleak enough when we got there. My grandfather's homestead was about eighteen miles from Red Cloud—a little town on the Burlington, named after the old Indian Chief who used to come hunting in that country, and who buried his daughter on the top of one of the river bluffs south of the town. Her grave had been looted for her rich furs and beadwork long before my family went West, but we children used to find arrowheads there and some of the bones of her pony that had been strangled above her grave" (Bohlke 9).

11. Archeology is also used to interesting effect in *The Professor's House.* Although in *The Professor's House* the relics are Ancestral Puebloan (Anasazi), they are interpreted Eurocentrically.

12. At the time Jim told "the girls" this tale, Charley was a midshipman at the U.S. Naval academy (*My Ántonia* 166).

13. Cather has used the legend of Coronado similarly in other texts. In "The Enchanted Bluff" (1909), Cather invokes the same legend, having Arthur Adams, the oldest boy in the story, inform the other Nebraskan boys that Coronado and his men "were all over this country [central Nebraska] once" (73).

14. In the 1890s the U.S. Navy was revitalized in part because of the convincing argument of Naval War College instructor Alfred Thayer Mahan, who recommended a large navy and overseas bases and coal stations to protect American interests (Brands 294). The popular reception of Mahan's *The Influence of Sea Power upon History, 1660–1783* (1890) in expansionist circles during the last decade of the nineteenth century directly contributed to assembling a respectable navy, which proved decisive in defeating the Spanish in 1898. Mahan's influential text and its recommendations for a revitalized navy were preceded in 1882 by similar recommendations made by a youthful Theodore Roosevelt in his influential history *The Naval War of 1812,* which he wrote while studying law at Columbia University. Roosevelt's study became required reading on all naval vessels, shortly after its publication (Morris 599). In view of their similar interests, it is little surprise that Roosevelt and Mahan became friends, correspondents, and political confidants.

15. For a detailed discussion of Cather's employment of Virgil, see chapter 3 of Guy Reynolds' book, *Willa Cather in Context: Progress, Race, Empire* (1996). In it, Reynolds discusses Cather's use of Virgil in relation to *O Pioneers!*

WORKS CITED

Anderson, Benedict. *Imagined Communities: Reflections on the Origin and Spread of Nationalism*, revised ed. New York: Verso, 1991.

Berkhofer, Robert F., Jr. "White Conceptions of Indians." *Handbook of North American Indians.* Ed. William C. Sturtevant. Vol. 4: *Indian–White Relations.* Ed. Wilcomb E. Washburn. Washington DC: Smithsonian, 1988. 522–547.

Bohlke, L. Brent, ed. *Willa Cather in Person: Interviews, Speeches, and Letters.* Lincoln: University of Nebraska Press, 1986.

Brands, H. W. *The Reckless Decade: America in the 1890s.* New York: St. Martin's Press, 1995.

Cather, Willa. "The Enchanted Bluff." *Harper's* April 1909: 774–778, 780–781.

———. *My Ántonia.* 1918. Willa Cather Scholarly Edition. Ed. Charles Mignon and James Woodress. Lincoln: University of Nebraska Press, 1994.

Fischer, Mike. "Pastoralism and Its Discontents: Willa Cather and the Burden of Imperialism." *Mosaic* 23.1 (1990): 31–45.

Gibbon, Guy E. *The Sioux: The Dakota and Lakota Nations.* New York: Blackwell, 2002.

Hodge, Frederick Webb, ed. Preface. *Handbook of American Indians North of Mexico.* Bureau of American Ethnology. Bulletin 30. Washington DC: GPO, 1907. v–ix.

Horwitz, Howard. "Selling Relics, Preserving Antiquities: *The Professor's House* and the Narrative of American Anthropology." *Configurations* 3.3 (1995): 349–389.

Hunt, Michael. "American Ideology: Visions of National Greatness and Racism." *Imperial Surge: The United States Abroad, the 1890s–Early 1900s.* Ed. Thomas G. Paterson and Stephen G. Rabe. Lexington: Heath, 1992. 14–31.

Karush, Deborah. "Innocent Voyages: Fictions of United States Expansion in Cather, Stevens and Hurston." Diss. Yale University, 1997.

Larson, Robert W. *Red Cloud: Warrior-Statesman of the Lakota Sioux.* Norman: University of Oklahoma Press, 1997.

Lepore, Jill. *The Name of War: King Philip's War and the Origins of American Identity.* 1998. New York: Vintage, 1999.

Limerick, Patricia Nelson. *The Legacy of Conquest: The Unbroken Past of the American West.* New York: Norton, 1987.

Michaels, Walter Benn. *Our America: Nativism, Modernism, and Pluralism.* Durham: Duke University Press, 1995.

Milton, John. *Paradise Lost.* New ed. Ed. Merritt Y. Hughes. New York: Macmillan, 1986.

Morris, Edmund. *The Rise of Theodore Roosevelt.* 1979. Revised ed. New York: Modern Library, 2001.

Nies, Judith. *Native American History: A Chronology of a Culture's Vast Achievements and Their Links to World Events.* New York: Ballantine, 1996.

Parks, Douglas R. Synonymy. "Sioux until 1850." Raymond J. DeMallie. *Handbook of North American Indians.* Ed. William C. Sturtevant. Vol. 13: Plains. Part 2. Ed. Raymond J. DeMallie. Washington DC: Smithsonian, 2001. 718–760.

Reynolds, Guy. *Willa Cather in Context: Progress, Race, Empire.* New York: St. Martin's Press, 1996.

Roosevelt, Theodore. Foreword. 1900. *The Winning of the West*. Vol. 1. 1889. Presidential ed. New York: Putnam's, 1900.

Rosowski, Susan J. *The Voyage Perilous: Willa Cather's Romanticism*. Lincoln: University of Nebraska Press, 1986.

Slotkin, Richard. *The Fatal Environment: The Myth of the Frontier in the Age of Industrialization*. New York: Atheneum, 1985.

Sollors, Werner. *Beyond Ethnicity: Consent and Descent in American Culture*. New York: Oxford University Press, 1986.

Stephanson, Anders. *Manifest Destiny*. New York: Hill & Wang, 1995.

Stout, Janis P. *Willa Cather: The Writer and Her World*. Charlottesville: University Press of Virginia, 2000.

Urgo, Joseph. *Willa Cather and the Myth of American Migration*. Urbana: University of Illinois Press, 1995.

Vimnor, Gerald. *Manifest Manners: Narratives on Postindian Survivance*. 1994. Lincoln: University of Nebraska Press, 1999.

DIANA H. POLLEY

Americanizing Cather:
Myth and Fiction in My Ántonia

In 1924, Willa Cather denounced "this passion for Americanizing everything and everybody," calling it a "deadly disease" (qtd. in Reynolds 73).
Although Cather was specifically referring to the nationalistic impulse to
transform ethnic immigrants into "Americans," her protest is relevant today.
As Susan J. Rosowski notes, "a writer is important not because she represents transcendent values or universal truths, but because she is inscribed
into a culture" (147). In attempting to understand how Cather's *My Ántonia*
"fits" into American literary culture, the critic, it would seem, is participating in exactly this type of "diseased" activity.

It is difficult, however, to read *My Ántonia* without acknowledging its
ties to a national identity. Indeed, the text has repeatedly been read in terms
of classic American myths, often as a longing for an earlier, more innocent
America. For example, David Stouck has read it as an American pastoral,
James E. Miller as a "commentary on the American experience" (112), Harold
Bloom as "an intense vision of a lost America" (1), and Robert E. Scholes as
"the myth of Adam in America" (19). Even more contemporary critics who
have acknowledged the novel's counter-cultural ties have reconfigured American myths to incorporate these new ideologies; thus, Mary Paniccia Carden
suggests that *My Ántonia* "recasts the starring role in the national romance

Willa Cather Newsletter and Review, Volume 49, Number 3 (2006): pp. 61–64. © 2006

with pioneering women . . ." (295). The subject positions may shift, but the overall identification with American mythology remains.

In examining the development of Cather criticism, these readings of *My Ántonia* make sense. Guy Reynolds explains that early critics, such as Van Wyck Brooks, overlooked Cather as worthy of canonicity because they felt that she wrote against the "significant tendencies" of current American ideology (35). In a 1995 *New Yorker* article, Joan Acocella argues that Cather finally gained attention in the academy when her literature began to "fit" and affirm new critical trends (65). Thus, in part, Cather has been canonized as critics have been able to write her into changing grand narratives of American culture. In a sense, we help to transform Cather into a cultural icon by Americanizing her, by inscribing her into a dominant national discourse.

It may not be possible to avoid this critical paradox in reading Cather's work. It is important, however, to qualify Cather's relationship, specifically in *My Ántonia,* to American mythology. *My Ántonia* clearly employs and even celebrates certain core American myths. In particular, the text pays homage to the philosophical teachings of Ralph Waldo Emerson; through setting, symbolism, character, and plot, *My Ántonia* applauds such classic American ideals as self-reliance, spiritual independence, and nature. As so many critics have noted, Jim's story mourns the loss of this epic Emersonian tradition. In *My Ántonia,* however, Cather also writes *against* these cultural myths; it is not that she denies the ideals inherent in the myths but, rather, that she recognizes them as fictions.

In *The Sense of an Ending,* Frank Kermode distinguishes between myth and fiction:

> Fictions can degenerate into myths whenever they are not consciously held to be fictive.... Myth operates within the diagrams of ritual, which presupposes *total* and adequate explanations of things as they are and were; it is a sequence of radically unchangeable gestures. Fictions are for finding things out, and they change as the needs of sense-making change. Myths are the agents of stability, fictions the agents of change. Myths call for absolute, fictions for conditional assent. (my italics 39)

In *My Ántonia,* Cather writes two stories: one of myth and one of fiction. Jim's story is the story of American myth, which celebrates the Emersonian vision of an American Adam and laments the intruding machine in the garden. Against this epic ideal, however, Cather offers us another story, one that honors Jim's vision but also understands it as fiction. Specifically, this larger story questions Jim's narrative by recognizing him as an unreliable narrator. The text distances itself from Jim's story in two ways. First, it questions the myth of the American Adam; through the characters of Ántonia and Lena, it applauds Emersonian heroism but reads such ideals as fictive. Second, the text critiques Jim's mythic reading of the machine in the garden; although Jim chooses to naturalize the loss of innocence onto the inevitable passage of time, the text ultimately suggests that the American individual is not the passive victim of history but, rather, the enabler of his own destruction. By fictionalizing the myth, Cather inscribes herself into American mythology but also writes against it. While Jim's narrative is an agent of stability, Cather's narrative is an agent of change. While Jim calls for absolute, Cather calls for conditional assent.

When we first meet Jim Burden in the Introduction, our external narrator, presumably a fictional version of Willa Cather, makes it clear that the elder Jim lives a sterile and far from romantic life. He has moved from the "freemasonry" of the West to the urban metropolis of New York, he is married to a cold and detached woman, and, "as legal counsel for one of the great Western railways," he has aided in the development of the land he loves (711). While Jim's spirit is still considered "naturally romantic and ardent," his romance finds its home in memory and desire (712). We learn that he has written a narrative about his childhood friend, Ántonia Shimerda. His narrative, not *Ántonia* but *My Ántonia,* will act as a remembrance of things past, a personal, unorganized recollection of "what Ántonia's name recalls to me" (714). Although this story will be about Ántonia, we sense that it will also be about American possibility and loss.

In Book I, we become immersed in Jim's Emersonian childhood. The Book begins when Jim, an orphan at age ten, moves from Virginia to Nebraska to live with his grandparents. His first encounters with the land seem to come right out of the pages of Emerson's philosophy, his descriptions "enumerating the values of nature and casting up their sum" (Emerson 8). Emerson's concept of the "transparent eye-ball" is notoriously difficult to express or conceive of within the realm of experience.

And yet, Jim's descriptions of Nebraska embody just this concept. Bumping along the road to his grandparents' farm, Jim notes the empty landscape:

> There was nothing but land: not a country at all, but the material out of which countries are made. . . . The wagon jolted on, carrying me I knew not whither. I don't think I was homesick. If we never arrived anywhere, it did not matter. Between that earth and that sky I felt *erased*, blotted out. (my italics 718)

Jim literally seems to "become a transparent eye-ball," where, as Emerson explains, "I am nothing; I see all; the currents of the Universal Being circulate through me; I am part or particle of God" (10); "mean egotism vanishes," the past is forgotten, and Jim experiences an "original relation to the universe" (7).

This first romantic encounter with nature continues throughout Book I, as Jim explores the prairie with his new Bohemian friend and neighbor, Ántonia. Although they come from remarkably different cultures, in childhood, they share this same freshness, vitality, and spiritual awareness of landscape. For both, the land acts as material out of which to shape self. Book I comes to embody each of the central tenets of Emerson's "Nature": nature becomes commodity, beauty, language, discipline, idealism, spirit, and prospects. The story of Jim and Ántonia's childhood is a story based on this classic American mythology; Emersonian possibility comes to life through their "unaffected, unbiased, unbribable, unaffrighted innocence" (Emerson 261).

Books II through V chart another American myth, what Harold Bloom calls "an intense vision of a lost America" (1); as Jim grows up, life continually seems to pull him further away from this Emersonian possibility. In Book II, his grandparents retire to the town of Black Hawk and send Jim to a local school. An older and more restless Jim expresses the town's sterility:

> People's speech, their voices, their very glances, became furtive and repressed. Every individual taste, every natural appetite, was bridled by caution. . . . The growing piles of ashes and cinders in the back yards were the only evidence that the wasteful, consuming process of life went on at all. (851)

It is not simply that Jim loses all sense of his childhood idealism. He still maintains his pastoral vision of America. He laments "the lost freedom of the farming country" and remembers weather on the farm as "the great fact" (805). This "great fact," however, now becomes recast, in Black Hawk, as a "bitter song" (823). Country life is seen as fruitful, town as "wasteful" and "consuming."

It may seem ironic, therefore, that, at the end of Book II, Jim decides to move further away from the country, to the city of Lincoln to continue his education. Jim, however, does not view this move as ironic but, rather, as the unavoidable process of growing up. Soon before Jim leaves Black Hawk, he spends a day in the country with the three "hired girls": Tiny, Ántonia, and Lena. Jim's description of a plough joins man and nature in one stunning image:

> There were no clouds, the sun was going down in a limpid, gold-washed sky. Just as the lower edge of the red disc rested on the high fields against the horizon, a great black figure suddenly appeared on the face of the sun. . . . Magnified across the distance by the horizontal light, [the plough] stood out against the sun, was exactly

contained within the circle of the disc; the handles, the tongue, the share—black against the molten red. There it was, heroic in size, a picture writing on the sun. (865–866)

This beautiful image is ephemeral: "even while [they] whispered about it, [the] vision disappeared." As natural as the sun setting, Jim must grow up, and the vision must recede. Jim laments: "When boys and girls are growing up, life can't stand still, not even in the quietest of country towns; and they *have* to grow up, whether they will or no" (my italics 835).

In Book II, Jim's personal narrative is cast against the continued story of Ántonia. Like Jim, Ántonia moves to town, not for school but financial necessity. Unlike Jim, however, Ántonia does not seem to mourn the loss of her childhood but adapts well to changing circumstances; despite her new surroundings, she displays the same level of vitality and Emersonian self-reliance. Her spiritual individualism is now associated with a larger group of Bohemian and Scandinavian women, all of whom live outside of the strict conventions of American society and exhibit "a positive carriage and free-dom of movement" (838). As a result of their "vigor," they are "considered a menace to the social order"; Jim tells us that "[t]heir beauty shone out too boldly against a conventional background" (840). In fact, Ántonia loses her job when she continues to attend the forbidden Vannis dances; she makes the important choice to overcome social and financial pressure in order to main-tain her self-determination. Ántonia seems to acknowledge, as does Emerson, that "nothing is at last sacred but the integrity of your own mind" (Emerson 261).

It is interesting that critics have viewed Lena Lingard as Ántonia's foil (Bowden 16). Although Ántonia's and Lena's desires suggest certain binaries, they share many values in common. Jim explains his earliest memories of Lena as "out among her cattle, bareheaded and barefooted, scantily dressed in tattered clothing, always knitting as she watched her herd." He describes her as "something wild," quite unabashed about her "ragged clothes," with an "easy" and "gentle" disposition matched equally against her ruggedness (817). Although she ultimately comes to represent an urban contrast to the earthy Ántonia, they both share the same heroic individualism, the same fierce sense of self-reliance that privileges personal integrity and independence above conformity and social convention. Jim explains how Lena manages to suc-ceed in Lincoln business without giving into the capitalist American model: "Lena's success puzzled me. She was so easy-going; had none of the push and self-assertiveness that get people ahead in business"; even in the urban world, Lena manages to translate her country qualities into a "blissful expression of countenance" (885). Rather than a foil, one might say that Lena Lingard is Ántonia's doppelganger; their paths may diverge, sending one out into the world and the other back to the earth, but their similar spiritual drive renders them complementary Emersonian heroines.

This idea is fostered by the fact that Jim comes to idealize and love them both. Rather than translate his ideals into reality, however, Jim distances himself from these two women. In Books III and IV, Jim has the opportunity to connect with each of these Emersonian heroines, but, instead, turns away. In Book III, he becomes physically and spiritually close to Lena. Yet, at a critical moment, Jim chooses to detach. He has the choice to remain in the West or to move East and study at Harvard. He seems to make this decision during a conversation with Lena. Lena teases Jim: "What's on your mind, Jim? Are you afraid I'll want you to marry me some day?" (893). Jim's response is telling: "Then I told her I was going away." Although Lena has made it clear that she has no intention of getting married, the juxtaposition of the two lines reflects Jim's fear, not necessarily his fear of marriage but, rather, his fear of embracing that Emersonian sensibility that he has already written off as lost.

In Book IV, we find Jim in a similar circumstance, this time with Án-tonia. Having gone away and finished his studies at Harvard, he returns to Black Hawk for the summer and learns that Ántonia has been deserted by her American beau and is now unmarried with a baby girl. Despite her hardship, Ántonia retains a calm and "deep-seated health and ardor" (909). Recognizing the beauty and vitality intrinsic in her character, Jim confesses:

> 'Do you know, Ántonia, since I've been away, I think of you more often than of any one else in this part of the world. I'd have liked to have you for a sweetheart, or a wife, or my mother or my sister—anything that a woman can be to a man. The *idea* of you is a part of my mind; you influence my likes and dislikes, all my tastes, hundreds of times when I don't realize it. You really are a part of me' (my italics 910).

The obvious question is: why does he not, then, choose to "have" Ántonia for a "sweetheart, or a wife"? He even admits that he feels the "old pull of the earth," and yet he still decides to return back East, away from the country, towards the center of sterile materialism (910). Rather than admitting his failure, however, Jim deflects his loss onto the landscape; as they walk "homeward across the fields," he describes the setting sun and rising moon as "resting on opposite edges of the world," as if to elegize and naturalize the position in which Ántonia and Jim now find themselves (910).

Jim relieves himself of the "burden" to act by relegating Lena and Ánto-nia to the world of ideas and assigning them the status of Muse. Specifically, Jim inscribes these women into the "poetry of Virgil," and, as he reads, actually sees the image of Lena "float[ing] before [him] on the page like a picture"

(880). Blanche Gelfant reads this as evidence of Jim's fear of sexuality, which acts, she argues, as "a determining force in his story" (62). I agree with Gelfant when she suggests that "by relegating Lena to the ideal but unreachable world of art he assures their separation" (69). However, rather than associating this with Jim's fear of sexuality, I understand it in terms of his allegiance to American mythology. Ántonia's and Lena's ability to maintain their vitality and independence threatens Jim's *inability* to maintain such ideals; thus, he views them as inherently impalpable, intangible. By recasting them into the role of Muse and himself into the role of epic poet, he, in effect, rewrites Virgil into his own American myth of possibility and loss. His failure suddenly becomes heroic.

Nowhere is this tendency more obvious than in the last paragraph of Book V. It is here that Jim's role as unreliable narrator becomes solidified, and the essence of his story can be understood. In one of the most beautiful passages of the book, Jim explains the "circle" of man's experience:

> For Ántonia and for me, this had been the road of *Destiny;* had taken us to those early accidents of fortune which *predetermined* for us all that we can ever be. Now I understood that the same road was to bring us together again. Whatever we had missed, we possessed together the precious, the incommunicable past. (my italics 937)

Despite the brilliant poetics of the language, there are certain troubling inconsistencies in Jim's seeming "epiphany" (Helmick 113). In particular, the words "destiny" and "predetermined" are completely out of synch with Jim's story. In this passage, Jim naturalizes his failure; his empty marriage, his destructive job, and his overall parasitic relationship to society get displaced onto some larger force that lies beyond individual choice. Jim's narrative, of course, undermines this notion. Beginning in Book II, each Book begins with a choice that moves Jim further and further away from the land he loves. In Book II, Jim's grandparents *choose* to move to town, in part to send Jim to school and help him integrate into American society. Book III opens with Jim's move to Lincoln, where he *chooses* the realm of ideas over experience. At the end of Book III, Jim *chooses* to leave Lena and follow his teacher East to the center of urban life. At the end of Book IV, Jim *chooses* to return to Harvard, to go to law school rather than stay in the country with Ántonia. And now, Jim *chooses* to romanticize and mythologize his loss in order to make sense of his empty life. In *The American Adam*, R. W. B. Lewis addresses the myth that Jim embraces: "Instead of looking forward to new possibilities, we direct our tired attention to the burden of history, observing repeatedly that it is later than you think" (196). This is precisely the myth that Cather understands as fiction. Jim Burden may envision himself as the symbolic "burden of history," but, instead, he represents the "burden" of all Americans who blame external forces on their own spiritual failures.

Although Cather recognizes that the "burden" of Emersonian possibility rests with the individual, she also recognizes that the myth of the American Adam is, itself, a fiction. The text certainly celebrates Lena and Ántonia as Emersonian figures and applauds their persistence, despite all odds, to preserve their individualism. Their lives, however, are far from ideal. If Lena and Ántonia act as complementary heroines, they also lack what the other manages to incorporate. Thus, although Ántonia is often cited as an Earth Mother goddess, by the end of the text, she is "battered [if] not diminished"; Jim describes her as "a stalwart, brown woman, flat-chested, her curly brown hair a little grizzled" (914). Likewise, while Lena maintains her independence and, as Tiny explains, is "the only person . . . who never gets any older," she sacrifices community and family in order to maintain her spiritual integrity (896). Any sense of pure idealism is mitigated by stark reality. More importantly, even this tempered vision of Emersonianism is figuratively relocated outside America: neither Lena nor Ántonia is American born, and Ántonia, ultimately reintegrates herself back into Bohemian culture. These "new Americans" give up that American myth of unadulterated idealism because they are willing to transform the "ideal" into the "real." Thus, the myth of the American Adam, the possibility of mapping the Emersonian self onto an empty landscape, is applauded, but it is also fictionalized.

There is much resistance to the idea that Cather does not fully embrace Jim's vision. Hermione Lee, for example, states that "Jim's elegiac pastoral expresses Cather's deepest feelings: it would be *perverse* to argue that his reading of Ántonia is meant to be distrusted" (my italics 150). Lee argues that Jim's story is Cather's story and, in many ways, it is. Cather does seem to "trust" Jim's mythological reading and to identify with the characters she introduces. After all, the novel's epigraph repeats a quote used by Jim in Book III, a quote by Virgil that mourns the inevitable passage of time. In this way, Cather inscribes herself into Jim's story, into American mythology, and into a national discourse. However, she also writes against this discourse; she affirms the national myths, but, at the same time, consciously holds such myths "to be fictive."

WORKS CITED

Acocella, Joan. "Cather and the Academy." *New Yorker* November 27 1995: 56–71.

Bloom, Harold. "Introduction." *Major Literary Characters: Ántonia.* Ed. Harold Bloom. New York: Chelsea, 1991. 1–3.

Bowden, Edwin T. "The Frontier Isolation." *Major Literary Characters: Ántonia.* Ed. Harold Bloom. New York: Chelsea, 1991. 14–18.

Carden, Mary Paniccia. "Creative Fertility and the National Romance in Willa Cather's *O Pioneers!* and *My Ántonia.*" *Modern Fiction Studies* 45: 2 (Summer 1999): 275–302.

Cather, Willa. *My Ántonia. Cather: Novels & Stories 1905–1918.* Ed. Sharon O'Brien. New York: Library of America, 1987. 707–937.

Emerson, Ralph Waldo. *Essays and Lectures.* New York: Library of America, 1983.

Gelfant, Blanche H. "The Forgotten Reaping-Hook: Sex in *My Ántonia.*" *America Literature* 43:1 (March 1971): 60–82.

Helmick, Evelyn. "The Mysteries of Ántonia." *Willa Cather's "My Ántonia."* Ed. Harold Bloom. New York: Chelsea, 1987.

Kermode, Frank. *The Sense of an Ending: Studies in the Theory of Fiction.* London: Oxford University Press, 1966.

Lee, Hermione. *Willa Cather: Double Lives.* New York: Vintage, 1989.

Lewis, R.W.B. *The American Adam: Innocence, Tragedy, and Tradition in the Nineteenth Century.* Chicago: University of Chicago Press, 1955.

Miller, James E. "*My Ántonia* and the American Dream." *Prairie Schooner* 48: 2 (Summer 1974): 112–123.

Reynolds, Guy. *Willa Cather in Context: Progress, Race, Empire.* New York: St. Martin's Press, 1996.

Rosowski, Susan J. "Prospects for the Study of Willa Cather." *Resources for American Literary Study* 22:2 (1996): 147–165.

Scholes, Robert. E. "Hope and Memory in *My Ántonia.*" *Major Literary Characters: Ántonia.* Ed. Harold Bloom. New York: Chelsea, 1991. 18–22.

Stouk, David. "An American Pastoral *Readings on* My Ántonia. Ed. Christopher Smith. San Diego, CA: Greenhaven, 2001.

ANN ROMINES

Why Do We Read—and Re-read—My Ántonia?

I was a relatively elderly first-time reader of *My Ántonia*. I had the idea that
it was one of those canonical American "classics," with the smell of slightly
stale bread, and I put off reading it until my late twenties, when the title
appeared insistently (as the *only* title by Willa Cather) on my Ph.D. reading
list. So, in 1972, I finally settled down dutifully with a dusty brown library
copy, whose crumbling pages did indeed smell like bread. Of course, I fell in
love. And I began plotting ways to *re-read* this extraordinary book: I'd write
a dissertation chapter about it, I'd assign it to my students, I'd give copies to
friends and family on the very next birthday or Christmas. . . . More than
thirty years later, I am still plotting.

My topic for this essay was an assignment from the Cather Founda-
tion. At the 2005 Willa Cather Spring Conference in Red Cloud, we were
to celebrate the culmination of a Nebraska-wide project, "One Book/One
State," as readers all over the state gathered to discuss Willa Cather's beloved
Nebraska novel. And I—not even a Nebraskan!—was to talk about "Why We
Read *My Ántonia*"? As I struggled with this thoroughly daunting assignment,
I began to suspect that many of us read this novel for the first time because
we are compelled by circumstance of various kinds—an assignment, a cur-
riculum, a dazzling billboard like those that dotted the Nebraska landscape
in 2005, proclaiming "Nebraska Reads *My Ántonia!*"—or because we are the

*In the First Fifty Years: A Celebration of the Cather Foundation's Promotion and Preservation
of the World of Willa Cather,* edited by Virgil Albertini, Susan Maher, and Ann Romines
(Red Cloud, N.E. The Willa Cather Pioneer Memorial and Educational Foundation,
2006): pp. 21–31. © 2006

recipients of somebody else's enthusiasm. But the choice to *re*-read is a far more individual commitment. And that's where I'd like to begin.

I re-read *My Ántonia* because this book keeps surprising me. So much is in it—and so much isn't. It keeps generating questions. For example: What does it mean to move—from a Bohemian town with flowering trees and gardens where musicians gather for "beautiful talk" or from a Virginia country house with generations of family portraits and family recipes and rituals—to land "as bare as a piece of sheet iron" where the sod only recently had been broken? What if one is, like Ántonia Shimerda, at the center of a needy, conflicted nuclear family, soon to be wrenched by a suicide? Or what if one, like Jim Burden, is suddenly orphaned in Virginia and then thrust back a generation, to be raised in a new country by old grandparents, who almost never speak of one's parents? How can these two uprooted children, Ántonia and Jim, find a common language, much less a common culture—especially as adolescents in a mean-spirited little town that doesn't even want them to dance together? (Surely Red Cloud was never that mean-spirited!) Inevitably we see Jim and Ántonia fall under the spell of their new country—and then they work out very different ways to shape their adult lives to express that love. Their choices separate them, at least physically—even though their shared Nebraska childhood is a bond, a "kind of freemasonry," as Jim's companion passenger in the book's introduction (*is* she Willa Cather?) says (x). It is Ántonia who is able to express openly the power of that bond: "Ain't it wonderful, Jim, how much people can mean to each other?" she says (312).

Jim and Ántonia begin to discover what they will mean to each other in their first, partially shared months in Nebraska. These first chapters have an unqualified intensity that's unlike anything else in the book. The strong colors, the overwhelming sensations leap off the page. Even the smallest features of the new country get the close scrutiny of children's eyes—closer to the ground than our adult eyes, they pick up on the smallest bits of life. On his first day in Nebraska, Jim braves the threat of rattlesnakes to sit surrounded by large yellow pumpkins and note the patterns on the backs of the tiny red and black bugs that march around him. "That is happiness," he thinks, "to be dissolved into something complete and great" (18). But when Jim is with Ántonia, things are often more complicated than that gratifying sense of union and dissolution. When she rescues another insect—the last, frail grasshopper of summer—the children are forced to remember that death is a part of the beautiful prairie autumn they are experiencing, and that the coming winter is a force that this last singer cannot survive. Furthermore, the grasshopper reminds Ántonia of an old storyteller in her Bohemian village, and—as her father joins the children—memory and homesickness complicate and deepen the children's discovery. On another foray, as they try to prod their way into a prairie dog's home, Jim is a reluctant "dragon-slayer" in an encounter with a fat old rattlesnake, becoming the hero of a story that he will later re-read as a "mock adventure" (48).

By the time of the first snowfall, Ántonia has translated for Jim the appalling tale of their Russian neighbors, Pavel and Peter, who sacrificed a wedding party to a pack of wolves, back home—and the very landscape of Jim's dreams has changed. When he arrived, the dark Nebraska country seemed undifferentiated, "nothing but land." Now, "At night, before I went to sleep, I often found myself in a sledge drawn by three horses [like that of Pavel and Peter], dashing through a country that looked something like Nebraska and something like Virginia" (59). Jim's old country—Virginia—and his vivid perceptions of his new home have merged with the stories that his immigrant neighbors brought with them, to become the very stuff of his consciousness. Ten years later, when he has already been away from Nebraska for two years, he says to Ántonia, "The idea of you is a part of my mind" (219). That part of Jim's mind—so precious to him—finally becomes a readable text, his manuscript of *My Ántonia*, which Willa Cather offers to us.

One of the first things we learn about Jim, once he meets the Shimerdas, is that he becomes a reading teacher, tutoring Ántonia in English, at her father's request. Although he is the younger of the two children, Jim's native English-speaking heritage gives him the cultural authority of the teacher. Except for a few words—one of which is *kolache!*—no one expects Jim to learn Bohemian, and his first feelings about Ántonia's native language are suggested when he yells at her, after she has excitedly tried to warn him about the rattlesnake, "What did you jabber Bohunk for?" (44). Yet Ántonia becomes Jim's translator and teacher as well, and what she teaches him almost always complicates his view of the world. Without her, he could not have understood the haunting tale of Pavel and Peter and the wolves or fully apprehended the poignancy of the dying grasshopper.

As his first year in Nebraska moves from fall to winter, Jim realizes that even the now-familiar fields of his grandparents' farm can be re-read with every change of weather. This is what he sees when the first snow falls:

> Beyond the pond, on the slope that climbed to the cornfield, there was, faintly marked in the grass, a great circle where the Indians used to ride. Jake and Otto were sure that when they galloped round that ring the Indians tortured prisoners, bound to a stake in the center; but grandfather thought they merely ran races or trained horses there. Whenever one looked at this slope against the setting sun, the circle showed like a pattern in the grass; and this morning, when the first light spray of snow lay over it, it came out with wonderful distinctness, like strokes of Chinese white on

canvas. The old figure stirred me as it had never done before and seemed a good omen for the winter. (83)

Although he has only been in Nebraska a few weeks, Jim has already grown practiced in re-reading "the old figure" in the grass. Among his grandfather and the hired men, he notes the controversies about how to read the Indians' uses of this circle, and he sees how their partially effaced history—and the problems of reading it—are a part of the Burdens' present experience of this place, an insistent "pattern in the grass," "like strokes of Chinese white" in the new snow. The ten-year-old child Jim surely did not know what "Chinese white"—an artist's pigment—was; that language is the product of a well-educated and sophisticated adult who lives in New York City with a wife who is a patron of artists. In this early image of the Indian circle— which is never mentioned again in the novel—we can see how the process of reading and re-reading "his country" permeates Jim Burden's experience, and this book, from the boy's first sighting of the figure to the distant adult's decision to describe it in terms of "Chinese white."

The first snowfall is soon followed by a blizzard, and by Jim's first Christmas in Nebraska, one of the most inclusive and beautiful scenes in this novel. Snowed in, the Burdens bring out treasures that are normally kept hidden to create their own "country Christmas." Grandmother gets out "her fancy cake-cutters" and bakes decorated cookies, as she did in Virginia. Since Jim wanted to buy picture books for his pupils, Ántonia and Yulka, she helps him to make cloth pages and to cut illustrations from the household's store of "good old family magazines," pasting them into his book along with Sunday school and advertising cards from his own "old country," Virginia. So Jim makes his first book, patching together the resources of his own American popular culture for the Bohemian children to read. And then the hired man Jake brings in a surprise—a little cedar Christmas tree, a rarity in Nebraska—because "he used to help my father cut Christmas trees for me in Virginia, and he had not forgotten how much I liked them" (79). This is the first mention of Jim's dead father since the day of his arrival in Nebraska. The whole household throws itself into decorating the little tree with popcorn, the gingerbread cookies, and homemade candles. Jake brings a little mirror out of his dark pocket "for a frozen lake" under the tree. And the hired man Otto brings out a surprise treasure of splendid decorations from his cowboy trunk:

a collection of brilliantly colored paper figures, several inches high and stiff enough to stand alone. They had been sent to him year after year, by his old mother in Austria. There was a bleeding heart, in tufts of paper lace; there were the three kings, gorgeously appareled, and the ox and the ass and the shepherds; there were

camels and leopards, held by the black slaves of the three kings.
Our tree became the talking tree of the fairy tale; legends and
stories nestled like birds in its branches. Grandmother said it
reminded her of the Tree of Knowledge. (80)

For Christmas, these immigrants have put aside their suspicions, con-
straints, and silences. They have brought their treasures out of their trunks and
combined them with the resources of Nebraska to create a beautiful, shining
multi-cultural text that honors both the old countries and the new one; both
their present companionship and the beloved persons who are far away or
dead, such as Otto's mother and Jim's father. When Ántonia's father comes
for a Christmas call, he is so moved by the tree that, as a Roman Catholic,
he kneels before it to pray, making the sign of the cross in the very Baptist
Burden household. But even this does not dim the spell of the Christmas
tree, and for a little while, Mr. Shimerda seems to break through his numbing
homesickness, displacement and despair. A scene like this seems to illustrate
all the rich possibilities of reading and re-reading that *My Ántonia* has to
offer, and each time I return to it I find another detail nestled in the green
branches of the Tree of Knowledge.

However, one of the hardest truths of this novel is that such moments
cannot heal everything. In a country without a priest, without the friendships, music, work, and familiar places that have meant so much to him, Mr.
Shimerda was cheered and warmed to see cherished symbols—even a Catholic bleeding heart—lovingly displayed in his Protestant American neighbors'
home. Nevertheless, in less than a month he is dead, a suicide.

And without her beloved father, Ántonia has no more time for reading
lessons. She and Jim will never again share the day-to-day intimacy of their
first weeks in Nebraska. Ántonia works in the fields to support her family
and grows strong, brown, and vigorous; Jim goes to a country school with
other English-speaking children. In midsummer, when Ántonia is hired for a
few weeks to help Jim's grandmother during the threshing, they are together
again briefly, in a memorable scene that ends the novel's first, longest book.
Companionably, they watch the drama of a prairie thunderstorm and enjoy
the beauty and promise of a fruitful growing season. Ántonia says, "I wish my
papa live to see this summer. I wish no winter ever come again." Jim replies,

"It will be summer a long while yet," I reassured her. "Why
aren't you always nice like this, Tony?"
"How nice?"
"Why, just like this; like yourself. Why do you all the time try
to be like Ambrosch [her gruff older brother]?"
She put her arms under her head and lay back, looking up at the

sky. "If I live here, like you, that is different. Things will be easy for
you. But they will be hard for us." (134–135)

Jim's impulse is to resist change and difference. "It will be summer for
a long while yet," he reassures his friend. And he wants her to always
be "nice," as she seemed to him in their first months together, when her
"genteel" father was alive. This tanned, muscular girl, who prefers outdoor to indoor work and won't wear the sunbonnet Grandmother Burden
gives her, is problematic for Jim. She is not acceptably feminine in ways he
has been taught to value. Again, Ántonia challenges Jim to complicate his
static reading of her—as she will continue to do throughout this book. He
is a boy, she an adolescent girl. His American family is already prosperous and established in Nebraska; her immigrant Bohemian family, newly
fatherless, is struggling to survive. Ántonia insists that Jim recognize
present realities of economics and social class: "Things will be easy for
you. But they will be hard for us."

In the following three books of *My Ántonia*—each shorter than the
last—the re-readings continue. When the Burdens move to town, Ántonia
soon follows, to work as a hired girl, and Jim is initiated into the schoolboy
culture of Black Hawk. Soon he is "quite another boy, or thought I was"
(141). In town, Ántonia's outdoor vigor is translated into her new pleasure
in dancing and friendships. Jim loves to dance with her and be with her.
When he kisses her in a decidedly unschoolboyish way, he is delighted
that she rebuffs him—because it means she is "still my Ántonia," with the
"warm, sweet face . . . kind arms, and . . . true heart" he first knew in their
childhood prairie days. As for Ántonia, it begins to be clear that she has
her own version of "my Jim," as well, who must be protected from sexual
entanglements with hired girls that might tie him down. She instructs
him, "Now, don't you go and be a fool like some of these town boys. You're
not going to sit around here and whittle store boxes and tell stories all your
life. You are going away to school and make something of yourself. I'm just
awful proud of you" (217–218).

Near the end of "The Hired Girls," the memorable scene of Jim's picnic
with the girls becomes another occasion for re-reading the prairie. As they eat
their lunch on a high bluff,

> Below us we could see the windings of the river, and Black Hawk,
> grouped among its trees, and, beyond, the rolling country, swelling
> gently until it met the sky. We could recognize familiar farmhouses
> and windmills. Each of the girls pointed out to me the direction in
> which her father's farm lay, and told me how many acres were in
> wheat that year and how many in corn. (231)

The vast "land" of Jim and Ántonia's first night in Nebraska is now an arranged landscape, including a town, and the houses and windmills have names and stories attached to them—in fact, each hired girl can point to a family farm that her own labors in town are helping to support. Just as Jim speculated years earlier about the Indian circle in his grandfather's field, he now tells the girls about the Spanish relics found in nearby fields, which seem to suggest that Coronado once explored this country, in the sixteenth century. The girls add bits of their own family histories to the story—the homesick grandmother, the new farm machinery, the twenty acres of rye planted so that Tiny's homesick mother can make "old country" bread. Collectively, just as any group of attentive readers might, they pull together the layers of meanings that span centuries:

> The girls began to wonder among themselves. Why had the Spaniards come so far? What must this country have been like, then? Why had Coronado never gone back to Spain, to his riches and his castles and his king? I couldn't tell them. I only knew the school books said he "died in the wilderness, of a broken heart." "More than him has done that," said Ántonia sadly, and the girls murmured assent. (180)

Of these readers, Ántonia makes the longest leap of imagination, connecting the homesickness of a Spanish nobleman who died in 1554 to her own Bohemian father's recent death in Nebraska.

Suddenly, as the sun sets, the readers have a moment of revelation, a symbol that spotlights the history of human labors in this place: the famous image of the plow against the sun.

> . . . a great black figure suddenly appeared on the face of the sun. We sprang to our feet, straining our eyes toward it. . . . There it was, heroic in size, a picture writing on the sun.
>
> Even while we whispered about it, our vision disappeared; the ball dropped and dropped until the red tip went beneath the earth. The fields below us were dark, the sky was growing pale, and that forgotten plough had sunk back to its own littleness somewhere on the prairie. (237–238)

This great image, which has been celebrated by so many readers of this book—and which, incidentally, has been the symbolic logo of the Cather Foundation for fifty years—is a celebration of collaborative reading, of the layers of meaning that a group of readers can achieve, putting their heads together.

    As *My Ántonia* moves toward its end, Jim continues his sporadic
efforts to re-read the prairie and Ántonia herself. At twenty, just before
traveling east to continue his education at Harvard, he makes a visit to
Black Hawk and sees a large photograph of Ántonia's first child, born out
of wedlock, in the local photographer's studio. He reads it as a "depressing"
image in a tasteless frame of a "round-eyed baby in short dresses . . . Tony,
of course must have its picture on exhibition at the town photographer's,
in a great gilt frame. How like her! I could forgive her, I told myself, if she
hadn't thrown herself away on such a cheap sort of fellow" (195–196). Jim's
snobbery and disapproval are palpable here; "his" Ántonia has violated his
standards of "nice" behavior, and it is impossible for him to see the photograph as evidence of a young mother's loving pride in a beautiful, healthy
first child. This failure of reading can be corrected, at least partially, only by
an experienced older woman's sympathetic view of Ántonia, related by the
Widow Steavens in "The Pioneer Woman's Story." The Widow evokes an
Ántonia who returned home chastened, humiliated, and pregnant after her
marriage did not materialize, and went resolutely to work on the Shimerda
farm. In the fall, she watched her cattle and took in the landscape that had
become so familiar, as she tells the Widow:

> "It seems such a little while ago when Jim Burden and I was playing
> all over this country. Up here I can pick out the very places where
> my father used to stand. Sometimes I feel like I'm not going to live
> very long, so I'm just enjoying every day of this fall." (307–308)

Waiting for her first childbirth, and obviously fearing that she might not
survive it, Ántonia is re-reading her "new" country, now marked with the
history she has shared there, with her dead father and absent Jim.
    When Jim finally goes to see Ántonia again, briefly, it is to tell her good-
bye: they both know he will never return to live in Nebraska again. His farewell
is partly a renunciation, in the past tense: "I'd have liked to have you for . . .
anything a woman can be to a man." And it is a qualified affirmation: "The idea
of you is a part of my mind" (312). In his mind, "my Ántonia" is safe.
    Ántonia answers Jim ardently, "Ain't it wonderful, Jim, how much peo-
ple can mean to each other? I'm so glad we had each other when we were
little. I can't wait till my little girl's old enough to tell her about all the things
we used to do" (312–313). Ántonia's response is different because, although
Jim obviously means as much to her as she does to him, she has no intention
of keeping him locked in her mind. She plans to tell the stories of their childhood in the new country, adding another layer to its accruing history. This
scene ends with another sunset, almost like a reprise of the plow against the
sun. But this time there are two great globes in the sky:

the sun dropped and lay like a great golden globe in the low west. While it hung there, the moon rose in the east, as big as a cartwheel, pale silver and streaked with rose color, thin as a bubble or a ghost-moon. For five, perhaps ten minutes, the two luminaries confronted each other across the level land, resting on opposite edges of the world. I [Jim] felt the old pull of the earth, the solemn magic that comes out of those fields at nightfall. I wished I could be a little boy again, and that my way could end there. (313)

Obviously, we are meant to read this scene with the earlier, plow-against-the-sun sunset in mind, and its suggestions of rich collectivity and connection. Here the two orbs, sun and moon, suggest both direct and reflected light, male and female, as well as confrontation from "opposite edges of the world," where Jim and Ántonia will soon be—at least physically. The point of view is Jim's alone, not the collective view of the earlier passage. For a moment, at least, he wishes for a return to childhood (as Ántonia never wishes) and perhaps even for death ("that my way could end there"), suggesting that there is something dangerous and potentially annihilating about his internalization of Ántonia.

That may be one of the reasons why Jim waits twenty years to return for a visit to Ántonia. One of the striking things about *My Ántonia*—which makes it meaningful to so many kinds of readers—is that the book suggests there is more than one way to know a place. In this interval of twenty years, Ántonia and Jim have worked out their own ways. She has stayed on the Nebraska farmland she came to love, raising crops, orchards, and a large family of bilingual children with her Bohemian immigrant husband, Anton Cuzak. "I belong on a farm," she tells Jim (332). Jim, a railroad lawyer married to a wealthy New Yorker, spends much of his life traveling through the West: "He loves with a personal passion the great country through which his railway runs and branches. His faith in it and his knowledge of it have played an important part in its development" (xi). Ántonia expresses her love by putting down roots; Jim expresses his in mobility. We readers have long debated about which of these expressions is better, more authentic. Sue Rosowski, for example, spoke eloquently for Ántonia's rooted life; Joe Urgo makes a strong case for Jim's mobility. At this point in my own re-readings, what seems to me remarkable about this book is that it endorses both ways of knowing a place. Jim Burden's way is obviously closer to Willa Cather's own—and yet the subject of this book was inspired by her dear friend Annie Sadilek Pavelka, who was as rooted as Ántonia, and is buried in Webster County, Nebraska, where she spent her entire American life.

In the early pages of *My Ántonia*, we noticed the vivid colors and intensity of Jim and Ántonia's first childhood responses to Nebraska. On Jim's return visit, those images recur in the famous fruit cave scene, as Ántonia's children "all came running up the steps together, big and little, tow heads and gold heads and brown, and flashing little naked legs; a veritable explosion of life out of the dark cave into the sunlight. It made me dizzy for a moment," Jim says (328). All this is no surprise to Ántonia; she lives her life surrounded by these lively children. But Jim is a childless city man; such an "explosion" is a threat to his equilibrium, making him dizzy. No wonder he chooses to enjoy these children in smaller doses—sleeping in the barn with just two boys; planning a camping trip with two more, and "city tramps" with their father. (Rather as Willa Cather often seems to have dealt with her beloved nieces and nephews, spending "quality time" with one or two at a time.) As Jim reflects, alone in his bed in the Cuzak barn, we see how he is processing the overwhelming impressions of his long-delayed visit with Ántonia:

> That moment, when they all came tumbling out of the cave into the light, was a sight any man might have come far to see. Ántonia had always been one to leave images in the mind that did not fade—that grew stronger with time. In my memory there was a succession of such pictures, fixed there like the old woodcuts of one's first primer. Ántonia kicking her bare legs against the sides of my pony when we came home in triumph with our snake; Ántonia in her black shawl and fur cap, as she stood by her father's grave in the snowstorm; Ántonia coming in with her work-team along the evening sky-line. She lent herself to immemorial human attitudes which we recognize by instinct as universal and true.... She still had that something which fires the imagination, could still stop one's breath for a moment by a look or gesture that somehow revealed the meaning in common things. She had only to stand in the orchard, to put her hand on a little crab tree and look up at the apples, to make you feel the goodness of planting and tending and harvesting at last. All the strong things of her heart came out in her body, that had been so tireless in serving generous emotions. (341–342)

All the dazzling energy and color of the children in the fruit cave are acknowledged, but Jim's Ántonia is still "a part of his mind," and stripped of color—like woodcuts that illustrate reading lessons in a primer or the black-and-white Benda drawings that Cather insisted upon as illustrations for this novel. Jim's mental pictures reinforce the images of "his Ántonia" that he most wants to preserve—even though we may miss some of the vivid variety of the young girl we met at the beginning of this novel. Nevertheless, Jim acknowledges what has been problematic for him before: that Ántonia's "generous emotions" are grounded in her bodily life, including her sexuality, which had been difficult for him to accept. Now he can recognize the fullness and the unity of his friend's life: "All the strong things of her heart came out in her body."

As I have read this beautiful passage before, I have always thought of the black/white palette of Jim's memories as a kind of a loss. But on this re-reading, I'm also thinking in another way. Black and white is the palette of printing, and Jim thinks of his mental images in terms of a book: "one's first primer." We know from Cather's introduction that what lies ahead for Jim Burden is the writing of his own book—the book we are reading now. Earlier, Jim kept, "my Ántonia" locked inside, as a part of his mind, while Ántonia put her memories into circulation, as tales for her large, voluble family. Now, with the encouragement of his companion on the train, Jim is writing "My Ántonia," and he assumes that his old friend, the narrator of the novel's introduction, is also writing her own version of Ántonia. By writing Ántonia, he unlocks her from the prison of his mind and puts her into circulation among readers. The black-and-white of *print* returns her to *color*, in our minds.

My Ántonia does not end with Jim's farewell to the Cuzak family. Instead, it concludes with one more (solitary) lesson in re-reading. Walking alone outside Black Hawk, Jim seeks out rough pastures that have never been cultivated, and thus look much as the land looked when he first saw it. Then, he says,

> I had the good luck to stumble upon a bit of the first road that went from Black Hawk out to the north country; to my grandfather's farm, then on to the Shimerdas'. . . .
>
> This was the road over which Ántonia and I came on that night when we got off the train at Black Hawk . . . wondering children, being taken we knew not whither. I had only to close my eyes to hear the rumbling of the wagons in the dark, and to be again overcome with that obliterating strangeness. . . . I had the sense of coming home to myself, and of having found out what a little circle man's experience is. (359–360)

Jim Burden is still re-reading, just as he read the Indian circle in the pasture at the age of ten. The first sensation he felt on this road is still accessible to him, that unforgettable "obliterating strangeness." But the new sensations here—of having come home to himself, and recognized "what a little circle man's experience is"—are the product of an adult's willingness to return, again and again, to the beloved figures in a rich, familiar text. They are the rewards of Jim Burden's re-readings—and of ours.

Works Cited

Cather, Willa. *My Ántonia.* Scholarly Edition. Ed. Charles Mignon with Kari Ronning. Lincoln: University of Nebraska Press, 1994.

Rosowski, Susan J. *The Voyage Perilous: Willa Cather's Romanticism.* Lincoln: University of Nebraska Press, 1986.

Urgo, Joseph. *Willa Cather and the Myth of American Migration.* Urbana: University of Illinois Press, 1995.

Chronology

1873	Born December 7, near Winchester, Virginia, to Charles F. Cather and Mary Virginia Boak Cather. Will a was to be the oldest of seven children.
1884	Moves with her parents to a ranch in Webster County, Nebraska.
1885	Family moves to Red Cloud, Nebraska.
1890	Cather moves to Lincoln to complete preparation for entering the University of Nebraska.
1891–1895	Attends University of Nebraska, paying her way by working as a newspaper columnist during her two final years.
1895–1896	Stays at home in Red Cloud.
1896–1897	Goes to Pittsburgh to work as a magazine editor.
1897–1901	Works as a newspaper editor and drama reviewer for Pittsburgh's *Daily Leader*.
1901–1902	Teaches English and Latin at Central High School in Pittsburgh.
1903	*April Twilights* (a book of poems)
1903–1906	Teaches at Allegheny High in Pittsburgh.
1905	*The Troll Gardens* (short stories).
1906–1912	Moves to New York city to join editorial staff of *McClure's Magazine*.
1908	Moves into apartment with Edith Lewis, subsequently her lifelong companion.

1912	*Alexander's Bridge* (her first published novel)
1913	*O, Pioneers!*
1915	*The Song of the Lark*
1918	*My Ántonia*
1920	*Youth and the Bright Medusa* (stories)
1922	*One of Ours*
1923	*A Lost Lady*
1925	*The Professor's House*
1927	*Death Comes for the Archbishop*
1931	*Shadows on the Rock*
1932	*Obscure Destinies* (stories)
1935	*Lucy Gayheart*
1936	*Not Under Forty* (essays)
1940	*Sapphira and the Slave Girl*
1947	Dies at her home in New York City on April 24.
1948	*The Old Beauty* (stories)
1949	*Willa Cather on Writing* (essays)

Contributors

HAROLD BLOOM is Sterling Professor of the Humanities at Yale University. He is the author of 30 books, including *Shelley's Mythmaking* (1959), *The Visionary Company* (1961), *Blake's Apocalypse* (1963), *Yeats* (1970), *A Map of Misreading* (1975), *Kabbalah and Criticism* (1975), *Agon: Toward a Theory of Revisionism* (1982), *The American Religion* (1992), *The Western Canon* (1994), and *Omens of Millennium: The Gnosis of Angels, Dreams, and Resurrection* (1996). *The Anxiety of Influence* (1973) sets forth Professor Bloom's provocative theory of the literary relationships between the great writers and their predecessors. His most recent books include *Shakespeare: The Invention of the Human* (1998), a 1998 National Book Award finalist, *How to Read and Why* (2000), *Genius: A Mosaic of One Hundred Exemplary Creative Minds* (2002), *Hamlet: Poem Unlimited* (2003), *Where Shall Wisdom Be Found?* (2004), and *Jesus and Yahweh: The Names Divine* (2005). In 1999, Professor Bloom received the prestigious American Academy of Arts and Letters Gold Medal for Criticism. He has also received the International Prize of Catalonia, the Alfonso Reyes Prize of Mexico, and the Hans Christian Andersen Bicentennial Prize of Denmark.

BLANCHE H. GELFANT is Robert E. Maxwell Professor of Arts and Sciences and Professor of English Emerita at Dartmouth College. In 1995, she won the Jay B. Hubbell Medallion for excellence given by the American Literature Section of the Modern Language Association. The citation reads, in part, "Her books range from her pioneering study *The American City Novel* (1954) to *Women Writing in America: Voices in Collage* (1985) and *Cross-Cultural Reckonings: A Triptych of Russian, American, and Canadian*

165

Texts, issued this year by Cambridge University Press. She has published articles and book chapters on such diverse authors as Jack Kerouac, Joan Didion, Emma Goldman, James T. Farrell, William Faulkner, John Dos Passos, Tillie Olsen, Margaret Mitchell, and Willa Cather."

DEBORAH G. LAMBERT has taught at Merrimack Valley College. She has written articles on Edith Wharton and Roland Barthes.

SALLY ALLEN MCNALL is on the faculty in the honors program at the University of California, Chico. She wrote *Who Is the House? A Psychological Study of Two Centuries of Women's Fiction in America, 1795 to the Present* (1981).

PAULA WOOLLEY has studied for her Ph.D. at Tufts University, where she taught writing.

SUSAN J. ROSOWSKI was a central figure in Cather Studies. She was Adele Hall Professor of English at the University of Nebraska and general editor with James Woodress of the *Cather Edition,* published by the University of Nebraska Press. Her books include *The Voyage Perilous: Willa Cather's Romanticism* (1986) and *Birthing a Nation: Gender, Creativity, and the West in American Literature* (1999). She died in 2004.

PATRICK SHAW was professor of English at Texas Tech University. He wrote *Willa Cather and the Art of Conflict: Re-Visioning Her Creative Imagination* (1992) and *The Modern American Novel of Violence* (1999).

STEVEN B. SHIVELY is associate professor of English at Northwest Missouri State University. He is co-editor of the journal *Teaching Cather* and serves on the Board of Governors of the Willa Cather Pioneer Memorial.

JANIS P. STOUT is former dean of faculties and associate provost at Texas A&M University. Her books include *Strategies of Reticence: Silence and Meaning in the Works of Jane Austen, Willa Cather, Katherine Anne Porter and Joan Didion* (1990), *Through the Window, Out the Door: Women's Narratives of Departure, from Austin and Cather to Tyler, Morrison, and Didion* (1998); and *Willa Cather: The Writer and Her World* (2000).

MICHAEL GORMAN teaches English and American literature at Hiroshima University in Japan. He completed his dissertation, "Versed in Country Things: Pastoral Ideology, Modern American Identity, and Willa Cather," at the University of Tulsa in 2005.

DIANA H. POLLEY teaches in the School of Liberal Arts at Southern New Hampshire University. She has written for the *Willa Cather Newsletter & Review*.

ANN ROMINES is professor of English at George Washington University, where she directs the graduate program in English. Her books include *The Home Plot: Women, Writing and Domestic Ritual* (1992) and *Constructing the Little House: Gender, Culture, and Laura Ingalls Wilder* (1999). She edited *Willa Cather's Southern Connections: New Essays on Cather and the South* (2000).

Bibliography

Al-Ghalith, Asad. "Willa Cather: Light and the Mystical Journey." *International Fiction Review*, 22:1–2 (1995): 31–36.

Amos-Bankester, Anthea E. "Teaching *My Ántonia:* The 'Introductions' and the Impact of Revisions." *Nebraska English Journal*, 37:1 (Fall 1991): 99–109.

Blackburn, Timothy C. "'Have I Changed So Much?' Jim Burden, Intertextuality, and the Ending of *My Ántonia.*" *Cather Studies*, 7 (2007): 140–164.

Bloom, Harold. "Ántonia." *Major Literary Characters*. New York: Chelsea House, 1991.

Bradley, Jennifer L. "Inviting Narratives: Willa Cather's Childhood Scrapbook and *My Ántonia.*" In *The Scrapbook in American Life*, edited and introduced by Tucker, Susan, Katherine Ott, and Patricia P. Buckler. Philadelphia: Temple University Press, 2006, pp. 174–192.

Cather, Willa. *My Ántonia*. Edited by Mignon, Charles, Kari Ronning, James Woodress, W. T. Benda, Kathleen Danker, and Emily Levine. Lincoln: University of Nebraska Press, 1994.

Davis, James L., and Nancy H. Davis. "Persons, Place, and the Frontier Experience in Willa Cather's *My Antonia.*" *Journal of the American Studies Association of Texas*, 20 (October 1989): 53–60.

Dillman, Richard. "Imagining the Land: Five Versions of the Landscape in Willa Cather's *My Ántonia.*" *Heritage of the Great Plains*, 22:3 (Summer 1989): 30–35.

Fetterley, Judith. "*My Ántonia*, Jim Burden, and the Dilemma of the Lesbian Writer." In *Gender Studies: New Directions in Feminist Criticism*, edited by Spector, Judith. Bowling Green, OH: Popular, 1986, pp. 43–59.

Goggans, Jan. "Social (Re)Visioning in the Fields of *My Ántonia*." *Cather Studies*, 5 (2003): 153–172.

Glover, Angela. "Using Willa Cather's *My Ántonia* as a Collection of Short Stories to Teach How to Write a First Person Narrative." *Eureka Studies in Teaching Short Fiction*, 6:1 (Fall 2005): 40–59.

Hill, David. "The Quotidian Sublime: Cognitive Perspectives on Identity-Formation in Willa Cather's *My Ántonia*." *Arizona Quarterly: A Journal of American Literature, Culture, and Theory*, 61:3 (Autumn 2005): 109–127.

Holmes, Catherine D. "Jim Burden's Lost Worlds: Exile in *My Ántonia*." *Twentieth Century Literature: A Scholarly and Critical Journal*, 45:3 (Fall 1999): 336–346.

Irving, Katrina. "Displacing Homosexuality: The Use of Ethnicity in Willa Cather's *My Ántonia*." *MFS: Modern Fiction Studies*, 36:1 (Spring 1990): 91–102.

Kleiman, Ed. "Bipolar Vision in Willa Cather's *My Ántonia*." *English Studies: A Journal of English Language and Literature*, 82:2 (April 2001): 146–153.

Lindemann, Marilee, ed. *The Cambridge Companion to Willa Cather.* Cambridge Companions to Literature. Cambridge, England: Cambridge University Press, 2005.

Loges, Max. "Jim's Changing Perception of Ántonia in Willa Cather's *My Ántonia*." *Mount Olive Review*, 6 (Spring 1992): 122–126.

Lucenti, Lisa Marie. "Willa Cather's *My Antoniá:* Haunting the Houses of Memory." *Twentieth Century Literature: A Scholarly and Critical Journal*, 46:2 (Summer 2000): 193–213.

McElhiney, Annette Bennington. "Willa Cather's Use of a Tripartite Narrative Point of View in *My Ántonia*." *CEA Critic*, 56:1 (Fall 1993): 65–76

Murphy, John J. My Ántonia: *The Road Home*. Boston: Twayne, 1989.

Pala Mull, Çigdem. "*My Ántonia:* Betrayed by Everyone, Author Included." *Interactions: Aegean Journal of English and American Studies*, 13:1 (Spring 2004): 71–79.

Palmer, Scott. "'The Train of Thought': Classed Travel and Nationality in Willa Cather's *My Ántonia*." *Studies in American Fiction*, 29:2 (Autumn 2001): 239–250.

Piacentino, Edward J. "A Study in Contrasts: Impressionistic Perspectives of Ántonia and Lena Lingard in Cather's *My Ántonia*." *Studies in the Humanities*, 12:1 (1985 June): 39–44.

Polley, Diana H. "Americanizing Cather: Myth and Fiction in *My Ánntonia*." *Willa Cather Newsletter & Review*, 49:3 (Winter–Spring 2006): 61–64.

Prchal, Tim. "The Bohemian Paradox: *My Ántonia* and Popular Images of Czech Immigrants." *MELUS: The Journal of the Society for the Study of the Multi-Ethnic Literature of the United States*, 29:2 (Summer 2004): 3–25.

Rosowski, Susan J. "Approaches to Teaching Cather's *My Ántonia.*" *Approaches to Teaching World Literature.* Volume 22. New York: Modern Language Association of America, 1989.

Ryder, Mary R. "'Our' Ántonia: The Classical Roots of Willa Cather's American Myth." *Classical and Modern Literature: A Quarterly,* 12:2 (Winter 1992): 111–117

Schwind, Jean. "The Benda Illustrations to *My Ántonia:* Cather's 'Silent' Supplement to Jim Burden's Narrative." *PMLA,* 100:1 (1985 Jan): 51–67.

Selzer, John L. "Jim Burden and the Structure of *My Ántonia.*" *Western American Literature,* 24:1 (1989 May): 45–61

Shaw, Patrick. "Marek Shimerda in *My Ántonia:* A Noteworthy Medical Etiology." *ANQ: A Quarterly Journal of Short Articles, Notes, and Reviews,* 13:1 (Winter 2000): 29–33.

Swenson, Jeffrey. "Art and the Immigrant: The Other as Muse in Cather's *My Ántonia* and Rólvaag's *Boat of Longing.*" *Midamerica: The Yearbook of the Society for the Study of Midwestern Literature,* 32 (2005): 16–30.

Swift, John N. "Willa Cather's *My Ántonia* and the Politics of Modernist Classicism." In *Narratives of Nostalgia, Gender, and Nationalism,* edited by Pickering, Jean and Suzanne Kehde. New York: New York University Press, 1997, pp. 107–120.

Tellefsen, Blythe. "Blood in the Wheat: Willa Cather's *My Ántonia.*" *Studies in American Fiction,* 27:2 (Autumn 1999): 229–244.

Trout, Steven. "Seeing the Rattlesnake in Willa Cather's *My Ántonia.*" *Isle: Interdisciplinary Studies in Literature and Environment,* 12:1 (Winter 2005): 99–114.

Woolley, Paula. "'Fire and Wit': Storytelling and the American Artist in Cather's *My Ántonia.*" *Cather Studies,* 3 (1996): 149–181.

Acknowledgments

Blanche H. Gelfant, "The Forgotten Reaping-Hook: Sex in *My Ántonia*"; *American Literature*, Volume 43, Number 1 (1971): pp. 60–82. © Copyright 1971, Duke University Press. All rights reserved. Used by permission of the publisher.

Deborah G. Lambert, "The Defeat of a Hero: Autonomy and Sexuality in *My Ántonia*"; *American Literature*, Volume 53, Number 4 (1982): pp. 676–690. © Copyright 1982, Duke University Press. All rights reserved. Used by permission of the publisher.

Sally Allen McNall, "Immigrant Backgrounds to *My Ántonia:* 'A Curious Social Situation in Black Hawk'"; *Approaches to Teaching Cather's* My Ántonia, edited by Susan J. Rosowski (New York: MLA, 1989): pp. 22–30. © 1989 Modern Language Association.

Paula Woolley, "'Fire and Wit': Storytelling and the American Artist in Cather's *My Ántonia*"; Reprinted from *Cather Studies*, Volume 3, edited by Susan J. Rosowski by permission of the University of Nebraska Press. © 1996 by the University of Nebraska Press.

Susan J. Rosowski, "Pro/Creativity and a Kinship Aesthetic"; Reprinted from *Birthing a Nation: Gender, Creativity, and the West in American Literature* by Susan J. Rosowski by permission of the University of Nebraska Press. © 1999 by the Univeristy of Nebraska Press.

Acknowledgments

Patrick Shaw, "Marek Shimerda in *My Ántonia:* A Noteworthy Medical Etiology"; *American Notes & Queries,* Volume 13, Number 1 (2000): pp. 29–33. Reprinted with permission of the Helen Dwight Reid Educational foundation. Published by Heldref Publications, 1319 Eighteenth Street, NW, Washington, D.C. 20036-1802. © 2000.

Steven B. Shively, "*My Ántonia* and the Parables of Sacrifice"; From *Willa Cather and the Culture of Belief,* edited by John J. Murphy (*Literture and Belief,* volume 22). © 2002 by Brigham Young University.

Janis P. Stout, "The Observant Eye, the Art of Illustration, and Willa Cather's *My Ántonia*"; Reprinted from *Cather Studies,* Volume 5, edited by Susan J. Rosowski, by permission of the University of Nebraska Press. © 2003 by the Board of Regents of the University of Nebraska.

Michael Gorman, "Jim Burden and the White Man's Burden: *My Ántonia* and Empire"; Reprinted from *Cather Studies,* Volume 6, edited by Stephen Trout, by permission of the University of Nebraska Press. © 2006 by the Board of Regents of the University of Nebraska.

Diana H. Polley, "Americanizing Cather: Myth and Fiction in *My Ántonia*"; *Willa Cather Newsletter & Review,* Volume 49, Number 3 (2006): pp. 61–64. © 2006 The Willa Cather Pioneer Memorial and Educational Foundation.

Ann Romines, "Why Do We Read—and Re-read—*My Ántonia?*"; *In the First Fifty Years: A Celebration of the Cather Foundation's Promotion and Preservation of the World of Willa Cather,* edited by Virgil Albertini, Susan Maher, and Ann Romines (Red Cloud, N.E.: The Willa Cather Pioneer Memorial and Educational Foundation, 2006): pp. 21–31. © 2006 The Willa Cather Pioneer Memorial and Educational Foundation.

Index